T3-BOG-542

OF DEAD KINGS AND DIRGES

SBL

Society of Biblical Literature

Academia Biblica

Saul M. Olyan,
Old Testament Editor

Mark Allan Powell,
New Testament Editor

Number 11

OF DEAD KINGS AND DIRGES

OF DEAD KINGS AND DIRGES
Myth and Meaning in Isaiah 14:4b–21

R. Mark Shipp

Society of Biblical Literature
Atlanta

BS
1515.52
.S55
2002b

OF DEAD KINGS AND DIRGES

Copyright © 2002 by the Society of Biblical Literature

All rights reserved. No part of this work may be reproduced or transmitted in any form or by any means, electronic or mechanical, including photocopying and recording, or by means of any information storage or retrieval system, except as may be expressly permitted by the 1976 Copyright Act or in writing from the publisher. Requests for permission should be addressed in writing to the Rights and Permissions Office, Society of Biblical Literature, 825 Houston Mill Road, Atlanta, GA 30329, USA.

Library of Congress Cataloging-in-Publication Data

Shipp, R. Mark, 1953-
Of dead kings and dirges : myth and meaning in Isaiah 14:4b–21 / by R. Mark Shipp.
p. cm. — (Academia Biblica)
Includes bibliographical references and index.
ISBN 1-58983-038-5 (paper binding : alk. paper)
1. Bible. O. T. Isaiah XIV, 4b–21—Criticism, interpretation, etc. 2. Myth in the Old Testament. 3. Dirges. 4. Middle Eastern literature—Relation to the Old Testament. I. Title. II. Series: Academia Biblica (Series) ; no. 11.
BS1515.52 .S55 2002b
224'.1068—dc21
2002015095

07 06 05 04 03 02 5 4 3 2 1

Printed in the United States of America
on acid-free paper

Of Dead Kings and Dirges: A Poem

Of dead kings and dirges
And gods of the night,
Of night-barks and surges
Of stars taking flight;
Like heavenly horses,
The planets and spheres
Go forth in their courses
And then disappear
On rivers of darkness
As still as a tomb
And nocturnal journeys
In netherworld gloom—
The primitive ancients
In solemn delight
Looked upwards in awe
At the gods of the night.

But we in our caverns
Of concrete and steel,
And we with our modern
Technology feel
That they are the primitives,
We the advanced,
That we are enlightened
And they are entranced;
But never in our
Analytical frame,
Could we in our arrogance
Possibly name
Those marvelous
Manifestations of light—
Nor look up in awe
At the gods of the night.

R. Mark Shipp

Table of Contents

Acknowledgments

This volume is substantially the same as my dissertation submitted to the faculty of Princeton Theological Seminary in December 1997. The only changes are some minor revisions to chapter four. The sequence and argumentation of the dissertation have remained the same.

This work could not have been written without the unfailing patience and good humor of my wife, Sheree. If a degree were awarded for "patience under long term duress" she would be a recipient. Her faith and resilient spirit have sustained me countless times.

Also, this project could not have been undertaken without significant teachers from my past. Dr. James E. Priest, retired professor of Old Testament at Pepperdine University, was the first to motivate me to enter the field of Old Testament studies. Dr. Ronald Tyler and Dr. Randall Chesnutt of Pepperdine University were patient instructors of the text of the Bible, the Hebrew language, and the theology of the testaments.

I wish to acknowledge the patience, help, and friendly advice of my committee, Drs. J. J. M. Roberts, C. L. Seow, and Richard Whitaker. This work would never have seen the light of day without the careful reading and critical eye of Professor Roberts and the creative suggestions of Professor Seow. Professor Whitaker carefully read each revision of the Ugaritic translations and offered invaluable suggestions and critiques. Others at Princeton Theological Seminary have had a formative impact on this work and on my scholarship. They are Drs. Katharine Sakenfeld, Patrick Miller, Dennis Olson, and James Armstrong. This community continues to influence my understanding of scholarship, theology, and ministry in important ways. Of course, I take full responsibility for any errors or infelicities which remain in the text.

Two of my students at Austin Graduate School of Theology deserve special mention. My graduate assistant, Todd Hall, put in long hours proofreading the text and hunting down obscure references. Ron Hall also sacrificed his time checking bibliographic references and proofreading the final manuscript. I am indebted to both of them.

Finally, I would like to thank my colleagues at the Austin Graduate School of Theology in Austin, Texas for their support, collegiality, and friendship over the past several years.

Table of Abbreviations

ASJ	Acta Sumerologica Japonesa
AOAT	Alter Orient und Altes Testament
ANE	Ancient Near East
ANET	*Ancient Near Eastern Texts Relating to the Old Testament*
AfO	*Archiv für Orientforschung*
ALASP	Abhandlungen zur Literatur Alt-Syrien-Palästinas und Mesopotamiens
CAD	*The Assyrian Dictionary of the University of Chicago*
AS	Assyriological Studies
AuOr	*Aula Orientalis*
BAfO	Beihefte, Archiv für Orientforschung
BZAW	Beihefte zur Zeitschrift für die alttestamentliche Wissenschaft
BM	British Museum text
BASOR	*Bulletin of the American Schools of Oriental Research*
CBQ	*Catholic Biblical Quarterly*
CEPOA	Recueil de travaux et de communication de l'association des Études du Proche-Orient Ancien
CRAI	Comptes rendus de l'academie des inscriptions et belles lettres
ConBOT	Coniectanea biblica: Old Testament Series
COS	*The Context of Scripture*
CT	*Cuneiform Texts from Babylonian Tablets in the British Museum*
DN	divine name
ErIsr	*Eretz-Israel*
ETR	*Etudes théologiques et religieuses*
FOTL	Forms of the Old Testament Literature
HSM	Harvard Semitic Monographs
HTR	*Harvard Theological Review*
HAR	*Hebrew Annual Review*
HUCA	*Hebrew Union College Annual*

HUCAS	Hebrew Union College Annual: Supplement Series
HSAT	*Die Heilige Schrift des Alten Testaments*
ICC	International Critical Commentary
IB	*Interpreter's Bible*
JSOTS	Journal for the Study of the Old Testament: Supplement Series
JBL	*Journal of Biblical Literature*
JCS	*Journal of Cuneiform Studies*
JNES	*Journal of Near Eastern Studies*
JAOS	*Journal of the American Oriental Society*
KTU	*Die Keilalphabetischen Texte aus Ugarit*
LXX	The Septuagint
MT	Masoretic Text
MDOG	Mitteilungen der Deutschen Orient-Gesellschaft
NedTT	*Nederlands theologisch Tijdschrift*
NCB	New Century Bible
NICOT	New International Commentary on the Old Testament
OB	Old Babylonian Period
OTL	Old Testament Library
Or	*Orientalia* (NS)
PEQ	*Palestine Exploration Quarterly*
PN	personal name
RS	Ras Shamra
RSV	Revised Standard Version
RHR	*Revue de l'histoire des religions*
RIMA	Royal Inscriptions of Mesopotamia, Assyrian Periods
SJOT	*Scandinavian Journal of the Old Testament*
SBL	Society of Biblical Literature
SANE	Sources and Monographs on the Ancient Near East
SAA	State Archives of Assyria
SAAS	State Archives of Assyria Studies
SBT	Studies in Biblical Theology
VTSup	Supplements to Vetus Testamentum
TB	Theologische Bücherei: Neudrucke und Berichte aus dem 20. Jahrhundert
TGUOS	Transactions of the Glasgow University Oriental Society
UF	*Ugarit-forschungen*
UBL	Ugaritisch-biblische Literatur
VT	*Vetus Testamentum*
WMANT	Wissenschaftliche Monographien zum Alten und Neuen Testament
WBC	Word Biblical Commentary
ZAH	*Zeitschrift für Althebräistik*
ZA	*Zeitschrift für Assyriologie*
ZAW	*Zeitschrift für die alttestamentliche Wissenschaft*

Chapter 1
Survey of the Interpretation of Myth and Isaiah 14:4b–21 Since 1928

I. Introduction

> In Isaiah 14:12–21, Hêlēl son of Shahar is asserted to have said to himself: "I will go up to heaven, above the stars of God I will place my throne on high. I will sit on the Mount of Assembly in Saphon, I will rise above the heights of the clouds, I will make myself like the Most High." His presumption, instead, resulted in his translation to the very depths of the underworld, to be mocked as the erstwhile all-powerful tyrant. If there are mythological overtones, as is probable, it remains to be determined how the myth was transmitted to Isaiah and used by him.[1]

Since the discovery of the Babylonian and Assyrian mythological texts in the last century most commentators have been convinced that a myth, or myths, lie behind the poem in Isa 14:4b–21. Particularly vv. 12–15, with their vivid description of the attempt of Hêlēl ben Šaḥar to ascend to the heavens resulting instead in his ignominious fall to Sheol, have fascinated commentators. The imagery associated with Hêlēl, his attempted ascent and resultant descent to Sheol, and his aspiration to rise "above the stars of ʾEl" and take his seat with the divine assembly have raised significant questions. To what myth might this part of the poem be referring? Do these few verses refer to a single mythological account, or do they reflect or allude to several myths? What culture produced these allusions and why are they used in Isaiah? What is the relationship between

[1] W. G. E. Watson, "Helel," in *Dictionary of Deities and Demons in the Bible*, (eds. Karel van der Toorn et al.; Leiden: E. J. Brill, 1995), 747–748.

the myth or myths described in these verses and the historical "king of Babylon" mentioned in v. 4a?

Most scholars assume, therefore, that Isa 14:12–15 is in some way related to ancient Near Eastern mythology. This assertion, however, has not been matched by an equal confidence in ascertaining exactly what that relationship might be and which myth or myths lie in the background of the poem. Mesopotamian, Ugaritic, Arabic, and Greek myths have all been proposed as providing such a background. Currently there is no consensus relative to this issue.

While most attention has focused on vv. 12–15, there are other images in the poem which may reflect the language of mythology. Some scholars have found in the cedars of Lebanon in vv. 7–8 a reference to a myth about the "garden of the gods," hewn down by an arrogant and presumptuous human. But how does this image relate to vv. 12–15? Why would the author of the poem make reference to two or more myths?

Likewise, the fall of the king to Sheol and his greeting by the Rephaim in vv. 9–11 and 18–20a have occasioned a great deal of discussion. Who are the Rephaim and what is their function in Sheol? Do the sections of the poem which deal with the Rephaim relate to yet a third myth, or do these sections refer to general Near Eastern cosmology, not reflected in a "story about the gods," the usual definition of myth? The grounds for this separation of the poem into "mythological" and "non-mythological" sections are seldom made clear. On what basis is the cosmology reflected in vv. 9–11 and 15–17 kept distinct from the "mythology" of vv. 12–15? Relative to this last question, what is the relationship between myth and cosmology? What, in fact, do we mean when we say "myth," and what is the function of such myths in the poem?

In view of the continuing debate relative to the presence and function of myth in the poem, I will survey several representative views of myth in Isa 14 since the discovery of the Ugaritic mythological texts in 1928. I will begin with those approaches which minimize or deny the presence of mythical elements in the poem. Secondly, I will look at those approaches which find several mythical allusions or narratives represented in the poem. Thirdly, I will survey the myth and ritual approach and some of its variations. I will end this chapter with a discussion of myth and cosmology in general and a recommendation for the way myth impinges upon our understanding of Isa 14.

II. Approaches Which Deny Mythical Elements or Minimize Them

There have been two ways which this approach has been manifested most commonly. The first is the attempt to explain mythological elements, especially in vv. 12–15, by means of the occurrence of natural phenomena. The second suggests that the apparent use of myth is a rhetorical device used for illustrative purposes, but does not truly reflect mythological perspectives or ideologies. These approaches have in common a lack of confidence that the various images and allusions in the poem can be adequately explained by recourse to Near Eastern mythology or cosmology. The Rephaim, for example, may simply be the dead, without reflecting an ancient Near Eastern myth. The cedars of Lebanon may simply be trees, personified as humans expressing relief that their "hewer" is no more. Day Star, son of Dawn may simply be the fall of a meteor from the heavens. Mythical sounding terms, in other words, are simply ways of expressing realities by means of metaphors and primitive science.

The first of these approaches attempts to explain the references in vv. 12–15 by means of natural or historical phenomena. Thus, Johann Fischer thought the ruler mentioned in the poem must be a reference to Nebuchadnezzar, as no Babylonian or Assyrian king controlled the Lebanon at the time of Isaiah, but later this monarch did rule over the Lebanon to the Amanus mountains.[2] Only so, he thought, could the reference to the "cedars of Lebanon rejoicing" at the king's death be understood. Hence it is probably not a "nature myth" which lies in the background of the poem, but a "natural process" that is in the foreground:

> Daß dieser Schilderung ein Naturmythus zugrunde liegt, ist nicht sicher erweisbar, doch jedenfalls liegt ihr ein Naturvorgang, das Herabfahren der Meteore, zugrunde.[3]

Fischer thought that vv. 12–15 have nothing to do with a myth, therefore, but have to do with the fall of a meteor.

Such approaches falter on several grounds. First, "natural" processes, as opposed to "supernatural" processes, would not have been a meaningful category in the ancient world. The natural and the supernatural were so entwined in the ancient Near East as to make it impossible to say when "divine" causality ended and "natural" causality began. Second, the attempt to describe the fall of Hêlēl ben Šaḥar as depicting such a natural process does not account for the cosmological elements which abound in the rest of the poem (Rephaim, Sheol, cedars of Lebanon, etc.). How do these elements refer to "natural" phenomena in the

---

[2] This is a curious statement, considering that Assyrian monarchs had made military incursions or had claimed the Lebanon at least as far back as Tiglath-Pileser I. See "Tiglath-Pileser I" (Daniel D. Luckenbill, *Ancient Records of Assyria and Babylonia* [London: Histories & Mysteries of Man, 1989], 1:98). During Isaiah's day, Tiglath-Pileser III (*Ancient Records* 1:288-289), Sargon II (*Ancient Records* 2:3), and Sennacherib (*Ancient Records* 2:119) all claimed to have held the Lebanon.

[3] Johann Fischer, *Das Buch Isaias, I. Teil, Kapitel 1–39* (*HSAT* 7; Bonn: Peter Hanstein, 1937), 118–123.

poem and why are such images, found elsewhere in the Old Testament and in extra-biblical inscriptions, present here?

The second approach is that which minimizes the presence of myth in the poem by suggesting that it alludes to myth for rhetorical or illustrative purposes only. Important to such approaches is the understanding that Israel's conception of religion and the cosmos was categorically different from that of neighboring nations and cultures. Hence today, even in a sermon, a point might be made from *Aesop's Fables* without any necessity that the preacher subscribe to the thought world of ancient Greece. This position also allows some scholars to admit the presence of "mythology" in the text of the Old Testament while maintaining Israel's distinctiveness over against such "intrusions" into it. Perhaps the clearest presentation of this view was Brevard S. Childs, *Myth and Reality in the Old Testament.*[4] Childs asserted that mythological elements in the Old Testament were for illustrative purposes only. To Childs, the presence of mythological allusions in the Old Testament does not mean that Israel shared such a mythological world view or possessed similar narrative myths. Israel did, however, borrow stock themes and terminology from available mythologies.

Similarly, Edward J. Young clearly attempts to separate Israel from the mythologies of its ancient Near Eastern context and avoids any reference to mythology in Isa 14. He does, however, discuss in footnotes the Israelite notion of Sheol and the Rephaim.[5] Relative to vv. 12–15 he says:

> According to Jacob . . . and Childs . . ., Helel was certainly a divine person. Jacob says he was reduced to the proportions of an historic individual, and Childs thinks he was an upstart against ᵓEl who was thwarted. This is mere conjecture. Isaiah may simply use the phrase to indicate the morning star.[6]

Again, in another footnote,

> The pagan mythology best known to the Hebrews would be the Canaanitish. Hence, Isaiah places in the mouth of the king the language of Canaanitish paganism . . . that the men of Judah may learn the extent of his boastful pretensions. This would seem to militate against Babylon as the place of composition of Isaiah 14.[7]

Young's implicit attempt to deny a common, or similar, cosmology between Israel and her neighbors might be more convincing if it were not for the fact

---

[4] Brevard S. Childs, *Myth and Reality in the Old Testament* (SBT; London: SCM, 1960).

[5] Edward J. Young, *The Book of Isaiah, Volume 1, Chapters 1–18* (NICOT; Grand Rapids: Eerdmans, 1965), 438.

[6] Young, *The Book of Isaiah,* 440, 77n.

[7] Young, *The Book of Isaiah,* 441, 78n.

that virtually every "mythological element" of the poem—the Rephaim, Sheol, the holy mountain, the stars of ʾEl, the heights of the clouds, etc.—occur in non-polemical contexts elsewhere in the Old Testament. Also, Young has limited the "pagan mythology" to vv. 12–15, without commenting on shared cosmological elements elsewhere in the poem.[8]

John D. W. Watts is even more adamant in his view that Israel borrowed imagery and terminology from its Canaanite neighbors, but it did so "for lack of a specific doctrine of its own, . . . without enthusiasm or conviction."[9] After an analysis of two myths which he agrees lie behind the poem (the "divine forest and forester in Lebanon" and the "fall of Day Star," which he attributes to the god ʿAṯtar), he concludes that

> It is a masterful poem to be sung over a tyrant who has fallen victim to his ambition and pride. Its picture of death and the realm of the dead was common to the ANE. . . . The apparent reflection of a "Lucifer myth" in v. 12 is just that. It is a simile to picture the fall and disgrace of the tyrant.[10]

One cannot help but note an apparent contradiction in Watts's conclusion. If "its picture of death was common to the ANE," then on what grounds is Israel excluded from such a cosmology? If Israel lacked a "doctrine of the afterlife," why does the Old Testament retain so many references to "the pit," "Sheol," "Rephaim," the invoking of ghosts (1 Sam 28), the fate of the unburied dead (Ezek 32), etc.?[11] It would seem, rather, that the Old Testament texts have by and large "de-deified" the cosmos, particularly in the later period, but they still seem to function and be structured in a manner similar to prevalent understandings in Ugarit, Mesopotamia, and elsewhere in the ancient Near East.[12]

---

[8] In a similar fashion, Jean Steinmann, *Le prophète Isaïe: sa vie, son oeuvre et son temps* (Paris: Cerf, 1955), 319–322, does not himself espouse a position relative to the possible mythological background of Isa 14. He suggests, following Roland de Vaux, that the poem does not reflect Israelite understandings of myth or the cosmos, but rather imitates (and, one would assume, parodies) Canaanite poetry for rhetorical effect. Unlike many commentators of this period, Steinmann discusses the literary form of the piece (*qînāh*, or elegy), but presumes it to have been written much later than the time of Isaiah.

[9] John D. W. Watts, *Isaiah 1–33*, (WBC 24; Waco: Word, 1985), 212.

[10] Watts, *Isaiah 1–33*, 212.

[11] See Klaas Spronk, *Beatific Afterlife in Ancient Israel and in the Ancient Near East* (AOAT 219; Neukirchen-Vluyn: Neukirchener Verlag; Kevelaer: Butzon & Bercker, 1986), 237–346.

[12] See Deut 32:1–8, Ps 82, Ps 29, etc. Note that the picture of the underworld is quite similar to that portrayed in the *Death of Ur-Nammu*, *Gilgamesh* tablet 12, the *Descent of Ištar*, and many others. The major difference between Isa 14 and these texts is that they portray gods of the underworld and a presiding deity as king of the underworld, while Sheol

According to these views, Israel either did not participate in the mythological/cosmological world view of its neighbors, or, if it did, it did so for lack of its own cosmology and "without conviction." The abundance of cosmological imagery in the poem, however, and the unselfconscious utilization of such imagery in other Old Testament passages makes these positions unlikely.

III. The Mythological Fragment or Allusion Approach

Another prevalent view is that which finds no one particular narrative myth behind Isa 14:4b–21. Instead, scholars who hold to this position postulate a number of "mythological allusions" or images and references to a number of pre-existent myths. This approach has gained ground because scholars have not identified one specific narrative myth as the "torso" of the poem.[13] It suggests that Isa 14 does reflect myth, but only fragments of a mythological narrative or narratives are to be found in the poem.

Most often, those who espouse this view suggest that vv. 12–15 contain fragments of, or allusions to, an otherwise unknown myth about the fall of an arrogant deity from heaven. Terminology relating to the Rephaim, Sheol, the "mount of assembly," Saphon, etc., might also be references and allusions to other mythical narratives according to this view.

Allusions to myths also may appear elsewhere in the Old Testament. Thus Isa 27:1, Ps 74:14, Ps 104:26, and Job 3:8 all make reference to Leviathan without recounting or summarizing a mythical narrative about the sea monster. Likewise, Judg 5:20, "from heaven fought the stars," in the poetic account of Deborah and Barak's battle with Sisera, may reflect the language of myth in a similar way without recounting the mythical narrative to which it alludes.[14]

Two considerations should be raised relative to the presence of mythical allusions in a text. First, it is often difficult to determine whether myths are being referred to in a specific text or whether terminology reminiscent of myth has entered into common speech. Thus, Šahar in the Old Testament generally refers to "dusk" or "dawn," but once or twice may make reference to the deity,

---

in Isa 14 is either "Sheol personified" or a non-deified attendant whose job was to be door-keeper.

[13] W. S. Prinsloo, "Isaiah 14:12–15: Humiliation, Hubris, Humiliation," *ZAW* 93 (1981): 436.

[14] Another example of allusion to, or even borrowing imagery and terminology from, a myth is that of Ps 48:12–13. It may well be a literary borrowing from the *Gilgamesh Epic* tablet 1 i 11-19 and tablet 11 vi 300ff, where the brickwork and foundations of the walls of Uruk are examined, in a manner similar to the inspection of the walls of Zion in the psalm.

or at least to the personification of a natural process (see Job 38:12 and Ps 139:9). Second, even if the references are in some sense mythological, in what sense are they "myth" and why and how are these images being used in a particular writing? To state that "such and such is an allusion to a myth" does not explain why that reference is appropriate analogically in a particular writing nor how it functions in its literary context.

A middle ground between those approaches which deny the presence of myth in the poem and those which find in it allusions to myths is the approach of William F. Albright. Albright suggests that "this poem teems with mythological allusions,"[15] but that these allusions are "vestiges" of Canaanite myths which have been "de-mythologized" by the Old Testament writer or prophet. Albright says of the divine names in Isa 14:13–14 that

> In none of these cases is there any reason to suppose that the Hebrew writers were deliberately employing pagan expressions. Some of the names of pagan divinities have simply become secular Hebrew words with no pagan meaning; mythological expressions are used as poetic symbolism without indicating the slightest reverence for the original pagan deities, just as in many Christian poets of the fifteenth-seventeenth centuries A. D.[16]

The line between mythological allusion and myth, however, is a rather fine one. Granted that the author of Isa 14 is not showing reverence to Hêlēl ben Šaḥar, it does not necessarily follow that "names of pagan divinities have simply become secular Hebrew words." In further discussion of these "vestiges" of myth in the Old Testament, Albright says

> It is clear that Israelite thought was indeed influenced by Canaanite mythological patterns. It is noteworthy that such Canaanite patterns were depotentized and demythologized rapidly, so that by the end of Old Testament times official Yahwist religion had been demythologized to a rather extreme degree.[17]

It is clear that Albright does not entirely dispense with myth. There are vestiges and allusions to myths which by the end of the Old Testament period have been "demythologized." We are not, however, dealing with the end of Old Testament times, rather with a poem which in my opinion ought to be attributed to Isaiah of Jerusalem. If by the end of Old Testament times the poem had been demythologized, how might Isaiah have regarded these mythological allusions? How might they have functioned within his broader ministry and self-

---

[15] William F. Albright, *Yahweh and the Gods of Canaan: A Historical Analysis of Two Contrasting Faiths* (Garden City: Doubleday, 1968), 141n.

[16] Albright, *Yahweh and the Gods of Canaan*, 188.

[17] Albright, *Yahweh and the Gods of Canaan*, 192–193.

understanding? Are they mythological allusions at all? Finally, Albright nowhere suggests political or theological functions for these allusions, simply that they "are" and that they have been "demythologized" by the end of the Old Testament period.

Donald Gowan is more confident about the presence of allusions to myth in Isa 14.[18] Gowan evaluates Childs's understanding of the nature of myth in the Old Testament and finds it wanting. He thinks Childs is wrong in his assessment that "myth" in the Old Testament is for illustrative purposes only. Why then, Gowan asks, does the author use such bizarre images? Furthermore, are they necessary in order to say what the author intended? Finally, is it possible to demythologize them? His conclusion is that the use of such images is indispensable to the author's intended meaning and that "we are brought to the realm of myth when we enter the world of the gods in this poem."[19]

Gowan thinks that the attempts to find an underlying myth or myths for the poem in Isa 14 are inadequate inasmuch as they are not answering the right questions and make unwarranted assumptions about an original myth, reconstructed from a variety of backgrounds and sources.[20] This approach relies on two things according to Gowan: that there was an original myth, and that the theory of cultural diffusion of this myth is operative. Gowan says this theory is not proven, but that with the ancient Near East it is much more likely to be true in terms of basic terms, images, and motifs than it is with Greek myths, such as the myth of Phaethon. Gowan goes on to say, however, that even with the ancient Near East it is not possible to make assumptions that every culture evaluated and interpreted those motifs and images in the same way. Many cultures which existed side-by-side interpreted them in opposite manners. Therefore, "the precise significance of a given theme can be determined only by the way it is used in the myths of a certain culture."[21] Gowan concludes his analysis with the observation that no single myth is referred to in Isa 14, but rather allusions to numerous myths.[22]

---

[18] Donald E. Gowan, *When Man becomes God: Humanism and Hybris in the Old Testament* (Pittsburgh Theological Monograph Series 6; Pittsburgh: Pickwick, 1975), 45–67.

[19] Gowan, *When Man becomes God*, 46.

[20] Gowan, *When Man becomes God*, 52.

[21] Gowan, *When Man becomes God*, 53.

[22] John Oswalt is very close to Gowan when he observes, "Recent attempts to derive the Isaiah account from the Greek myth of Phaethon . . . suffer from the evidence that the Greek myth is derived from the Near Eastern stories rather than being the precursor of them. Once again, the indications are that the prophet was not dependent upon any one story, but used a number of current motifs to fit his own point." See Oswalt, *The Book of Isaiah, Chapters 1–39* (NICOT; Grand Rapids: Eerdmans, 1986), 321.

Similarly, Ronald Clements suggests that

> Vv. 12–15 appear to contain either a fragment of, or at least an allusion to, an ancient myth of the banishment of a divine being from heaven. . . . The title Day Star, Son of Dawn, must certainly be a reference to the morning star, the planet Venus, and the deity consistently associated in Canaanite mythology with this planet is ʿAṯtar. . . . Whether there is a coherent myth of the "fall" of a high god from the heavens to the underworld is not yet firmly established, although it appears plausible enough from various fragmentary echoes from the Old Testament and elsewhere.[23]

Clements, unlike Gowan and others, does not speculate about the presence of other mythological fragments or allusions in the poem. He states that vv. 12–15 suggest the existence of a narrative myth of the fall of a high god, hinted at elsewhere in the Old Testament and in the ancient Near East, but whose presence and exact characteristics have so far eluded researchers. Clements suggests that some such mythological narrative must have existed.

A more significant problem for Clements's analysis is his definition of myth. Apparently, he defines myth as "narratives about the gods" and finds only one such narrative reflected in the poem, vv. 12–15. But on what basis are the preceding verses (4b–11) excluded from being so considered?[24] What of references to the Rephaim, Sheol, and the other underworld terms abounding in the poem? What in fact are "myths"? The question ought to be raised about the nature of the surrounding text if only vv. 12–15 allude to a myth about the fall of a high god.

Even if one allows that there are several myths referred to in the poem, one still needs to explain why those images, and not others, have been included in it. Furthermore, when it is unclear whether we have identified the myths to which the allusions point, it is incumbent upon interpreters to be careful in assigning images to such myths.

IV. The "Narrative Myth" Approach

The "narrative myth" approach has predominated in this century. I mean by narrative myth that a coherent story about the gods and their relationship to a foundational event or events occurring on earth is presented. Thus, while the poem in Isa 14 is designated as a *mashal* about the king of Babylon in v. 4a, it also describes a story about a god or gods and their hubris, rebellion, and eventual fall from the divine realm to the underworld. Indeed, there is no particular *a priori* reason why this ought not to be the case. The boundary

---

[23] Ronald Clements, *Isaiah 1–39* (NCB; Grand Rapids: Eerdmans, 1980), 142.

[24] See below on Hans Wildberger, who suggests at least two such narrative myths.

between heaven and earth in antiquity was not as sharply defined as in modern times. "Microcosm" mirrored "macrocosm": Mesopotamian, Canaanite, and Egyptian inscriptions contain many examples of the correspondence between the divine and human realms, the one being a mirror of the other.[25] Those who suggest that a narrative myth or myths lie(s) behind the poem operate largely on the assumption that "myth" may be defined as a story about the gods and such a story is represented in our texts. They admit that no narrative about the gods is extant relative to Isa 14. They suggest, rather, that the poem reflects such a narrative myth.[26]

Thus Gen 6–9, the flood account, is analogous to and reflects the same flood story as that contained in the *Gilgamesh* and *Atrahasis* epics without coinciding in all its details. This is no simple literary allusion, but a parallel account of the myth of the flood. Similarly, according to this approach the account of Hêlēl ben Šaḥar in Isa 14:12–15 retells in summary fashion the chief events of the fall of an astral deity from the heavens due to his arrogance and presumption. Attention in this regard has focused upon vv. 12–15, but recently vv. 7–8 have also been suggested as reflecting or summarizing events in a myth about the "violation of the garden of the gods in the Lebanon."

Suggestions about the myth or myths which lie behind the poem have not been lacking. In this section we will look at several of the more influential theories regarding such myths: first at that of Hans Wildberger, who has suggested two narrative myths behind the poem, then at several theories which relate the fall of Hêlēl to the fall of a divine being or god from the heavens, and finally at an approach which relates the poem to a Greek myth.

Hans Wildberger finds at least two narrative myths which lie in the background of Isa 14:4b–21.[27] The first of these is a myth which Wildberger suggests lies behind the first part of the poem in vv. 7–8.[28] This myth has to do with the "invasion of the garden of God in the Lebanon" by "ein tollkühner Frechling" ("foolhardy impudent one"), who

---

[25] See, for example, the epics of *Keret* and *Aqhat*. Human politics, intrigue, dining, etc. are reflected among the gods, or maybe vice versa. See John Gibson, *Canaanite Myths and Legends* (Edinburgh: T & T Clark, 1977), 91.

[26] Of course, no one has suggested that the king of Babylon is actually a god. Rather, the king in his hubris is compared to such a god whose foolish arrogance gets him cast out of heaven.

[27] Hans Wildberger, *Jesaja, Kapitel 13–39* (Biblischer Kommentar 10.2; Neukirchen-Vluyn: Neukirchener Verlag, 1980).

[28] For this interpretation he is partially dependent upon F. Stolz, "Die Bäume des Gottesgartens auf den Libanon," *ZAW* 84 (1972): 141–156.

> Steigt in dem Libanon hinauf, dringt in dem Gottesgarten ein und begeht den Frevel . . . Bäume Els anzutasten. Nicht der "Baum," wie bei Ezechiel, sondern der von hubris getriebene Eindringling wird in die Hand eines Starken gegeben, der mit ihm verfährt nach seiner Bosheit.[29]

This invader trespasses on sacred territory and as a result is cast into the underworld. Wildberger suggests that this myth ("the invasion of the garden of God") and the myth of the fall of Hêlēl ben Šaḥar frame the entire poem. Both, to Wildberger, have to do with a person of reckless arrogance who takes upon himself divine prerogatives and as a result is cast into the underworld.

Wildberger seems, at first glance, to have a reasonable key to unlocking the poem. First, there are numerous accounts of Assyrian monarchs who made campaigns to the Lebanon to cut down cedars for their various building projects. This hypothetical myth would be the perfect analogy for arrogant Assyrian or Babylonian monarchs who trespass on a sacred grove resulting in judgment by the gods. Second, there is a myth which to some degree reflects the theme of invasion of the sacred forest (probably Lebanon) by an arrogant monarch: the *Gilgamesh Epic*, tablet 3. In this scene, Gilgamesh talks his comrade Enkidu into traveling with him to the "Cedar Mountain." The monstrous guardian of the Cedar Forest, Huwawa, is slain by Gilgamesh after a long struggle. Later, Enkidu's life is taken by Ištar and he goes down to the underworld.

On closer scrutiny, Wildberger's analysis raises questions. First, Mesopotamian monarchs clearly took cedars from Lebanon and just as clearly felt they had the divine right to do so. Nowhere, however, does Isa 14:4b–21 suggest that the reason the "king of Babylon" is going to Sheol is because he has violated the sacred precincts and chopped down the sacred trees. The trees merely rejoice that their "hewer" will no longer come and decimate them, due to his untimely death. If anything, the poem suggests that the reason the Lord has "broken the staff of the wicked" is because he "smote people with fury, an unceasing blow."

Second, the parallels with the *Gilgamesh Epic* are not as clear as Wildberger's analysis suggests. Enkidu, and not Gilgamesh, king of Uruk, is slain by Ištar. If anything, Enkidu is the more cautious, the less arrogant of the two. Also, the violation of the "Cedar Mountain" and the slaying of Huwawa did not immediately result in Enkidu's death, rather his slaying of the "bull of heaven," Ištar's pet. If the *Gilgamesh Epic* is the mythical background to vv. 7–8, the connection with Isaiah is still unclear and tenuous. If there is another narrative myth behind vv. 7–8, we do not possess such a myth. We are, therefore,

---

[29] Wildberger, *Jesaja, Kapitel 13–39*, 547.

no closer to the "mythological source" of vv. 7–8 than we are to the myth of Hêlēl ben Šaḥar.

Wildberger has attempted to read more of the poem as reflecting narrative myths, rather than focusing attention on vv. 12–15 as a "mythological torso." This approach has obvious advantages in that one does not have to determine in his presentation which sections of the poem are mythological and which are not. He has also performed a service in his presentation of Sheol and his judicious treatment of the Rephaim. He continues, however, to present two different views of myth: on the one hand, he suggests two narratives about the gods reflected in and underlying Isa 14, and on the other he speaks of the Rephaim and Sheol in a cosmological sense.

Another group of scholars devotes attention to vv. 12–15 and suggests that this passage reflects a myth of the fall of a divine being from the heavens. Included in this group are those who see the fall of Satan reflected in Isa 14, although some would be reluctant to apply the term "myth" to that account. On the other hand, several West Semitic deities have been suggested for the role of Hêlēl ben Šaḥar. Notable among these are ʾEl, ʿAṯtar, and Môt. Each of these suggestions will be surveyed in order.

The first approach, that Hêlēl ben Šaḥar is a reference to Satan, has a lengthy history. The Latin Vulgate translates Hêlēl ben Šaḥar with Lucifer, "Light Bringer." This rendering may have helped to further obscure the original meaning of the term.[30] The Church early on associated this passage with a primordial fall of Satan from heaven with other passages which seemed to suggest something similar (e.g., Luke 10:18, Rev. 12:7–9).[31] Early Church scholars

---

[30] In the Vulgate, "quomodo cecidisti de caelo lucifer qui mane oriebaris."

[31] This interpretation became common as early as St. Augustine. Note the following:

> For even as he who seduced him said of himself [i.e., Satan]: *I will set my throne towards the north*, so likewise he persuaded Adam, saying: *Taste, and you shall be as gods* (*St. Augustine on the Psalms* [trans. S. Hebgin and F. Corrigan; Ancient Christian Writers 30; New York: Newman, 1961], 245).

Likewise Jerome says with reference to Isa 14,

> Now the Sun of justice is rising in the West, but in the East, that notorious Lucifer, who had fallen, has exalted his throne above the stars (*The Letters of St. Jerome: Volume 1* [trans. Charles Mierow; Ancient Christian Writers 33: New York: Newman, 1963], 70).

The Church was by no means completely agreed on this interpretation. Theodoret of Cyrus, the last great theologian of Antioch, made no such association of Hêlēl ben Šaḥar with Satan, but associated the figure with Nebuchadnezzar. See *Theodoret of Cyrus on Divine Providence* (trans. Thomas Halton; Ancient Christian Writers 49; New York: Newman, 1988), 152. Much later, Luther and Calvin also repudiated any connection between Hêlēl ben Šaḥar and Satan. Luther made such a connection between references to a fall of Satan and Luke 10 and Revelation 20, but not, interestingly, with Isa 14. See *Lectures on Isaiah, Chapters 1–39*

thus could explain the passage in ways which made sense to them theologically. In so doing, they contributed to the development of medieval speculation about the primordial fall of Satan, a preeminent member of the divine court.[32]

It was only with the discovery of the Mesopotamian mythological texts, and especially the Ugaritic texts with their mention of a *hll*, that the consensus opinion of vv. 12–15 reflecting a primordial fall of Satan from heaven began to become less prevalent. The tradition of the association of this passage with the fall of Satan, however, survives to this day and has many adherents.

Illustrative of this approach is the dissertation by Jose Bertolucci in which he analyzes the history of the interpretation of Isa 14:12–15 and the various theories of myth which have been applied to it, and finally suggests that the traditional association of Hêlēl ben Šaḥar with Satan and his fall from heaven is the only viable alternative.[33] The association of Hêlēl with the malevolent Satan of the New Testament may be an appropriate theological analogy, but does not explain the presence of terminology which occurs outside of the Bible describing underworld (*rp'm*, see *KTU* 1.20–22) or astral (*hll*, see *KTU* 1.24) deities. While this approach has a great deal to say, therefore, about the Church's later appropriation of the poem, it does not advance our understanding of its details nor its literary function in Isaiah.

Resembling this approach, but also similar to the myth and ritual approach, is an article by Julian Morgenstern. Morgenstern thought all of the myths of the vanquished or fallen gods are one myth (i.e., Isa 14, Revelation, Enoch, etc.).[34] Furthermore, he wondered whether the myth of the fall of the Titans is associated. To Morgenstern, there were two original myths about the fall of divine beings which are both reflected in Isa 14:12–15. The first is a myth about the fall of a divine being (Satan, Lucifer, or הילל בן־שׁחר) who attempts to achieve power over God and is cast down to Hell. The second is a myth about divine beings who come down to earth of their own accord, are guilty of having relations with human women (Gen 6), and are therefore cast out from God's presence.[35]

(trans. Jaroslav Pelikan; Luther's Works 16; St. Louis: Concordia, 1969), 140 and John Calvin, *Commentary on the Book of the Prophet Isaiah* (trans. William Pringle; Calvin's Commentaries 7; Grand Rapids: Baker, 1979), 442.

[32] The Babylonian Talmud seems not to have made this connection. Of the three references to Isa 14:12–15 in the Babylonian Talmud, in every case Nebuchadnezzar is specified as the king. See *Ḥullin* (*b. Ḥul. 89b*), *Ḥagigah* (*b. Ḥag. 13a*), and *Pesaḥim* (*b. Pesaḥ. 94b*).

[33] Jose Bertolucci, "The Son of the Morning and the Guardian Cherub in the Context of the Controversy between Good and Evil" (Th.D. Diss., Andrews University, 1985), 301–303.

[34] Julian Morgenstern, "The Mythological Background of Psalm 82," *HUCA* 14 (1939): 29–126. See the "Myth and Ritual" section below for more on Morgenstern.

[35] Morgenstern, "The Mythological Background of Psalm 82," 107–108.

> Apparently Isa. 14:12–14 records both these versions of the fate of the rebellious divine being, for v. 12 pictures Helel ben Shahar as cast down to earth, while v. 14, on the other hand, pictures him in the very lowest depths of the abyss. All this evidence establishes with absolute certainty that the myth . . . of the fall of Satan and his associate angels from heaven to earth, or even into the abyss, is identical to the myth of Helel ben Shahar of Isa. 14:12–14.[36]

Morgenstern's approach is mainly speculation based on his combinations of various passages in the Bible with late Jewish traditions. Morgenstern assumes that the various texts which deal with the descent of a divine being from heaven to earth are variations of a single myth. His joining of these mythical texts without attention to the diversity of style, genre, and literary setting of each text does not inspire confidence in his synthetic treatment.

Several West-Semitic deities have also been mentioned as candidates for Hêlēl ben Šaḥar. In an important monograph,[37] Marvin Pope thinks that Isa 14 and apocalyptic literature in the Old and New Testaments reflect a myth about the fall of the gods from heaven. He thinks that the fall actually refers to ʾEl losing his place in the divine council and being cast down to earth.[38] There is no evidence, however, that ʾEl ever suffered such a rebellion and fall from his status as head of the Ugaritic pantheon, but rather that he was relegated to a "semi-retired" status of "head god emeritus."[39] If the notion of a divine rebellion and attempted usurpation of the throne of heaven by upstart deities must be questioned in Ugaritic mythology, then the analogy of such a rebellion with Isa 14 must likewise be questioned.

Ulf Oldenburg compared the fall of the Babylonian tyrant to a myth which he thought must have circulated throughout the ancient Near East.[40] We first encounter this myth in the Baʿal and Môt epics from Ugarit: Baʿal was

---

[36] Morgenstern, "The Mythological Background of Psalm 82," 109.

[37] Marvin Pope, *El in the Ugaritic Texts* (SVT 2; Leiden: E. J. Brill, 1955), 96–103.

[38] Pope, *El in the Ugaritic Texts*, 98–99. Pope also thinks that Ezek 28 is associated with this and has to do with the fall of ʾEl. He thinks the "Stones of Fire" in Ezek 28 are metals which are smelted and used as building material for Baʿal's mansion.

[39] Although this has been and remains a popular assumption, there is no indication in the epic that ʾEl loses his position as father of the gods or supreme deity. Indeed, Baʿal must get permission to build his palace from ʾEl and Anat must get ʾEl's permission to go in search of Baʿal and effect his restoration. It seems rather that these mythological narratives reflect the increasing popularity of Baʿal Hadad worship in the Levant in the second millennium. The kingship which is bestowed upon Baʿal in no way disqualifies ʾEl from ultimate authority. ʾEl was creator (*bny arṣ*) and father of the 70 *bny il*, the council of the gods.

[40] Ulf Oldenburg, "Above the Stars of El: El in Ancient South Arabic Religion," *ZAW* 82 (1970): 187–208.

defeated and killed and the call went out for someone to sit upon his throne and rule in his place. ʿAṯtar the "Terrible" was brought in to take the throne of Baʿal, but the throne was too big for him and so he was not able to retain it. Oldenburg suggests that this myth reflects the reality of 1) ʾEl's demotion and semi-replacement by Baʿal as functional king of the gods, a reality reflected in West-Semitic worship practices; and 2) the attempt on the part of many to replace ʾEl worship by the worship of ʿAṯtar, clearly the "morning star," or the planet Venus in Old South Arabic religion.[41] The former suggestion does seem to be reflected to some degree in the Baʿal and Môt epic, as Baʿal does take the kingship of the gods. The second assertion, that the reality of ʿAṯtar worship in South Arabia in the late first millennium is reflected initially in the Baʿal epic and the attempt by ʿAṯtar to usurp the throne as well as by the poem in Isa 14, rests on circumstantial evidence at best. First, ʿAṯtar does not usurp the throne in the Baʿal epic but is given a position unsuited for him. He descends from the throne, due to his lack of stature and inability to fill it, suggesting quite the opposite of hubris. Secondly, there is no evidence, as Oldenburg points out, that such a myth of ʿAṯtar's attempt to usurp, or actual usurpation, of the position of supreme god in a Semitic pantheon ever existed. We have only Oldenburg's conjecture that such a myth "must have existed." Furthermore, ʿAṯtar is nowhere mentioned in the Isa 14 text, unless one takes "Day Star son of Dawn" as a designation for ʿAṯtar, which may or may not be correct. All Oldenburg has done is provide evidence that ʿAṯtar was considered to be the planet Venus in ancient South Arabic religion and was worshipped as one of the chief deities, not proof that he was so regarded elsewhere in the ancient Near East.

Oldenburg has reminded us, however, that there is always a connection between the intrigues, relationships, and positions of the various deities in the ancient world and the political and social realities of the cultures which worshipped them. If ʾEl was replaced in South Arabic religion by the worship of ʿAṯtar, as Oldenburg has convincingly shown, it reflects the political and social reality of Arabia in the mid-first millennium B.C.E.

Similar to both Oldenburg and Pope is Theodore Mullen's analysis in his monograph, *The Assembly of the Gods*. As with Oldenburg and Pope, Mullen thinks Isa 14 has to do with a revolt among the gods in heaven. Unlike them, however, he does not equate such a rebellion with either Baʿal or ʿAṯtar, but rather Môt. He cites *KTU* 1.23 (*Šaḥar and Šalim and the Gracious Gods*), where Môt is called *Môtu-wa-Šarru*, which he takes to be a compound name of the same type as *Kôṯar-wa-Ḫāsis*. He also thinks that *šarru* is cognate with the Akkadian word *šarāru*, meaning "to shine." The connection with Isa 14 he feels

[41] Oldenburg, "Above the Stars of El," 24. See also Simon Parker, "Shahar," in *Dictionary of Deities and Demons in the Bible*, 1425.

to be that as Môt, the "Shining One," rules in the underworld, even so Hêlēl ben Šaḥar, the "Shining One," is cast down into the underworld, Môt's domain.[42]

Mullen's analysis raises many questions. First of all, nowhere is Môt specifically linked with dusk or dawn (שׁחר and שׁלם). The divine name *Môtu-wa-Šarru* occurs in the opening lines of the inscription as a "bereaver" and a "widower," but nowhere is he explicitly connected to the birth of the two "gracious gods." Mullen suggests that Môt the Shining One is the son of Šaḥar and Šalim, much as Hêlēl is the son of Šaḥar in Isa 14. It is possible that Môt is the child of the two gracious gods in this text, but if so that connection is not made explicit. Second, that *šarru* means "shining" is not clear. According to Gibson, *Môtu-wa-Šarru* is a double name meaning something like "Death (even) the Prince," although he recognizes that others have suggested other definitions.[43] It is likely that Gibson is correct and *šarru* here means "king" or "prince."[44] The *w* connecting *mt* and *šr* probably does not serve to connect two synonymous terms as it does in other compound names in Ugaritic (Kôṯar-wa-Ḫāsis, for example), regardless whether one translates *šarru* as "prince" or "shining one."

In what sense is Môt the "Shining One"? How is Hêlēl, possibly related to Akkadian *ellu*/*elīlu* and meaning "Shining" or "Brilliant One," related to Môt, the Shining (*šarru*) One? Even if Mullen is correct and both Hêlēl and *šarru* mean "shining," that may mean nothing more than they both have reference to divine beings and members of the heavenly court. There is no necessary connection between Môt and Hêlēl. Furthermore, it makes more sense to translate *Môtu-wa-Šarru* with something straightforward, such as "Prince Death," than to equate an Akkadian term with an Ugaritic one which normally means "prince" and relate both with Môt and Isa 14.

A radically different approach has been taken by Pierre Grelot towards the identity of Hêlēl ben Šaḥar and the myth behind vv. 12–15.[45] Grelot suggests that Hêlēl is to be identified with neither Baʿal nor ʿAṯtar. He suggests, following Gunkel, that Hêlēl is to be associated with Φαέθων (Phaethon) in Greek mythology. He identifies Phaethon as an impetuous youth, son of Eos and Helios, who desired to drive his father's chariot and horses of the sun on their daily course through the heavens. He prevailed upon his father, against the latter's better judgment, and was allowed to drive them. Because of his youth and inexperience,

---

[42] E. Theodore Mullen, *The Assembly of the Gods: The Divine Council in Canaanite and Early Hebrew Literature* (HSM 24; Chico: Scholars Press, 1980), 238–241.

[43] Gibson, *Canaanite Myths and Legends*, 28 and 123.

[44] If this is correct, then Môt is designated with authority and office with the term *šr* as he is with *il*, or as Baʿal is designated (*zbl*).

[45] Pierre Grelot, "Isaïe XIV 12–15 et son arrière-plan mythologique," *RHR* 149–150 (1956): 18–48.

when he was unable to control the horses and came perilously close to the ground, Zeus killed him with a thunderbolt. Grelot draws parallels between this myth and that of the Baʿal and Môt cycle (the story of ʿAṯtar and his inability to sit upon the throne of Baʿal) and the reflection of this myth in the story of Hêlēl ben Šaḥar. Finally, he suggests that the Greek myth came first and influenced both Ugaritic mythology and ultimately biblical texts such as Isa 14.

J. W. McKay questioned whether Grelot's main assertions (Isa 14 reflects the myth of Phaethon and that this myth originated in Greece and became prevalent throughout the Semitic East) were adequately supported. First, McKay noticed that שַׁחַר is a masculine noun in Hebrew, although Eos, whom Grelot equated with שַׁחַר, was a feminine deity. He attempted to provide evidence which would verify Grelot's positions from the text of the Old Testament: שַׁחַר may sometimes be a masculine noun and in the book of Job in particular may have had reference originally to a masculine deity שַׁחַר. Secondly, he attempts to provide a firmer basis for Grelot's supposition of cultural diffusion.[46]

These two articles have given rise to a flurry of responses. For Peter C. Craigie, the similarities between the story of ʿAṯtar in the Baʿal and Môt cycle and Isa 14 are clear and "undeniable":

> In spite of the extensive chronological gap between the extant form of the Ugaritic text and the adaptation of the themes in Jes 14, 12–15, the parallel seems to be undeniable.[47]

Craigie suggests that the older understanding that ʿAṯtar should be equated with Hêlēl is still viable. This conclusion is based partly upon his reading of the name of ʿAṯtar in the Ugaritic texts (he translates *ʿṯtr ʿrẓ* not as "ʿAṯtar the terrible," but as "ʿAṯtar the luminous"), partly on circumstantial evidence (ʿAṯtar is a warrior like the Babylonian king), and the assertion that Greek myths were influenced by, but did not influence, Canaanite myths.

Subsequent writers have by and large either been convinced by Grelot's hypothesis (that Isa 14 reflects the Greek myth of Phaethon), or by the ʿAṯtar hypothesis. As recently as 1984 Hubert Bost could confidently assert, "Il y a, derrière la satire d'Is. 14, un arrière-fond mythique dont l'origine cananéene ne fait pas de doute: le mythe d'Attar."[48]

---

[46] J. W. McKay, "Helel and the Dawn-Goddess: A Re-examination of the Myth in Isaiah XIV 12–15," *VT* 20 (1970): 451–464.

[47] Peter C. Craigie, "Helel, Athtar, and Phaethon (Jes 14, 12–15)," *ZAW* 85 (1973): 223.

[48] Hubert Bost, "Le chant sur la chute d'un tyran en Esaïe 14," *ETR* 59 (1984): 13. See also Nicholas Wyatt, "ʿAṯtar and the Devil," *TGUOS* (1973–74): 85, who says "The god in question is now generally agreed to be ʿAṯtar."

The narrative myth approach, while attempting to discern the reflection in summary form of a myth especially behind vv. 12–15, is subject to some of the same criticisms as the "mythical allusions" approach: there is no single, mythical narrative which has been discovered to date which actually mirrors the themes, terminology, and deities mentioned in Isa 14:12–15, let alone the entire poem. Suggestions about the deity in question are intriguing, but finally must be judged inadequate due to their lack of firm evidence. Second, too much attention has been given to the identity of the deity in question in vv. 12–15 and not enough to the form of the poem (a *mashal* based on the dirge form, see chap. 2) or to the fact that it is a human king who is aspiring to such superlative greatness. Finally, one might ask a similar question as Gowan asked of critics of those who find a myth or myths behind the poem: why such bizarre imagery applied *to the king*? What is it about the king in question which provokes such a response? Why is it that other, similar passages in the prophetic literature are also aimed directly at human kings (Ezek 32, a dirge against Pharaoh of Egypt and Ezek 28, against the king of Tyre)?

While there may be a narrative myth behind the poem, and there are certainly myths which contain similar motifs, none so far suggested closely resembles the terminology and motifs sufficiently to suggest it as its narrative background. Until and unless such a myth is discovered, therefore, judgment about assigning the poem to one of the current suggestions should be restrained.

V. The Myth and Ritual Approach

The final approach relative to myth which I will survey is that of "myth and ritual." Those who take this approach believe that there is a very close relationship between the myths of a culture and their enactment in rituals. Some "ritualists" go so far as to say that the mythical tale is a secondary development out of the ritual: it is an attempt to explain the ritual. Most of those who subscribe to the myth and ritual approach are not so extreme, but suggest that myths give rise to rituals and rituals reenact and interpret myths. Therefore, story and ritual go together in the Bible and the ancient Near East. The Passover celebration and the story of Israel's deliverance (Exod 12:3–10) and the *Enuma Elish* read on the occasion of the Babylonian *akitu* festival are outstanding examples of this common phenomenon.

Beginning prior to the discovery of the tablets in Ugaritic at Ras Shamra, but spurred on by their publication, was the "myth and ritual school," whose most prominent figure was S. H. Hooke. The myth and ritual program[49] presented

[49] Simply put, that of uncovering the supposed original cultic setting for many biblical narratives. While not denying an original historical core to Old Testament narratives,

its case in three collections of essays edited by Hooke: *Myth and Ritual*,[50] *The Labyrinth*,[51] and *Myth, Ritual, and Kingship*.[52] In *The Labyrinth* a definition of myth is given. Whereas in volume one he understands myth as derived from rituals (i.e., myths arose in order to explain rituals), in *The Labyrinth* he adjusts this definition:

> Hence the myth which is the object of our discussion is the product, not of reflection, but of action in response to a concrete situation. . . . The term is used to express the fact of the ever-recurring repetition of a situation in which human need is met by the life-giving potency of a sacral act.[53]

Hooke, therefore, is willing by the publication of the second volume of essays to admit that there is an "event" which gives rise to the myth, not identical to the ritual but embodied and repeated in the ritual. To the myth and ritual school, then, myth and ritual are inextricably joined, although the myth may have arisen outside of an explicitly ritual context.[54]

---

they assumed that many of the narratives we possess were originally dramatically portrayed at religious festivals, notably the New Year's Festival.

[50] S. H. Hooke, ed., *Myth and Ritual: Essays on the Myth and Ritual of the Hebrews in Relation to the Culture Pattern of the Ancient East* (London: Oxford University Press, 1933).

[51] S. H. Hooke, ed., *The Labyrinth* (New York: Macmillan, 1935).

[52] S. H. Hooke, ed., *Myth, Ritual, and Kingship: Essays on the Theory and Practice of Kingship in the Ancient Near East and in Israel* (Oxford: Clarendon, 1958).

[53] Hooke, *The Labyrinth*, x.

[54] It should be noted that from the outset many scholars were at odds with the myth and ritual position. In particular, Henri Frankfort and his colleagues in *Before Philosophy: The Intellectual Adventure of Ancient Man* (Chicago: University of Chicago Press, 1946) attacked the assumptions of the Myth and Ritual school. In 1958, in the *Myth, Ritual, and Kingship* volume, Hooke summarizes Frankfort's criticisms as follows:

> 1) Contributors to *Myth and Ritual* slavishly follow James Frazer (author of *The Golden Bough: A Study in Magic and Religion* [New York: MacMillan, 1922]).
>
> 2) Similarities between the myths of various ancient Near Eastern nations cannot be described as providing a pattern.
>
> 3) That differences are specific but similarities are generic is denied; in fact the similarities really do not exist.
>
> 4) Contributors to *Myth and Ritual* recklessly imposed their pattern on the religion of Israel (p. 4).

Hooke responds to each of these criticisms and then resorts to *ad hominem*: "He was really not an Old Testament scholar, and his excursion into that domain shows a complete ignorance of the state of modern Old Testament scholarship" (p. 9).

Hooke himself did not give an interpretation of Isa 14, being more interested in his "diffusionist" theory of Babylonian influence on the myths and rituals of the entire Near East.[55] The closest thing to an analysis of Isa 14 is his brief discussion of Ezek 28, in which he suggested that the mythical pattern of divine kingship was not unknown among the Israelites.[56]

In the earliest volume of essays, *Myth and Ritual*, Theodore Robinson briefly discusses Isa 14, connecting it with Ezek 28 and Hooke's analysis. Robinson suggests that Isa 14 is a "relic surviving from a story of war against the gods":[57]

> Here we have clearly a reminiscence of a "war in heaven." The morning star has sought presumptuously to take a dominant position among the celestial bodies, whose true rulers have been (presumably) the Sun and the Moon—more probably the latter, since it is the night sky that is in question. The rebel planet is forced to yield, and its light is extinguished. So it falls to a depth at least as great as the height to which it had aspired.[58]

He suggests it is a myth fragment referring to a war in heaven connected with creation accounts and similar to the myth of the "origin of the giants" in Gen 6. He connects such accounts with surviving traditions from astral cults, of which Isa 14 is an "isolated fragment which has no corresponding ritual in Israel."[59]

Aubrey Johnson is the only one of the contributors to *The Labyrinth* who briefly deals with possible connections between Isa 14 and the myth and ritual approach. In "The Rôle of the King in the Jerusalem Cultus," Johnson refers to the poem of the "Fall of Helal ben Shahar" as "an obvious fragment from the circle of mythology associated with ʿElyôn."[60] He is not, however, interested in this article in the use of mythopoeic language in Isa 14 in its own right, but rather with its supposed connections to a pre-Israelite cult of ʿElyôn in Jerusalem. Following Gunkel, he posits an original mythical narrative to which the poem alludes in which a "morning star" attempts to ascend to the zenith of heaven,

---

[55] See S. H. Hooke, *Middle Eastern Mythology* (Baltimore: Penguin, 1963); *Origins of Early Semitic Ritual* (London: Oxford University Press, 1938); and *Myth and Ritual*, 4. Many of the problems with the myth and ritual approach are treated admirably in John Rogerson, *Myth in Old Testament Interpretation* (BZAW 134; New York: Walter de Gruyter, 1974).

[56] Hooke, *Myth and Ritual*, 10–11.

[57] Theodore Robinson, "Hebrew Myths," in *Myth and Ritual*, 179–180.

[58] Robinson, "Hebrew Myths," 179.

[59] Robinson, "Hebrew Myths," 180.

[60] Aubrey Johnson, "The Rôle of the King in the Jerusalem Cultus," in *The Labyrinth*, 82.

represented by the sun with all its force. Johnson suggests that ʿElyôn was such a sun-god, revered in Jebusite Jerusalem, whose attributes were assumed by Yahweh and whose worship was reflected in the Solomonic temple:

> Solomon's temple was a Sun-temple and seems to have been built on the site of an earlier Sun-worship. Hence, when we find that in the Davidic Cultus Jahweh plays the part of a Sun-god and is himself known as ʿElyôn, it is only reasonable to assume that he has become the focus for ritual and mythology once associated with His traditional predecessor in Jerusalem.[61]

In *Sacral Kingship in Ancient Israel*,[62] Johnson has backed away entirely from the association of Yahweh with sun-worship, except in a "symbolic" sense. He still maintains that it is a "fragment from the cycle of mythology associated with the 'Most High'," but he goes on to make the interesting statement, "which has been preserved for us through its being given an historical application."[63] The question immediately arises as to the meaning and function of mythological texts in general. Are they attempts to transcend the historical setting out of which they arise and are only subsequently "historicized"? Or could the reverse be true (i.e., are they texts which attempt to apply concrete, historical reality to the cosmos and only subsequently become "universalized")? In any event, Johnson makes little attempt to deal with the poem on its own terms and less attempt to deal with its genre and function. In both of the works cited, Johnson does make an overt connection of this poem with rituals performed at the New Year's Festival, without demonstrating what such rituals may have been or how they are connected with this poem in particular.[64] Note also that Johnson alludes to the mythological fragment as consisting of only vv. 12–15. He makes no attempt to analyze the rest of the poem nor to explain the place of these verses within their literary setting.

More definite in his assertion of a ritual background to Isa 14 is Julian Morgenstern, treated briefly in the "Narrative Myth" section above. According to Morgenstern, Yahweh's day of judgment of divine beings or of humans was

---

[61] Johnson, "The Rôle of the King in the Jerusalem Cultus," 83.

[62] Johnson, *Sacral Kingship in Ancient Israel* (Cardiff: University of Wales, 1955), 84n.

[63] Johnson, *Sacral Kingship in Ancient Israel*, 85.

[64] Note the following: "The passages in the canonical prophets, particularly the book of Isaiah, which need to be seen against the background of this festival are so numerous that the writer refrains, for the most part, from drawing attention to them. . . . But the reader should compare at this point the fragment from the cycle of mythology associated with the' Most High' . . ., i.e., Isa 14:12–15" (*Sacral Kingship in Ancient Israel*, 85). As late as 1958, Johnson was still finding Babylonian backgrounds to Israelite royal ideology (see Hooke, *Myth, Ritual, and Kingship*, 165–170).

at a set time each year, namely New Year's day. Morgenstern thought that the divine beings, the *ʿdt ʾl* or *bĕnê ʾĕlōhîm*, appeared with Yahweh in judgment on this day when the fates and destinies of humans and divinities were decided. The day of Yahweh's visit was commemorated during the New Year's Festival. On this day, the temple doors would be thrown back so that the radiance of Yahweh, the sun, might enter into the very holy of holies. In pre-exilic Israel, specifically before the reform of Asa, Israelites shared with Phoenicians temple iconography and ideology, the notion of a high, solar deity and his council, and the New Year's Festival.[65]

It is puzzling why he makes no use of the Ugaritic material, which at the time of his writing was becoming available. Nevertheless, his approach is similar to the myth and ritual school in the sense that he places a great deal of emphasis upon the centrality of the New Year's Festival and attendant solar rituals for the explanation or clarification of ancient Israelite cosmology.

Following World War II there was renewed interest in the place of myth and ritual in the ancient Near East and the Old Testament. The primary exponent of this modified "myth and ritual" approach was Theodor Gaster, as especially exemplified in the two works *Thespis: Ritual, Myth, and Drama in the Ancient Near East*[66] and *Myth, Legend, and Custom in the Old Testament.*[67] In *Thespis*, Gaster thought that "Helal ben Shahar" is a direct allusion to ancient Near Eastern myth, analogous to the Šaḥar of *Šaḥar and Šalim and the Gracious Gods.*[68] To Gaster, Helal was a son of one of these two "comely" gods; he is a rebellious deity who was cast down from heaven in the same sense as the gods of Ps 82, the "Princes." He thinks *Šaḥar and Šalim and the Gracious Gods* is a ritual text for the feast of first fruits, the Feast of Weeks or Pentecost to the Jews. Isaiah 14 is a reflection of this myth. He suggested that the myth was widespread throughout the ancient world—it was known in Greece, Anatolia, Persia, Edessa, Syria, and elsewhere.

One of the strengths of Gaster's work is that he attempted to tie the myth in Isa 14 to a real setting in Israelite life. Nevertheless, that it was tied to the Feast of Weeks is speculative and goes well beyond the available data. Furthermore, if there is a ritual tied to a myth in Isa 14, it makes more sense to suggest it is one which the text seems to make more explicit: a funeral dirge for a dead king.

---

[65] Morgenstern, "The Mythological Background of Psalm 82," 59–66.

[66] Theodor Gaster, *Thespis: Ritual, Myth, and Drama in the Ancient Near East* (New York: Henry Schuman, 1950).

[67] Theodor Gaster, *Myth, Legend and Custom in the Old Testament* (New York: Harper & Row, 1969).

[68] Gaster, *Thespis*, 225–237. See also Gibson, *Canaanite Myths and Legends*, 123–127.

Theodore Lewis has recently analyzed the Niqmaddu funeral dirge from Ugarit and has found some points of contact with Isa 14. Some of the elements of the poem may be understood more clearly in light of *KTU* 1.161 (RS 34.126),[69] particularly the greeting of the king by the Rephaim, the invoking of the Rephaim, and the mention of thrones.[70] In his view, Isa 14 reflects the same general understanding as in Ugaritic literature of 1) the dead kings who sit on thrones in the underworld as they did in life;[71] 2) the agitation of the dead kings or inhabitants, which he compares to 1 Sam 28 (Saul and the witch of Endor); and 3) sacrifices made on behalf of the dead king. Further, he suggests that Šapšu, the sun, was the designated deity for the transporting of the dead to the netherworld, although this element is not reflected in the poem in Isa 14.

Lewis's analysis has much to commend it. He is one of the few scholars who has related Isa 14 to an actual funeral dirge. Furthermore, Lewis does not draw a dichotomy between narrative myth and "general cosmology" in Isa 14 or *KTU* 1.161. Lewis, however, has not recognized that the various components of the poem correspond to a Near Eastern dirge pattern (see chapter 2), nor has he fully recognized that the twin themes of the ascent of the king to heaven and descent to the netherworld, components of such dirges, are present in the poem.

The myth and ritual approach potentially has strengths lacking in other approaches. Its focus on the ritual and functional aspects of myths draws attention to their religious and social setting. Furthermore, Isa 14 is cast in the form of a dirge, further undergirding the value of a ritual approach to the poem. Nevertheless, ritualists have rarely dealt with the poem as a *mashal*, nor have they explained the various components of the poem and how they might be explained both by analysis of myth and of the dirge form.

In the foregoing, I have attempted to survey four different approaches to myth as applied to Isa 14. They range from approaches which deny or minimize the presence of myth in Isa 14 to those which not only affirm its presence but

---

[69] Pierre Bordreuil and Dennis Pardee, "Le rituel funéraire Ougaritique RS 34.126," *Syria* 59 (1982): 121–128.

[70] Theodore Lewis, *Cults of the Dead in Ugarit and Israel* (HSM 39; Atlanta: Scholars Press, 1989), 40–46.

[71] He refers to the GIŠ.GU.ZA, or "ghost throne" of Sumerian literature as evidence that dead kings were understood to retain some sort of royal status in the underworld. One might also mention Alexander Heidel, *The Gilgamesh Epic and Old Testament Parallels* (Chicago: University of Chicago Press, 1946), 198. Heidel refers to the thrones of the dead kings in Isa 14 as reflective simply of a parody. The Israelites would not have had such a conception, nor, apparently, did the Babylonians, for he says that the *Gilgamesh Epic* tablet seven says dead kings did not sit on thrones or wear crowns. Contrary to his view, the parody must be based on *something*. As we shall see in the next chapter, the Sumerians and Babylonians did indeed believe their kings retained royal status in the underworld.

attach it to specific rituals. If there has been a single common element to these approaches, it is that the term "myth" is not defined, or is ill-defined. Its relationship to narrative, cosmology, and ritual is rarely made explicit. We turn now, therefore, to an examination of the phenomenon of myth, its relationship to ritual, and how myth and ritual relate to Isa 14.

VI. Myth and Meaning: The Definition of "Myth"

There is no consensus relative to the presence, extent, or function of myth in Isa 14. Indeed, this lack of consensus or clarity relative to mythology in the Old Testament is not a new phenomenon, but there has been much speculation about the meaning and purpose of myth at least for the past two hundred years. The modern period of mythological analysis relative to the Old Testament may be said to have begun with Hermann Gunkel's classic *Schöpfung und Chaos in Urzeit und Endzeit*,[72] which set the tone for most research on myth as it pertains to the Old Testament down to the present.[73]

The discussion about myth and its relationship to the Old Testament has taken place in the past century within broader debates about myth as a general phenomenon of human culture. Many theories of myth have been advanced in this century. Ivan Strenski has recently insisted that myth is not a single identifiable or definable phenomenon. Those approaches which seek to reduce myth to a single purpose, background, or meaning are by definition incomplete.[74]

Strenski analyzes four modern philosophers and their views of myth: Ernst Cassirer, Bronislaw Malinowski, Mircea Eliade, and Claude Lévi-Strauss. They are broadly representative of four basic approaches to the study of myth and its relationship to history, ritual, politics, and the primordium. It will be useful, therefore, to place this discussion in the broader context of the philosophical and anthropological debates about myth, a procedure seldom followed by biblical scholars in their discussions about myth.[75]

---

[72] Hermann Gunkel, *Schöpfung und Chaos in Urzeit und Endzeit: eine religionsgeschichtliche Untersuchung über Gen. 1 und Ap. Joh. 12* (Göttingen: Vandenhoeck & Ruprecht, 1894).

[73] To Gunkel, myths were "stories about the gods." Gunkel understood, however, that there was a tendency in Israel to demythologize the content of "borrowed" myths in the development of Israel's history and theology (so Rogerson, *Myth in Old Testament Interpretation*, 60–61). This has been the predominant understanding of myth and the Old Testament in this century.

[74] Ivan Strenski, *Four Theories of Myth in Twentieth-Century History: Cassirer, Eliade, Lévi-Strauss and Malinowski* (London: MacMillan, 1987).

[75] I am partially dependent upon Ivan Strenski, *Four Theories of Myth*, for the order and basic interpretations of the four mythologists analyzed.

The name of Bronislaw Malinowski is associated with the "functional approach" to myth. Malinowski owed his greatest debt to Sir James Frazer,[76] to whom he dedicated his book *Myth in Primitive Psychology*.[77] Frazer is most commonly associated with the "ritual approach" to myth; as Robert Ackerman describes, Frazer's approach was "that religion originated in man's attempts to control the world by aiding the gods to do his bidding magically (that is, by means of ritual)."[78] Second, Ackerman describes Frazer as a ritualist in that Frazer believed that

> Man worshipping is first (and foremost) an actor. He does something to cause his gods to shine their countenances upon him; he may sing or chant and he will certainly dance. When he moves he acts out what he wants the gods to do for him.[79]

Frazer's ritualism is a kind of functionalism in that the myth is not intended to be primarily explanatory, but rather acted out in ritual so as to secure the gods' favor. While Frazer's ritualism was profoundly influential on Malinowski, Frazer himself was inconsistent in his application of this approach. According to Ackerman, he combines euhemerism (that myths are based upon real heroes and kings of antiquity), intellectualism (that myth is primitive philosophy, science, or reason), and ritualism.[80]

Malinowski objected strenuously to the common understanding that myths were explanatory tales (explanations of how things got to be the way they are) or primitive attempts at philosophy or science. After a prolonged study of the Trobriand islanders in the Western Pacific, and particularly their *lili'u* tales (which he classified as myths), he stated

> This definition would create an imaginary, non-existent class of narrative, the aetiological myth, corresponding to a non-existent desire to explain, leading a futile existence as an "intellectual effort" and remaining outside native culture and social organization with their pragmatic interests. The whole treatment appears to us faulty, because myths are treated as mere stories, because they are regarded as primitive

---

[76] Frazer is best known for his twelve volume work on anthropology, myth, and religion called *The Golden Bough: A Study in Magic and Religion*. For more on Frazer, see my discussion above.

[77] Bronislaw Malinowski, *Myth in Primitive Psychology* (New York: W. W. Norton, 1926). Malinowski is best known for his anthropological study of the Trobriand islanders, *Argonauts of the Western Pacific* (New York: E. P. Dutton, 1961).

[78] Robert Ackerman, *The Myth and Ritual School: J. G. Frazer and the Cambridge Ritualists* (Garland: New York, 1991), 55.

[79] Ackerman, *The Myth and Ritual School*, 55.

[80] Ackerman, *The Myth and Ritual School*, 55.

> intellectual armchair occupation, because they are torn out of their life context, and studied from what they look like on paper and not what they do in life.[81]

To Malinowski, myth is neither mere narrative, nor science, nor history, nor explanatory tale. He does not give a concise definition of myth, but rather several ways in which myth functions: "Myth . . . supplies a retrospective pattern of moral values, sociological order, and magical belief."[82] In the final analysis, myth functions to "strengthen tradition and endow it with a greater value and prestige by tracing it back to a higher, better, more supernatural reality of initial events."[83]

Malinowski did not only believe that myth has a sociological function. Ivan Strenski refers to Malinowski as a broad functionalist in the sense that he believed society is an "interdependent, organic whole."[84] He says, however, that Malinowski was a functionalist in a more narrow sense:

> For [Malinowski], to talk of the function of a social phenomenon, such as myth, was to concern oneself with "any significant but unobvious effect it has on the general condition or development of society." In *Argonauts*, Malinowski observes the way myth functions to fix custom, sanction modes of behavior, dignify institutions or found a system of magic—*even though the natives themselves may not be aware of these functions.*[85]

To Malinowski, then, myth always serves a function in society, but that function is largely unconscious even to the society which produces the myth.

In the final analysis, Strenski asserts that to Malinowski, myths are the *important stories* society has to tell, which serve a traditioning and socially cohesive function. "Malinowski calls for the study of myth within its 'context of living faith, social organization . . . morals . . . and customs.'"[86] In this attitude he is not far from Ernst Cassirer's understanding of myth as serving political functions.

For Ernst Cassirer, more could be said about myth than simply to talk about its function in a society. It is also a mode of *thinking* and *conceptualizing* the cosmos. Furthermore, for mythical thought there is no sense of history, of the passage of time, or the sequence of events. Events are collapsed into the one

---

[81] Malinowski, *Myth in Primitive Psychology*, 33–34.

[82] Malinowski, *Myth in Primitive Psychology*, 91.

[83] Malinowski, *Myth in Primitive Psychology*, 91–92.

[84] Strenski, *Four Theories of Myth*, 53.

[85] Strenski, *Four Theories of Myth*, 53.

[86] Strenski, *Malinowski and the Work of Myth* (Princeton: Princeton University Press, 1992), xxi.

Event.[87] Likewise, myth does not represent or symbolize some phenomenon, it *is* that phenomenon:

> If we examine myth itself, what it is and what it *knows* itself to be, we see that this separation of the ideal from the real, this distinction between a world of immediate reality and a world of mediate signification, this opposition of "image" and "object," is alien to it. The "image" does not represent the "thing"; it does not merely stand for the object, but has the same actuality, so that it replaces the thing's immediate presence.[88]

This has particular importance for his understanding of ritual. Ritual is not sympathetic magic, nor is it merely "functional." History and myth, image and object, become merged into a single identity:

> Seen in this light, rites are not originally "allegorical"; they do not merely copy or represent but are absolutely *real*; they are so woven into the reality of action as to form an indispensable part of it. . . . It is no mere play that the dancer in a mythical drama is enacting; the dancer *is* the god, he *becomes* the god.[89]

To Cassirer, language and myth are similar and both represent humanity's earliest attempts at conceptualizing thought by means of symbolic expression. Language and myth are, therefore, the two oldest *symbolic forms*, arrived at by intuition rather than by discursive logic:

> The intuitions about nature and man reflected in the oldest verbal roots, and the processes by which language probably grew up are the same elementary intuitions and the same processes which are expressed in the development of myth.[90]

Myth and language are two ways of expressing human thought symbolically. While myth never really broke out of the "magic circle of its figurative ideas,"[91] language could and did and eventually gave rise to "logical thought and the conception of facts."[92]

Cassirer also understood myth to be the justification for the state:

> In *Mythical Thought*, Cassirer notes with Schelling and the German romantic nationalists that myth lays the basis for nationhood. It is behind the feeling of nationality, and gives it its force. As Schelling says, in a remark Cassirer quotes but whose implications

---

[87] Ernst Cassirer, *The Philosophy of Symbolic Forms, Vol. II: Mythical Thought* (New Haven: Yale University Press, 1955), 34.

[88] Cassirer, *Mythical Thought*, 38.

[89] Cassirer, *Mythical Thought*, 39.

[90] Cassirer, *Language and Myth* (New York: Harper & Brothers, 1946), ix.

[91] Cassirer, *Language and Myth*, ix.

[92] Cassirer, *Language and Myth*, x.

> even he could not fully comprehend at the time, "It is inconceivable that a nation should exist without a mythology."[93]

To Cassirer, the myth which lays the basis for the state is essentially negative; the mythological world view is primitive and deals with ideologies which control society. As opposed to the social control inherent in the myth of the state, Cassirer suggests that science and scientific thought provide the way out of mythological mind set to true freedom.[94] While this characterization of science and the scientific method seems quaint to us now, his views on science and national ideology are understandable considering his experience with Nazi ideology in the 1940s.

Cassirer, while seeking to avoid prescribing a definition of myth and limiting himself to a descriptive enterprise, has nevertheless found a lowest common prescriptive denominator in his definition of myth: 1) that myths are symbolic and pre-logical modes of expression; 2) that myths are stories which serve political functions; and 3) that all myths are held together by the single principle of emotional unity. Strenski criticizes Cassirer on the grounds that even if such a monistic principle is applicable to every myth (a matter of some doubt), by advancing such a general *prescription* for understanding myth he has not really added to our understanding.[95]

Unlike Cassirer, Mircea Eliade does hazard a definition of myth. He understands a myth to be "before everything else, a tale. . . . Modern man's attraction to myths betrays his latent desire to be told stories."[96] These are, of course, more than just entertaining stories. Eliade defines myth as a narration of "sacred history; it relates an event that took place in primordial Time, the fabled time of the 'beginnings.'"[97] Myths also function concretely in society for Eliade as they do for Malinowski and Cassirer:

> The foremost function of myth is to reveal the exemplary models for all human rites and all significant human activities—diet or marriage, work or education, art or wisdom.[98]

Myths, to Eliade, are more complex than the socially functional stories of Malinowski. They have "no other function than to reveal how something came

[93] Strenski, *Four Theories of Myth*, 16.

[94] Cassirer, *The Myth of the State* (New Haven: Yale University Press, 1946), 348 ff.

[95] Strenski, *Four Theories of Myth*, 39.

[96] Strenski, *Four Theories of Myth*, 72.

[97] Mircea Eliade, *Myth and Reality* (New York: Harper & Row, 1963), 5.

[98] Eliade, *Myth and Reality*, 8.

into being. . . . How worlds are born and what happened afterward." [99] Strenski suggests three major properties and functions of myth operative in Eliade's work:

> 1. They are stories *about* origins, beginnings, creations.
> 2. They *function* to provide men with an existential, ontological orientation by narrating the sacred, external events of their own origins, beginnings, or creations.
> 3. They *originate* in a human *experience* of a yearning for such a fundamental orientation. To satisfy the yearning is to achieve a real appropriation of timelessness in the midst of history.[100]

To Eliade, myths are really only references to the *one* myth of the world's creation: "All myths participate in some sort in the cosmological type of myth . . ., how the world came to be." [101] Because all myths are derived from the one primordial myth in Eliade's thought, "Myth teaches the primordial 'stories' that have constituted [archaic man (sic)] existentially. . . . Myths constitute the paradigms for all significant acts."[102] Strenski alerts us to the connection between myth and existential orientation in Eliade's thought. To Eliade, this accounts both for the origin of myths in the human need to find existential orientation in a primal event and the timelessness of myths as vehicles to transport us back to the beginning through ritual and the repetition of the myth.[103] A strange sort of difference between Eliade and both Cassirer and Malinowski emerges at this point: what is existentially *and religiously* foundational to human life is the primal event of creation and its reappropriation in the myth. As opposed to important stories which legitimate human practices and political systems *within human history*, Eliade seems to have a distaste for the merely historical. His program is to transcend human history in the interest of the true and primal *Existenz.*

Claude Lévi-Strauss, like Cassirer, suggested that myth and language function in a very similar fashion:

> Myth is language, functioning at an especially high level where meaning succeeds practically at "taking off" from the linguistic ground on which it keeps on rolling.[104]

---

[99] Strenski, *Four Theories of Myth*, 72.

[100] Strenski, *Four Theories of Myth*, 72.

[101] Strenski, *Four Theories of Myth*, 73.

[102] Strenski, *Four Theories of Myth*, 74.

[103] Strenski, *Four Theories of Myth*, 75.

[104] Claude Lévi-Strauss, *Structural Anthropology* (New York: Basic Books, 1963), 210.

Myths operate by means of binary opposites and the main characters in the myth are "given roles to play in so far as each is worked into a binary opposition."[105] These binary oppositions depend on observable phenomena. Myth is, therefore, a sort of "hyper language," language operating above the level of the observable. Myths go beyond empirical deduction ("binarism"). Myths

> added a transcendental deduction which, going beyond any mere abstract concepts of arbitration between those supreme opposites, life and death, proceeds to create a whole series of images which it then reincorporates into the real world.[106]

Lévi-Strauss takes his understanding of myth much further than this, however. He finds that similar myths exist in widely divergent primitive cultures and these same myths exist in many variants even in the same culture. To Lévi-Strauss, all of the variants of a single myth are really a part of that myth.

For Lévi-Strauss, myth is a "strongly structured, important story."[107] Strenski notes a certain amount of circular reasoning in Lévi-Strauss's understanding of myth—only those stories are classified as myths which *are* strongly structured. Lévi-Strauss, according to Strenski, feels that structure has to do with "shaping and constraining human life in general. With structure we reach fundamental levels of human existence; in myth, says Lévi-Strauss with emphasis, '*Structure is a primordial fact.*'"[108] Structure to Lévi-Strauss has to do with the archetypal and universal patterns of the human mind. Only certain highly structured fields are subject to structural analysis. These are mathematics, music, natural languages, and myth.[109] To Lévi-Strauss they reflect the basic structures of the human psyche. In particular, myths

> teach us a great deal about the societies from which they originate, they help us lay bare their inner workings and clarify the *raison d'être* of beliefs, customs . . . and most importantly, they make it possible to discover operational modes of the human mind.[110]

Myths, to Lévi-Strauss, are important stories which not only reflect a culture's *important* beliefs and practices, but also reflect structured patterns of human existence.

---

[105] Lévi-Strauss, *The Naked Man* (Chicago: University of Chicago Press, 1971), 556.

[106] Lévi-Strauss, *The Naked Man*, 557.

[107] Strenski, *Four Theories of Myth*, 131.

[108] Strenski, *Four Theories of Myth*, 131.

[109] Strenski, *Four Theories of Myth*, 131.

[110] Strenski, *Four Theories of Myth*, 132.

According to Strenski, one of the modern debates about the meaning and significance of myth is that of the myth's relationship to ritual and history. It should be apparent from the foregoing discussion that two of the approaches mentioned above (Cassirer, Malinowski) are more likely to emphasize the political, functional, and historical reality represented by myths. In addition, Cassirer, Malinowski, and Eliade would emphasize the crucial relationship of the cult and ritual to myth-making. Eliade's purpose in doing this, as noted above, is to transcend the historical, to emphasize the myth's connection to the primordial beginning in the repetition of ritual acts. Finally, two approaches find little use in the "merely" historical or political (Eliade, Lévi-Strauss) as a viable explanation for myth. In the case of Lévi-Strauss, indeed, the purpose of myth may only be found in the trans-historical "deep structures" of the human psyche.

If one thing may be gleaned from the foregoing, it is that "myths" are *not* simply stories about the gods. All of the mythologists analyzed above would agree that myths are stories *central to a culture's self-concept* and that they often (Eliade would say always), at least, ground present understandings and practices in the past or primordial time. Less clear is the relationship of the current ritual, social practice, or political reality to the myth.

It is true that the term myth originally meant "story," but in every culture myth means far more than simply a story, even an important one. For the purposes of this study I shall define a myth as a narration of events which occurred at some point in the past or in the primordium in which the divine realm intrudes in such a way into the human realm that human behavior, institutions, or beliefs are forever altered. A myth is a story, but a story about the inbreaking of Eternity into history with implications for the future. If what one means by myth is an understanding of the universe and how it works, how it began and continues to function, then one can do justice to both the synchronic aspect of myth (relationship to the primordium) as well as diachronic aspects (changing political realities bringing about changes in myth and ritual). This approach will have implications for our understanding of Isa 14. For now, it is important to emphasize that the whole poem in Isa 14:4b–21 should be understood as "mythological," in the sense that it is a ritual text (albeit a parody of one) which is a reflection of ancient Near Eastern cosmology tied to a myth of the primordium. It is to this ritual and its reuse in a parody that we turn in chapter two.

Chapter 2
The Literary Genre of Isaiah 14:4b–21

I. Introduction

Much of the current debate surrounding Isa 14:4b–21 centers on a discussion of its genre (*Gattung*). The beginning of the poem, the exclamation אֵיךְ in v. 4b, is an exclamation commonly occurring in laments for the dead (*qînāh*, elegy or dirge), found elsewhere in the Old Testament (e.g., 2 Sam 1:19–27). The superscription of the poem, however, vv. 1–4a, refers to the poem as a *mashal*, prompting many scholars to refer to the poem as a "taunt song." If the poem were written upon the occasion of the death of the "King of Babylon," it could be a parody of the dirge. Nevertheless, while it does seem clear that a traditional style was used to parody the "mourning" for the death of the king, the structure and imagery of the poem do not correspond to those of the *qînôt* elsewhere attested in the Old Testament. It is difficult, therefore, to equate the genre of the poem with the *qînāh* in the Old Testament on formal grounds.

In light of these difficulties and the lack of clarity in the secondary literature, in this chapter I will survey various possibilities of genre with the end in view of situating the poem within its literary, ritual, and religious setting.

II. The Genre of the Poem

A. INTRODUCTION

The superscription to the poem describes it as a *mashal*, or "proverb," usually translated as a "taunt."[1] The term *mashal* does not connote a taunt, nor

---

[1] Gowan is unequivocal in his assessment of the genre of the poem: it is a parody of

does the *mashal* itself comprise a literary genre, but is rather a "formal comparison." The poem has some of the characteristics of a dirge in the Old Testament, but is dissimilar to dirges such as 2 Sam 1 or "city dirges" (laments for the death of a city) in Lam 1, 2, and 4. Donald Gowan has recently suggested that the poem is a parody of a dirge, much like the dirge fragment in Amos 5:2 over the fall of "virgin Israel" tantamount to a "taunt."[2] At stake here is whether the superscription to the poem (vv. 1–4a) should be considered a part of the original composition or whether someone subsequently added to it, giving it a somewhat different title and interpretation than it originally possessed. This question we will take up again in chapter five. In the next section we will look at various formal possibilities in order to say something more concrete about the *Gattung* of the passage.

B. THE *MASHAL*

The only formal designation which Isa 14 makes of the poem is that it is a *mashal* (v. 4). This is a less helpful designation than it might appear, as the term *mashal* is used to describe a number of speech forms: riddles, proverbs, "by-words," allegories, parables, etc. There are two lexical entries for the root משׁל given by Brown, Driver, and Briggs in their lexicon: משׁל I, with the meaning "to be like," and משׁל II, with the meaning "to rule." There have been a number of attempts to relate these two roots semantically (i.e., "to stand," "to speak with power," etc.), without much success.[3] William McKane has suggested that these roots must be considered separately, at least until further evidence comes to light.[4]

---

the dirge, therefore a "taunt." To make blanket statements such as this, however, does not explain the typical form of the dirge (or the taunt) or how much of Isa 14 actually fits into any of these categories. Gowan, *When Man becomes God*, 47.

[2] Gowan, *When Man becomes God*, 47–48.

[3] See J. Schmidt, *Studien zur Stylistik der alttestamentlichen Spruchliteratur*, (Alttestamentliche Abhandlungen 13; Münster: Aschendorffschen, 1936). Note that this attempt to relate the term to "to rule" is by no means a thing of the past. See R. N. Whybray, *Proverbs* (NCB; Grand Rapids: Eerdmans, 1994), 13: "In this sense these were 'powerful words.'" (It may be noted that this kind of power has been linked by some scholars to one of the etymologies proposed for the word *mashal*, that it is related to the verb *mashal*, "to rule.")

[4] Schmidt suggested we do have a case by which we can relate these two roots משׁל: the Arabic *mṯl*. McKane has responded to this by suggesting that if there is an etymological relationship, it can only be through *mṯl* in Arabic, but that even the Arabic root more likely derives from "to be like" than from "to rule": "It may be shown that the idea of 'perfection' or 'excellence' in *mṯl* is a development from 'exemplar' or 'model'. . . . It suggests that 'to be like' is more primary than 'to rule.'" See William McKane, *Proverbs: A New Approach*

A comprehensive survey of literature related to *mashal* and its meaning is not my intent in this study. It will suffice here to conduct a brief survey of important studies on the term since Eissfeldt's 1913 monograph in order to clarify issues and then relate these studies to Isa 14 and its classification as a *mashal*.

The classic study of the meaning of *mashal* in the Old Testament is that of Otto Eissfeldt.[5] Eissfeldt was among the first to suggest that two roots must be posited for *mashal* in the Old Testament and that the basic meaning of משל I is "to be like." [6] Furthermore, Eissfeldt proposed that the earliest *mĕšālîm* were simple folk proverbs, without *parallelismus membrorum*, in the manner of 1 Sam 10:12 or 24:14. These folk sayings were followed by poetic wisdom sayings, crafted by wisdom writers, in parallel stichs. Finally comes the lengthy instruction or discourse literature.[7] Eissfeldt's study has been the point of departure for most recent treatments of *mashal* in the Old Testament.

H. J. Hermisson and Gerhard von Rad, on the other hand, thought that wisdom writings did not so evolve in Israel's history. For them, wisdom, whether of the short proverb or of the lengthy instruction, was a product of wisdom "schools."[8] Von Rad and Hermisson are not interested in the varying types of wisdom literature which may have developed over a lengthy period of time. In fact,

> It should be stated here that, as a matter of principle, we do not see it as our task to go behind the didactic poems in the book of Proverbs to enquire whether perhaps here and there forms of a much older wisdom may be discerned. We accept the material as it is presented by the collectors, and we are justified as understanding it, in that form, as school wisdom.[9]

They are not interested, therefore, in the preliterary form of the *mashal* or its various permutations in Israelite literature.

More recent work on the *mashal* in the Old Testament will tend to follow one or the other of these two approaches, with the caveat that most are not really interested in the *mashal* per se, but in the origins of Israelite wisdom in

---

(OTL; Philadelphia: Westminster, 1970), 25.

[5] Otto Eissfeldt, *Der Maschal im Alten Testament* (BZAW 24; Gießen: Alfred Töpelmann, 1913).

[6] Eissfeldt, *Der Maschal im Alten Testament*, 2, 4.

[7] Eissfeldt, *Der Maschal im Alten Testament*, 43.

[8] Gerhard von Rad, *Wisdom in Israel* (London: SCM, 1972), 16 and Hans Jürgen Hermisson, *Stüdien zur israelitischen Spruchweisheit* (WMANT 28; Neukirchen-Vluyn: Neukirchener Verlag, 1968), 122–136.

[9] von Rad, *Wisdom in Israel*, 11–12.

the popular folk proverb or the wisdom "school." There have not been, consequently, many studies on the *mashal* as an inner-biblical designation for various genres of literature. Some have thrown up their hands in despair of ever finding an underlying or unifying meaning for *mashal*, while others continue to search for such a meaning.

William McKane is heavily indebted to Eissfeldt for his discussion of *mashal*. McKane advances the discussion about the root by maintaining that all of the various genres designated *mashal* must be related to each other in the sense that each may be said to be a "model," "paradigm," or "exemplar."[10] After establishing that the meaning "to rule" was limited to the Hebrew language and that "to be like" is basic to the meaning of √ משל and is distributed thoughout the Semitic languages, he goes on to analyze several examples of one line wisdom sentences, which he takes to be the original form of the *mashal*. Proverbs, characterized by *parallelismus membrorum*, came next, and only later the other longer literary *Gattungen* labeled *měšālîm* (allegories, discourses, etc.). By this time, the term *mashal* had lost its original concreteness.[11] Specifically, the instructions of Prov 1–9 originally have nothing to do with either popular wisdom or the *mashal*, even though they begin a work which bears the title *měšālîm*.[12]

The *mashal* provides a model of behavior which may be laid alongside other phenomena or behaviors. According to McKane,

> The effectiveness of a *mashal* derives from its concreteness and from the circumstances that a model of a general truth stimulates the imagination and clamors for attention, as a matter of fact statement would not.[13]

McKane follows Eissfeldt's undertanding of the development of wisdom from the popular wisdom sentence to instructions and longer discourses. As such, he is really not interested in allegories, parables, prophetic discourses, etc., which are called *měšālîm* but do not demonstrate the same compactness of comparison. This approach has been largely discarded by more recent writers on the meaning of *mashal*, while they tend to keep his and Eissfeldt's understanding that the *mashal* is not a specific *Gattung* and that it implies a comparison.

George Landes was one of the first to attempt to bring all occurrences of the term *mashal* under a common umbrella. He explored all of these occurrences in the biblical text and suggested that the *mashal* aspect of these texts was not in their *Gattung*, but in the fact that they all made literary comparisons (proverbs,

---

[10] McKane, *Proverbs*, 32.

[11] McKane, *Proverbs*, 31–32.

[12] McKane, *Proverbs*, 23.

[13] McKane, *Proverbs*, 28.

parables, allegories), pointed people out as negative comparisons (by-words, taunts), or set forth a discourse or a song comparing one state of being with another (Balaam oracles, Num 23–24; Job's "discourses," Job 27–31).[14] To Landes, one cannot speak of literary characteristics relating to the *mashal*. They are *měšālîm* only in the sense that comparisons are being made:

> Thus once again we see the *mashal* functioning to get its hearers to draw a comparison between the situation adumbrated in its content and their own relation to that situation in order to respond in some appropriate way.[15]

While Landes was one of the first to attempt to organize all references to *mashal* in the Old Testament under one rubric in an intelligible way, one must question whether all occurrences of *mashal* can be so categorized without further nuancing. Granted that comparisons are made (although he possibly stretches the point in his analysis of the Song of Heshbon, Job's discourses in Job 27–31, and the Balaam oracles),[16] is there not a distinction between genres which *imply* comparisons and those in which comparisons might be found? It is this criticism which David Suter makes of Landes's approach.

Suter accepts Landes's proposal in general, but is not happy with his (and Jeremias's) disregard for matters of literary form relating to the *mashal*:[17]

> His [Jeremias's] solution, to define *mashal* as "figurative forms of speech of every kind" is overly colored by the varieties of figures of speech in rabbinic usages cited and fails to account for the fact that, at least in earlier usage, the term usually identifies a speech form of some sort rather than a figure of speech or the presence of figurative language. . . . While Landes's approach is designed to deal with a composition . . . that appears to be different in form from the traditional *měšālîm*, he fails to clarify sufficiently the role of form in the *mashal*.[18]

In his survey of the *Similitudes of Enoch* Suter suggests that there are formal criteria for a text to be considered a *mashal*. In the first place, he suggests that some forms *always* imply a formal comparison (proverbs, allegories, parables), and therefore are always *měšālîm*. In other cases, the comparison is not integral

---

[14] George M. Landes, "Jonah: A *Māšāl*?" in *Israelite Wisdom: Theological and Literary Essays in Honor of Samuel Terrien* (ed. John Gammie et al.; Missoula: Scholars Press, 1978), 137–146.

[15] Landes, "Jonah: A *Māšāl*?" 146.

[16] Landes, "Jonah: A *Māšāl*?" 141–145.

[17] David Suter, "Māšāl in the Similitudes of Enoch," *JBL* 100 (1981): 196. See also J. Jeremias, *The Parables of Jesus* (2nd rev. ed.; New York: Charles Scribner's Sons, 1972), 20.

[18] Suter, "Māšāl in the Similitudes of Enoch," 196–197.

to the genre (discourse, song, oracle). In these cases, the comparison is rhetorical and involves certain topics or themes, such as the comparison between the righteous and the wicked, or Israel's present and future state in the Balaam oracles.[19] In the case of the *Similitudes of Enoch*, he posits an "eschatological/cosmic" element which suggests that the comparison to be made is between a cosmic exemplar and mundane phenomena.

> The pattern proves to be the common thread that runs through the cosmological and eschatological elements of the work, coordinating and uniting them. The ultimate justice of God is defended by establishing a comparison, a *mashal*, between his ordering of the cosmos and the inevitability of the ordering of society that will take place at the last judgment. The result is similar to an allegory in that comparison occurs at a number of points within the work. The righteous and the kings and the mighty of the earth both have their counterparts in the heavenly world—the stars, the angels and the elect on the one hand, and the fallen angels on the other—and the action of God, depicted through the metaphors of weighing and measuring, is applied to both cosmos and society.[20]

Not every comparison to be made is a *mashal*. Phenomena to be compared may simply be similar and invite such comparisons. To Suter, the *Similitudes of Enoch* comprise a *mashal* only in the sense that there is a comparison of cosmic, paradigmatic phenomena to earthly reality:

> The function of the cosmological material in the Similitudes is mythological in character: the creative activity of the deity in defeating the powers of chaos and establishing order is transferred from cosmos to society through a *mashal*.[21]

There is a connection between Suter's paradigm model and the approach to myth taken in this analysis of Isa 14. Indeed, Suter even uses the term "mythological" with respect to the *mĕšālîm* of the *Similitudes of Enoch*. Myths are narratives which link current societal practices with events and personages of the primordium. *Mĕšālîm*, according to Suter, invite comparison of divine exemplars with current observation and experience.

Timothy Polk [22] builds on the work of Landes and Suter. He suggests that Landes and Suter are essentially correct in suggesting that the *mashal* is not a *Gattung* but rather a designation for formal comparisons, paradigms, and models. He furthers their work by suggesting that these comparisons lend themselves to

---

[19] Suter, "Māšāl in the Similitudes of Enoch," 200.

[20] Suter, "Māšāl in the Similitudes of Enoch," 208.

[21] Suter, "Māšāl in the Similitudes of Enoch," 211.

[22] Timothy Polk, "Paradigms, Parables, and *Mĕšālîm*: On Reading the Māšāl in Scripture," CBQ 45 (1983): 564–583.

religious discourse by involving all readers or hearers in parables and paradigms of human behavior which force decisions and bring judgment.[23] Indeed, he calls this approach to *mashal* the "paradigmatic-parabolic" approach.[24] Polk applies Suter's and Landes's analyses and takes them a step further: to Polk, all *měšālîm* are models and paradigms of reality, inviting comparison by the reader and affecting decision in that reader's life:

> The comparisons . . . must have been thought to model a reality always capable of impinging upon a particular readership. Hence, when the elements of the passage turned metaphorical, then the depiction of Israel's history as one of judgment and salvation became paradigmatic such that Israel's history becomes *trans*historical and the passage can say, "Here is Israel's life and death and destiny, and not just sixth-century Israel's."[25]

In important ways, McKane, Landes, and Suter all help us understand that the term *mashal* designates "model" or "paradigm." This designation is not limited to a particular *Gattung* (Landes, McKane), but is usually restricted to certain literary forms or thematic content (Suter). Finally, *měšālîm* are paradigmatic in the sense that they are transhistorical: they are models of behavior which may be based in cosmological reality and force decisions upon the hearer/reader (Suter, Polk). The historical/developmental model of the *mashal* favored by Eissfeldt and McKane would seem to be totally eclipsed by the "paradigmatic/transhistorical" model.

Susan Niditch attempted to reintegrate, to some degree, the historical dimension into the *mashal*. She raises several appropriate questions in her chapter on the *mashal* in *Folklore and the Hebrew Bible*:

> How does one define and understand the Israelite term *mashal*? Is the *mashal* a meaningful literary category in Israelite tradition? Does a genre recognized among the Israelites lie behind the Bible's many invocations of the term?[26]

Niditch answers these question in the affirmative. She suggests that *mashal* is an "ethnic genre," that which is "passed down through generations, inherited knowledge."[27] She follows Eissfeldt closely in her understanding that *mashal* derives from a root "to be like," in the sense that the *mashal* is "something

---

[23] Polk, "Paradigms, Parables, and *Měšālîm*," 565, 570.

[24] Polk, "Paradigms, Parables, and *Měšālîm*," 565, 573.

[25] Polk, "Paradigms, Parables, and *Měšālîm*," 583.

[26] Susan Niditch, *Folklore and the Hebrew Bible* (Minneapolis: Fortress, 1993), 71–72.

[27] Niditch, *Folklore and the Hebrew Bible*, 75.

which evokes something else. It is similar to the real thing, but not the real thing, a model."[28] Finally, she attempts a definition of *mashal*:

> Drawn from personal memory and experience and built upon the traditions that are claimed by a folk group to be its collective memory, the *mashal* is a form of oblique and artful communication that sets up an analogy between the communication . . . and the real-life settings of the listeners. The *mashal* provides a model of and a model for reality. . . . Abstract and compact, in its ambiguity of meaning, the *mashal* allows for varying responses and a wide range of applicability.[29]

Niditch's analysis is insightful and has advanced the discussion of *mashal* beyond the single defintion for the term provided by most earlier commentators. However, her definition of *mashal* as an "ethnic genre" may suffer from being too broad. She builds on Eissfeldt's (comparison arising from proverbs and similitudes) and McKane's (*mashal* as model or exemplar) understanding of *mashal* and she accepts Polk's definition (that *mashal* is a "model of " and a "model for" a cosmogonic worldview). She suggests that the synchronic approach to *mashal* has much to commend it over the diachronic, evolutionary approach of Eissfeldt.

It is doubtful whether every usage of the term *mashal* can be understood in these terms, however. Why, for example, does the writer or compiler of Job only refer to the speeches in Job 27 and 29 as *měšālîm* (see 27:1 and 29:1)? Why not the wise sayings and discourses of the preceding three cycles of speeches? Are Job 27 and 29 cosmogonic models in a way that Job's other speeches are not? I suggest that, while Niditch's model has much to commend it, one ought not to overlook entirely Eissfeldt's evolutionary model. In Job, for example, there are several references to *mashal* used in the sense of a negative or positive likeness (Job 13:12, "proverb"; 17:6, "by-word"; 30:19, *hitpael* verbal form, "to be like," and 41:25, "likeness"). The other two occurrences (27:1 and 29:1) seem to introduce extended wisdom discourses.

I will build on Eissfeldt's analysis by suggesting that the occurrences of *mashal* in the instances cited above are older than the introductory statements in chapters 27 and 29 and can be understood as negative or positive models. As most commentators on the book of Job have seen, however, the text of Job has been disturbed at 27:1, after short, and probably disturbed, speeches by Bildad. Also, Job 27:1 anomalously begins with ויסף איוב שאת משלו ויאמר, as opposed to the normal introduction of the discourses, יען PN ויאמר. Job 27:1–12 begins Job's protestations of innocence, taken up at more length in chapter 31. Job 27:13–23 may well be either Zophar's "missing" third speech, or the continuation of Bildad's third speech, as it is reflective of thoroughgoing

[28] Niditch, *Folklore and the Hebrew Bible*, 76.

[29] Niditch, *Folklore and the Hebrew Bible*, 86.

retribution theology as opposed to Job's otherwise consistent protests of innocence and criticism of such thought. With the breakdown of the dialogues, the editor has apparently attached separate speeches of Job by means of the introductory formula given above. My suggestion is that this formula is reflective of later wisdom terminology, when *mashal* has ceased to mean a model or paradigm and simply means "wise saying" or "wisdom discourse." This is particularly helpful when looking at the instructions, proverbs, wisdom sayings, etc. of Proverbs, all of which fall under the broad umbrella of *mĕšālîm*. By the compilation of Proverbs, the term *mashal* had come to be applied to any wisdom utterance, whether maxim, riddle, instruction, discourse, allegory, or proverb.

In general, however, Niditch's approach is correct and helpful. Particularly when one looks at Ezekiel and compares the fifteen occurrences of the term, one is confronted with a wide semantic range, utilized by a single author (12:22–23; 14:8; 16:44; 17:2; 18:2–3; 21:5; 24:3). These run the gamut from single line folk sayings (12:22), to by-words (14:8), to riddles (17:2), to allegories (21:5). One's definition of the term must be commensurate with its semantic range, particularly by a single author in one historical period.

Several conclusions may be drawn from the surveys of the literature above: 1) *mĕšālîm* do not themselves comprise a formal literary genre. 2) *mĕšālîm*, whether in short proverbs or lengthier allegories or parables, are intended to provide models, exemplars, or paradigms for the comparison of experienced or observed phenomena. 3) If *mĕšālîm* provide such exemplars or paradigms, their exemplary nature is due to processes or phenomena observed in the natural order, based in creation, and having their inception in the primordium. 4) Myths, while not identical with *mĕšālîm*, function similarly by providing paradigms of behavior in the primordium which are reflected in society in the ages which ensue. It is perhaps for this very reason that Isa 14:4b–21, while replete with mythopoeic images, is called a *mashal*.

We have noted above that the term *mashal* does not specify a particular *Gattung*, but may be used of any number of formal genres. The question is, in what sense does the author of Isa 14:4b–21 understand the poem to be a *mashal*? He is obviously intending to make a comparison, but what kind of comparison is being made? How close is the analogy which he intends to draw?

There is at least one clue internal to the poem and indicating the author's intent in calling it a *mashal*. V. 10 quotes the Rephaim gaping in wonder at the once mighty monarch and saying, "you have become like us!" (*nimšāltā*), referring to his newly won status as a denizen of the netherworld, but one who has come without benefit of proper burial and netherworld credentials. The comparison is both positive and negative. On the one hand, he is a king and is indeed dead. On the other hand, he does not have a sepulcher nor a throne in Sheol, so he is unlike those dead kings of past generations who had an honorable burial and continue to receive honor in Sheol.

This, however, does not explain how the entire *poem* is a *mashal*, rather than some of the elements in the poem.[30] If *měšālîm* provide models of behavior or comparisons of earthly traits or behaviors with cosmic exemplars (Suter, Polk), the reason for the designation of the poem as a *mashal* becomes clear. Insofar as the *mashal* is a comparison it must have both a "referent" (the behavior, story, ritual, etc. actually referred to) and the "analogy" (the metaphorical comparison, the *mashal*). Suter, Landes, and Polk's suggestion that *měšālîm* provide paradigmatic/cosmic exemplars at times, at least, tied to a mythological world view, is particularly helpful in the case of Isa 14. The referent in Isa 14 is the king of Babylon in all his presumptuousness and arrogance and his resounding fall from the position he had arrogated to himself. The analogy is provided by the dirge sung over the demise of the king with its attendant cosmology.

Further discussion of the dirge form and its relationship to the *mashal* in Isa 14 must wait until chapter five. It is important for now to underscore the exemplary, cosmological nature of the dirge in Isa 14. It does not depict a literal dirge ritual any more than Ezek 32 does, or than Jer 17 depicts true trees and eagles. The king in all his arrogance attempts to take upon himself divine prerogatives. He wishes supreme dominance ("above the stars of ʾEl I will set my throne") and authority rivaling the gods ("I will sit in the mount of assembly in the heights of Saphon"). His fall to the depths and loss of all power and prestige will mirror his desire for supreme power and authority. The analogy to the king's arrogance and judgment is provided by the parody of the dirge. The imagery associated with the dirge is the imagery of death, Sheol, and other cosmological elements. Thus the dirge provides a particularly suitable vehicle for the *mashal* as "cosmic exemplar." It provides a warning to all would-be tyrants that their fall and shame will exactly correspond to the heights and glory to which they aspire.

---

[30] The typical approach is to see only certain elements as pertaining to the *mashal*, such as the ascent/descent terminology in vv. 12–15, or to translate *mashal* as "taunt" or "song." If the entire poem is viewed as a *mashal*, its parabolic and exemplary character become clear. The poem fits the category of parody. It is cast in the form of a funeral dirge for a dead king, but the intent of the dirge is to ridicule. Parodies only work if the intended audience is aware of 1) both components of the formal comparison (the royal and exalted king of Babylon and a maggot-covered corpse), and 2) the fact that this is a parody of, and not a true, funeral dirge. By the same token, the poem is not a proverb because another *Gattung* (the dirge) is used and parodied. It is not an allegory because the king of Babylon is always presented as the king of Babylon and not as a tree, or an eagle, or some other symbolic object or being. It is not a riddle, because both the comparison and the parody are clear.

In summary, it is important to keep in mind what the introduction to the poem itself has to say about its genre. First, the designation of the poem as a *mashal* does not in itself connote a particular *Gattung*. It is rather an indication that a formal comparison is about to be made. That formal comparison may take many forms; in this case, it is a "lament for the dead," or dirge. Second, when the *mashal* uses formal *Gattungen* in order to parody them, the intent is usually to ridicule or taunt. It is to the "taunt song" that we now turn.

C. THE *MASHAL* AS PARODY OR "TAUNT SONG"

Otto Eissfeldt considered the *Spottgedicht* (taunt song) to be derived from the "folk proverb."[31] Most commentators today would agree with Eissfeldt that Isa 14:4a refers to a type of *mashal* known as a "taunt song." A negative proverb or saying, therefore, is a taunt or "by-word" much as we today refer to a traitor as a "Benedict Arnold." As we have seen, however, a *mashal* is a formal comparison. That comparison may be positive or negative in tone and may be short (proverbs, maxims) or extended (allegories, parables). To refer to the poem in Isa 14:4b–21 as a "taunt" to some degree prejudges the nature of the comparison to be made and also leaves many questions unanswered. In what sense is it a taunt song? Is the object of the taunt (ostensibly the king of Babylon) still alive (and is therefore sent to Sheol before his time in a most impolite manner), or is he already dead (in which case this taunt is the ancient equivalent of spitting on his grave)? These questions will be taken up at greater length below, but for now it is important to stress that "taunt song" is not a formal *Gattung*, but one may taunt or be taunted by any number of formal media.

If the *mashal* against the king of Babylon is a parody, what is being parodied? I suggested above that the *mashal* is not a specific *Gattung* but uses other *Gattungen* to make formal comparisons. Likewise, a parody relies on the unexpected or humorous "misuse" of an established form. These points raise at least two questions. First, how does Isa 14 function as a parody? Second, are there other examples of such unexpected use of established forms in the Old Testament or literature from the ancient Near East? I will reserve comment on the first question until my discussion of the dirge below.

The second question may be answered in the affirmative, although we are somewhat hampered by the lack of specific examples from the ancient Near East. This lack is due to a host of factors, but a significant one is that we do not thoroughly comprehend established forms of discourse in the ancient world and

---

[31] Eissfeldt, *Der Maschal im Alten Testament*, 43.

therefore the parodies of such forms escape us. Fortunately, some are too blatant to miss. We possess a Neo-Assyrian inscription, previously unpublished but now made available in the *State Archives of Assyria* series.[32] I include a translation of the text below, taken from this volume.

1. K 1351

Open the tablet container and [re]ad the stele, [learn the fate] . . . like a dog, Bel-eṭir, the son of Ibâ:

When Ṣallâ had not yet met his fate, he, a lowly [ ], the king did not know him, a slave waiting upon Šamaš-Ibni, the son of a lowly fisherman n[ot . . . king-]ship, the shit-bucket (sic) of Zeru-kinu, an empty talker, a raped comrade of Nummuraya, said:

"In Assyria and Babylonia there is no one equal to me. The woman . . . has praised me. Where in the whole world is my rival?"

[ ] her, who did not [ ] to him reverently. [ ] did not drink, did not [ ] feared his lady, the lady Hulalitu. [ ] was greener than all of these [ ] a mare they pass the street [ ] does not [under]stand does not see, does not [ ] the horizon, a mare in [ ] a mare [ ] bread [ ] his marsh in [ ] when in his fishery [ ] scandalous [ ] let us [ ] [. . . spo]ke foolishness with him:

"Who has taken from me the son of Bibie, who has darkened your radiant countenance?"

Later, by way of purification, she called his name "angry Pazuzu, the son of Hanbi." In the face of this, mankind humbly bowed down, saying: "This is correct behavior, reverence!"

"This is the stele which the prostitute set up for the son of Ibâ, the farter (sic), and left for posterity."

Indeed, in the whole, in the heart of this, there is this teaching for the future: like one who is lacking in understan[ding, in]competent, he praised himself, [ ] his endless obscenities from [his] heart.

He himself did the talking, he himself did the praising, he himself did the saying, he himself did the [glor]ifying, and became a proverbial expression and obscenity in the mouth of mankind.

And as for him, he did not know [ ] with his heart.

It is not a (deeply) incised hand, this which I wrote, very tiny [ ].

---

[32] K 1351 (Alasdair Livingstone, *Court Poetry and Literary Miscellanea* [SAA 3; Helsinki: Helsinki University Press, 1989], 64–66.

K 1351 is clearly a parody of a memorial stele, written on a clay tablet. It is a classic case of being "damned by faint praise": it refers to a memorial stele set up in "honor" of a man whose only claim to public praise was that which he so richly endowed upon himself. Alasdair Livingstone in his introduction suggests that this is an example of a farce, which "plays on the genre of *narû* literature."[33] He further suggests that there are a number of allusions in this text to historical events having to do with rebellious activity against Assyria. The particular *narû* which K 1351 parodies is the *Cuthean Legend of Naram-Sin.*[34] Note that a formal comparison is made with *narû* literature, but the comparison is a parody, damning rather than praising the subject of the memorial stele. As a formal parody, the analogy with the original is quite close. Note the formal opening line of the stele,[35] the discussion of past "accomplishments," and the scribal colophon at the end.[36]

Two other features of K 1351 need to be mentioned. First, the inscription leaves us with no indication whether Bel-eṭir had already died. We simply do not know enough from this inscription to say one way or the other, except that a memorial stele is referred to. This is in itself no necessary indication that Bel-eṭir had already died, as the inscription is a parody of *narû* literature. One might assume that a parody intended to ridicule a person would be much more effective if that person were still alive. Indeed, Livingstone assumes that Bel-eṭir is very much alive and labels the inscription, "Warning to Bel-eṭir."[37] Note how similar this "monument" to a vain leader, whether dead or alive, is to Isa 14:4b–21.

---

[33] Livingstone, *Court Poetry*, xxviii.

[34] Livingstone, *Court Poetry*, xxviii. For a more or less complete transcription and translation of the Standard Babylonian version of the *Cuthean Legend of Naram-Sin*, see "Cuthean Legend of Naram-Sin" (Joan G. Westenholz, *Legends of the Kings of Akkade: The Texts* [Mesopotamian Civilizations 7; Winona Lake: Eisenbrauns, 1997], 300–331).

[35] Compare with the *Cuthean Legend of Naram-Sin*: "Open the tablet box and read out the stele."

[36] Compare with the *Cuthean Legend*, ("Cuthean Legend of Naram-Sin," 327 and 331), lines 151, 154–155, and 177–180:

I have made a tablet-box for you and inscribed a stele for you . . .
Read this stele!
Hearken unto the words of this stele!
You who have read my inscription
and thus have gotten yourself out (of trouble),
you who have blessed me, may a future (ruler)
Bless you!

Note that the intent of the inscribing (and the adding of the colophon at the end) of K 1351 is certainly not to bless Bel-eṭir.

[37] K 1351, 64.

Second, the writer of the inscription suggests that all of Bel-eṭir's bravado had made him a "proverb and obscenity in the mouth of mankind" (til-te u_3 bil-te ina KA UN.MEŠ). As in Isa 14, Bel-eṭir is ostensibly mourned and remembered via a formal literary medium. The net result of such a parody, however, is to underscore the total incongruity between the elegy form and the actual desserts of the individual in question (one is reminded of the song, "Pore Jud is Daid" in the musical "Oklahoma," by Rodgers and Hammerstein).[38] Not only has Bel-eṭir made himself a proverb (*tiltu*, parallel to *mashal* in Isa 14:4a), but the function of the memorial stele is to accentuate such a reputation.

2. Ezekiel 32:18–32

Another biblical dirge parody besides Isa 14:4b–21 is found in Ezek 32:18–32. Here Ezekiel uses the form of the dirge to send the Egyptian king to the deepest and least desirable abode in Sheol, rather than use the form to bless and speed him on his way to bliss and a throne in the underworld. It is curious that Ezek 32 is introduced as a "lamentation (*qînāh*) for Pharaoh, king of Egypt," though there is really no lament in form or content until v. 18. Vv. 2–15 appear to be a typical "oracle against a foreign nation," but this oracle begins with the designation of lament and ends in v. 16 with the comment, "this is a lamentation; it shall be chanted. The women of the nations shall chant it, over Egypt and all its hordes they shall chant it." The lament proper is in vv. 18–32, which resembles the lament for the dead Ugaritic king Niqmaddu (see below on the dirge). What makes this passage a parody is that its form is that of the dirge, with the commandment to "wail" over him (v. 18), yet the content does not reflect the intent of the form: v. 19, "Who do you surpass in beauty?" (i.e., no one, a reversal of a typical burial eulogy; see 2 Sam 1:19, 23) and "Go down, be laid to rest among the uncircumcised" (a parody of the ceremony of an apparent ritual of sending the dead king to his rest among the dead kings who have gone before; see the Niqmaddu burial below and the tragedy of death among the uncircumcised in 2 Sam 1:20). See also v. 31: "When Pharaoh sees them (i.e., all of the uncircumcised kings of various nations with their armies who have gone down to the pit in shame), he will be consoled for all his hordes." It is obvious that this "consolation" he will experience is the consolation of knowing that Pharaoh is only one among the many dead kings who reside in shame in the realm of the dead.

---

[38] Richard Rodgers and Oscar Hammerstein II, *Oklahoma! A Musical Play* (New York: Williamson Music, 1943), 93.

3. Conclusion

This passage, as with the Bel-eṭir inscription, uses a traditional form (*qînāh*) and parodies it. Also, as is probable with Bel-eṭir, the king of Egypt is not dead, but is "mourned" with a funeral dirge before his death. Isa 14 also uses a traditional form, in this case much like Ezek 32. Whether the king who is mourned in Isa 14 is alive or dead on the occasion of the delivery of the dirge is another matter and will be taken up in chapter 5.

D. The Various Forms of Laments for the Dead

1. Introduction

There are a number of examples of laments for the dead, also known as dirges or elegies, in the Old Testament. There are certain elements characteristic of the dirge, although in many cases the dirge is attenuated and not intended to convey the entire form (see 2 Sam 3:33–34). Other forms show similarity to the dirge and seem to have formal characteristics in common with it. These are the city lament and, some have argued, the *hôy* oracle.[39] Of these, the city lament most closely corresponds to the form of the Old Testament dirge. The *hôy* oracle contains a similar exclamation, "ah!" (see *ʾêḵ*, "how!" in many Old Testament dirges), but will not be treated here, as it does not share the same background, function, or formal characteristics with the lament for the dead to warrant inclusion. I will briefly mention city laments in the Old Testament and the ancient Near East, but concentrate my attention on elegies for private individuals and for kings.

2. City Laments

The city lament is a well-represented genre in the ancient Near Eastern corpus of literary remains and is found in the Old Testament as well. At least

---

[39] See J. J. M. Roberts, *Nahum, Habakkuk, and Zephaniah* (OTL; Louisville: Westminster/John Knox, 1991), 118. Roberts suggests that the *hôy* oracle is simply an attention-getting exclamation, much like the English "hey!" Waldemar Janzen, *Mourning Cry and Woe Oracle* (BZAW 125; Berlin: Walter de Gruyter, 1972), 1–6, 27–34, had previously proposed that the *hôy* oracle was a cry of mourning for the dead. He suggests that the cry *hôy* originated in the funeral dirge, although only 1 Kgs 13:30 connects *hôy* with a funeral dirge or funerary context. Roberts quotes Isa 55:1, where *hôy* is used in a specifically non-mourning context, as evidence that the background and function of the *hôy* oracle is other than Janzen supposed. I follow Roberts rather than Janzen in excluding the *hôy* oracle from consideration.

five of these laments are extant from Sumer, dating to the period immediately following the destruction of the Ur III civilization.[40] These five are the *Lament Over the Destruction of Ur,*[41] the *Lament Over the Destruction of Sumer and Ur,*[42] the *Eridu Lament,*[43] the *Uruk Lament,*[44] and the *Lament Over Nippur.*[45] Other "canonical" laments are known from Sumer, some with some of the characteristics of the city lament, such as *The Curse of Agade,*[46] *Oh Angry Sea (a-ab-ba hu-luh-ha)*[47] and possibly others. Mark Cohen has suggested that the *balag* lament, so called because of the use of the *balag* instrument in its performance, and the city lament are quite close. He does not equate these, however. The city laments seem to have been laments intoned over the destruction of important Sumerian cities, especially with reference to temples in those cities, and the invocation for the god or goddess to return to the city and temple. *Balag* laments, on the other hand, were used in rituals in Mesopotamia for hundreds of years, without the necessity of the actual destruction of a city. They were used especially when old temples were razed and new ones erected, or for major repairs on temples. The main difference, according to Cohen, is that the *balag* has no reference to an actual historical event (the destruction of a city by a real enemy), while the city laments always do. Accordingly, the *balag* is not actually a "dirge," but a "congregational ritual lament." [48] The reason to include

---

[40] Mark Cohen suggests that the city lament and the general, "canonical" laments written in Sumerian and Akkadian down to the Seleucid period (the so-called *balag* laments) are quite similar. See Cohen, *The Canonical Lamentations of Ancient Mesopotamia* (Potomac: Capital Decisions Limited, 1988), 15, 24, 33–39.

[41] "The Lament Over the Destruction of Ur," translated by Samuel N. Kramer (*ANET*, 455).

[42] Piotr Michalowski, *The Lament Over the Destruction of Sumer and Ur* (Winona Lake: Eisenbrauns, 1989).

[43] M. W. Green, "The Eridu Lament," *JCS* 30 (1978): 127–161.

[44] M. W. Green, "The Uruk Lament," *JAOS* 104 (1984): 253–279.

[45] Samuel N. Kramer, "The Lamentation Over the Destruction of Nippur," ASJ 13 (1991): 1–26.

[46] Jerrold Cooper, *The Curse of Agade* (Baltimore: Johns Hopkins University Press, 1983), 20 has suggested that the *Curse of Agade* is neither *balag* nor city lament nor historical narrative, but a combination of all these.

[47] The author mentions the five canonical city laments, as well as the *Curse of Agade*, as the extant city laments, but then includes *Oh Angry Sea* as a "congregational lament" over a city. See A ABBA HULUHA in Mark Cohen, *Canonical Lamentations*, 272–318, 374–400.

[48] See F. W. Dobbs-Allsopp, *Weep, O Daughter of Zion: A Study of the City-Lament Genre in the Hebrew Bible* (Biblica et Orientalia 44; Rome: Pontifical Biblical Institute, 1993), 13–14. Dobbs-Allsopp has suggested, following Cohen and others, that first millennium B.C.E. *balags* and *eršemmas* are the genetically linked successors of the earlier city laments,

city laments in this analysis is that they show formal similarities to the dirge in the Old Testament.

The Old Testament itself contains a number of city laments.[49] Of course, the most well-known example of city laments in the Old Testament is that of the book of Lamentations (chaps. 1, 2, and 4).[50] One might characterize the city lament as a "lament for the death of a city."[51] As such, one ought to expect certain formal similarities between city laments and elegies, as I have suggested. City laments tend to follow a regular pattern whether Sumerian or biblical. These laments are poetic, literary productions, not *ad hoc*. They are easily analyzed in terms of structure, as they tend to be quite repetitive. The structure of the Sumerian city lament is simple, according to M. W. Green: all city laments possess the common themes of the destruction of cities and temples in Sumer, assignment of responsibility, abandonment by the gods, restoration of the cities and temples, and the return of the gods.[52] Note the similarity to the biblical book of Lamentations:

1) The destruction of Jerusalem: 1:1–7, 10–13, 15, 2:1–9, 17, 21–22, 3:1–20 (portrayed in a "personal lament"), 43–48, 4:1–12, 17–20, 5:2–6, 8–16a.

2) Assignment of responsibility: 1:8–9, 18–19, 2:14–16, 3:37–42, 4:13–16, 5:7, 16b.

---

being produced and copied down to the Seleucid period.

[49] See Dobbs-Allsopp, *Weep, O Daughter of Zion*, 97–155, where he analyzes the city lament genre in the Hebrew Bible. He concludes that the "city lament genre's existence outside of Lamentations would seem to be established" (p. 156).

[50] See especially Claus Westermann, *Lamentations: Issues and Interpretation* (Minneapolis: Fortress, 1994), especially p. 18, where he finds very close parallels between the *Lament Over the Destruction of Ur* and the biblical book of Lamentations.

[51] Westermann, *Lamentations*, 1–23.

[52] M. W. Green, "The Uruk Lament," 253. Dobbs-Allsopp suggests the presence of a few more structural elements: "subject and mood," "structure and poetic technique," "divine agent of destruction," and "weeping goddess." Green's analysis is simpler and adequate to demonstrate both the similarities and the differences between city laments and other *qînôt*. Note also the discrepancy between Green's analysis (that the city laments are intended to undergird and legitimate the current royal regime in the Isin-Larsa period, after the devastation of the Ur III empire and the rebuilding of the cities and the temples of Sumer) with that of Thorkild Jacobsen, *The Harps That Once . . .: Sumerian Poetry in Translation* (New Haven: Yale University Press, 1987), 447. Jacobsen suggests that the cities and temples were not yet rebuilt and that the purpose for the writing of the laments was to "calm the disturbed, turbulent, suffering soul of Nanna, the god of Ur, so that he can regain his composure and think of rebuilding his destroyed home" (p. 447). Jacobsen does not focus his analysis upon the political legitimation of the Sumerian ruler effected by the production and acceptance of the city lament, on the part of both gods and people, as Green does.

3) Abandonment/judgment by God: 1:12–15, 2:1–8, 17, 22, 3:1–18, 3:43–45, 4:11, 16, 5:20–22.

4) Restoration of Jerusalem/return of God: there is no specific mention of a restored Jerusalem in the book. There is explicit reference to an end to exile: 4:22. The place of the restoration of the city and the return of God to it seems to be taken in the book of Lamentations by prayers for God to restore his people and look again with favor on them: 1:21–22, 2:18–19, 3:21–42, 49–51, 55–66, 4:22a, 5:19–21.

In broad terms, there is a reflection of Green's analysis in the book of Lamentations and, according to Dobbs-Allsopp, in other Old Testament passages.[53] This even carries over into the actual ordering of the themes, although such ordering is general and not uniform: destruction tends to come first, followed by assignment of blame, followed by God's abandonment of the city (taking the form of his active judgment), followed by prayers for God's renewed favor and presence.

One aspect of these city laments which Green does not pick up and which directly relates to biblical dirges is their relation to the dirge. City laments and dirges in the Old Testament are very similar. Note the following motifs present in Lamentations and in many other dirges:

1) Exclamation: "How (אֵיךְ) lonely sits the city" (1:1); "How like a widow" (1:1); "How the gold has grown dim" (4:1). Note the relationship between this type of expression and virtually all of the other individual or city dirges, as well as its relationship to Sumerian laments.

2) Summons to mourn: 2:18–19.

3) The "Contrast Motif":

- Memory of past glory/beauty: 1:1, 7, 2:1–3, 15b, 4:1–2a, 5a, 7, 10a.
- Present reality of destruction/death: 1:1–6, 2:2ff, most of chapter 4, 5:1–18, etc.

4) Affect of the death upon bystanders: 1:7, 12, 21, 2:10, 15–16.

5) Bewilderment that the death could have occurred: 1:12–17, most of chapter 2 (see especially 2:13, 20–22).[54]

---

[53] Dobbs-Allsopp, *Weep, O Daughter of Zion*, 100–153, has identified some fragmentary "city laments," laments containing many of the motifs of the ancient Near Eastern city lament, in the Old Testament outside of the book of Lamentations, mostly in the prophetic literature. These include Isa 1:7–9, 21–26, 3:25–4:1, 13, 14:28–32, 15–16, 22:1–14, 23:1–14, 47:1–15, 52:1–2, Jer 4–6, 8–10, 46–48, 49:1–6 and 23–27, chaps. 50–51, portions of Ezek 26–28 and 32, Mic 1:2–16, 4:9–10, Nahum, Zeph 2:13–15, 3:14–20, and most of Amos 5.

[54] This category is less clear, but I think justifiably present in Lamentations.

These are the elements which occur in dirges in the Old Testament, according to Claus Westermann (see more on the dirge form below). They are the themes which make it a dirge or *qînāh*, together, often, with its 3/2 "dirge" meter. True laments for the dead, however, do not include the restoration of the dead to life, nor do they typically include statements concerning abandonment by God or the gods, nor a request for them to return to the deceased. We see, then, that city laments are similar to dirges in some formal characteristics, but their purpose and structure vary from that of the dirge.[55]

3. The *Qînāh* or Funeral Dirge

Most scholars up to the present have assumed that Isa 14:4b–21 is a *qînāh* and that this is a form well-attested in the Hebrew Bible. Claus Westermann has recently suggested that there are no complete *qînôt* in the Hebrew Bible and that only 2 Sam 3:33–34 and Jer 38:22—along with 2 Sam 1:19–27 and Jer 9:16–21, which are "artistic imitations" of true dirges in Westermann's view—even come close to being true dirges.[56] Other laments designated as *qînôt* in the Bible are "communal laments" or prophetic judgment speeches with one or two dirge-like elements embedded in them, according to Westermann. To use the term *qînāh* is, therefore, a misnomer. According to Westermann, the true *qînāh* has an identifiable and fixed structure and was originally quite short and oral. Based on Hedwig Jahnow's seminal work on the dirge form, *Das hebräische Leichenlied im Rahmen der Völkerdichtung*,[57] Westermann sees the following elements as constitutive of a dirge: the mourning cry ("ah," "alas," "how"), the summons to mourn, the notice that a death has occurred, the contrast motif, the effect of the death upon bystanders, and bewilderment or questions that the death could have happened to the deceased.

Jahnow's categories have been very influential upon succeeding generations of scholars' analyses of the dirge form, as evidenced recently by Westermann. None of the dirges Jahnow allows in the Old Testament, nor the attenuated imitations of these dirges, possess all of these dirge elements. Certain of Jahnow's elements are commonly attested, however, in the true dirges and in the prophetic reappropriation of dirge elements, themes, and structure. Correspondingly, I

---

[55] This analysis agrees with that of Dobbs-Allsopp, who understands the city lament and the dirge to be related, but distinct, genres. See Dobbs-Allsopp, *Weep, O Daughter of Zion*, 9.

[56] Westermann, *Lamentations*, 1–2.

[57] Hedwig Jahnow, *Das hebräische Leichenlied im Rahmen der Völker-dichtung* (Gießen: Alfred Töpelmann, 1923).

will focus attention upon those elements which more commonly occur in Old Testament dirges or dirge-like literature.

Furthermore, the themes and structure of dirges within and outside of the Old Testament would appear to be more complex than Jahnow and Westermann allow. Certain dirges, in particular those for dead kings, exhibit few of the themes outlined above and, indeed, introduce other elements not included in the typical dirge pattern as presented by Jahnow and Westermann. I will look at several examples of dirges in the ancient Near East and in the Old Testament, therefore, in order to build on the work of Jahnow and Westermann relative to the form and ideology of the dirge.

a. Dirges outside of the Old Testament

There are few preserved funeral laments which may shed light on the analysis of the dirge in Isa 14. Among these are 1) two Sumerian elegies in the Pushkin Museum, 2) RS 34.126/*KTU* 1.161, an actual royal funeral lament from Ugarit on the occasion of the death of king Niqmaddu and the accession of his son ʿAmmurapi, and 3) and *The Death of Ur-Nammu and his Descent into the Underworld.*

i. *Funeral Dirges in the Pushkin Museum*

Important to the ascertaining of the form of the funeral dirge is the translation and notes of two Sumerian funeral dirges at the Pushkin Museum in Moscow, translated and analyzed by Samuel N. Kramer.[58] These are among the few "private" dirges so far extant from the Sumero-Akkadian corpus. As such, they are important for the comparative analysis of dirges in the Old Testament. They are both written by a certain Ludingirra, whose father Nanna was killed in battle. He was also the husband of a certain Nawirtum, who apparently fell victim to a sudden illness. As such, they are "private," or "common" (i.e., non-royal) dirges, intended to eulogize, lament, and pray for the welfare of the deceased.

Both dirges follow a similar pattern. They begin with a number of lines which eulogize the deceased (lines 1–15 and 113–120, although the latter is broken and its transition to the second section uncertain). Each line of section

[58] Samuel N. Kramer, *Two Elegies on a Pushkin Museum Tablet: A New Sumerian Literary Genre* (Moscow: Oriental Literature, 1960). This tablet is now extant in 5 copies, described by Åke Sjöberg in "The First Pushkin Museum Elegy and New Texts," *JAOS* 103 (1983): 315–320.

one mentions a memorable and positive attribute of the deceased, each also ending with a statement concerning the reason for lament:

> "Who was wise of plan, highly-qualified for the assembly, had become ill,
> Who was a man of truth, god-fearing, had become ill." (lines 7–8)

Section two is the lament proper. In both sections (lines 16–62, 121–150 [?]) there is an extended description of the mourners, family, servants, and townspeople, who lament without cease. In the lament for Nanna, there is a third section (lines 63–85) which calls down vengeance upon Nanna's killers. The elegy for Nawirtum replaces this "cursing" section with one in which Ludingirra asks where his beautiful and sweet wife has gone. Both elegies have a final section of jussive prayers on behalf of the deceased (lines 86–112, 169–178).

One is struck by the similarity in form between these dirges and those found in the Old Testament. Old Testament dirges contain a memory of past glory or beauty, compared with the unpleasant reality of the present (contrast motif). They also often contain a statement about the mourners of the deceased and the depth of their grief. These two elegies do not contain any appreciable discussion about the underworld and its denizens, except for incidental mention of UTU, Etana, and the underworld in the sense of wishing the deceased pleasant habitation there.[59]

ii. RS 34.126/*KTU* 1.161
(*The Funeral Dirge for Niqmaddu of Ugarit*)

The next two examples are dirges for dead kings: the dirge for Niqmaddu of Ugarit and the lament for Ur-Nammu of Sumer. Presented here is my own translation of *KTU* 1.161, based upon Dietrich, Loretz, and Sanmartín's second, enlarged edition of *KTU*, with attention also to Bordreuil and Pardee's edition of this text.[60] Following this is a comparison of the structure of the dirge with

---

[59] Sjöberg, "The First Pushkin Museum Elegy," 320, also suggests that Etana is mentioned in line 97 of this text as . . . nu-banda$_3$-kur-ra-ke$_4$, the "steward" of the "Land" (the netherworld), in ZA 67, 14, 78 (UTU Hymn) where he is in charge of the gate (line 79). This position would put Etana in a similar category as Gilgamesh, high official in the underworld. See chapter three below for further discussion about Gilgamesh and Etana.

[60] A critical edition was made of this long-known liturgical text by P. Bordreuil and D. Pardee ("Le rituel funéraire Ougaritique RS 34.126"), based upon a careful examination of the original tablet. The text was translated and interpreted two years later by Baruch Levine and Jean-Michel de Tarragon, "Dead Kings and Rephaim: The Patrons of the Ugaritic Dynasty," *JAOS* 104 (1984): 649–659. Most recently, Manfried Dietrich, Oswald Loretz, and Joaquín Sanmartín have reexamined the Ugaritic texts, including 1.161. See "*KTU* 1.161"

that of Isa 14:4b–21. The mythological/cosmological concepts contained in this dirge are important, but these will be explored in following chapters.

1) The book of the sacrifice of the shades: [61] spr.dbḥ.ẓlm

2) You have called [62] the Rephaim of the

(Manfried Dietrich, Oswald Loretz, and Joaquín Sanmartín, *The Cuneiform Alphabetic Texts from Ugarit, Ras Ibn Hani, and Other Places* [2nd, enl. ed.; ALASP 8; Münster: Ugarit-Verlag, 1995], 150–151). This is the base text for my translation.

[61] Now read almost universally as *ẓlm*, although initially read by Pope and others as *qlm*, "intonation." See Marvin Pope, "Notes on the Rephaim Texts from Ugarit," in *Essays on the Ancient Near East in Memory of Jacob Joel Finkelstein* (Memoirs of the Connecticut Academy of Arts and Sciences 19; Hamden: Archon, 1977), 177. Conrad L'Heureux, *Rank Among the Canaanite Gods: El, Baʿal, and the Rephaʾim* (HSM 21; Missoula: Scholars Press, 1979), 187, reads *qlm* as an abstract noun from *qll*, "to fall," with the meaning "prostration." John F. Healey, "Ritual Text KTU 1.161—Translation and Notes," *UF* 10 (1978): 85, reads *spr dbḥ qlm* as the "ritual of the sacrificial meal of laments/invocations." He reads *dbḥ*, "sacrificial meal," in line with his understanding of the similarity of this ritual with the Akkadian *kispu*. See more on this below. Bordreuil and Pardee have produced several new and superior readings based on their analysis of the tablet, among which is *ẓlm* in line one. Their transcription and translation are based on analysis of the original tablet and this analysis is the basis for most subsequent work on the text. Wayne Pitard, "The Ugaritic Funerary Text RS 34.126," *BASOR* 232 (1978): 65, originally read "*q/ẓlm*," but in his most recent examination of the tablet itself, agrees with Bordreuil and Pardee. The question is now what it means. Pitard, Levine, and de Tarragon have suggested the basic meaning is not "spirits," but "protectors" or "patrons," as in Ps 121:5–6. These protectors are identical in this text to the Rephaim, according to these scholars.

In the Hebrew Bible, *ṣēl* can be symbolic of life's brevity and transitiveness. See in particular Job 17:7, "all my members are like a shadow," a description of Job's physical condition near to death. See also Ps 102:12, "My days are like an evening shadow, I wither away like grass." While admittedly the connection between *ṣēl* and the dead is tenuous, the connection between *ṣēl* and "benefaction" or "patronage" is even more tenuous. In the Hebrew Bible, shadows/shade may provide protection from the heat of the sun, or metaphorically provide protection under the shadow cast by a king or lord. The other meaning of *ṣēl* is that of insubstantiality and the intimate connection between life and death. To my knowledge, nowhere else are benefactors or patrons referred to as "shadows." Read here, rather, shadows as the insubstantial and underworld "double" of original physical existence on earth. This in no way diminishes the Rephaim as benefactors of Ugarit, but obviously suggests that John Gray's and Conrad L'Heureux's understanding that the Rephaim are comprised of cultic functionaries or a living aristocracy is incorrect. See John Gray, "The Rephaim," *PEQ* 81 (1949): 135–138 and Conrad L'Heureux, "The Ugaritic and Biblical Rephaim," *HTR* 67 (1974): 272.

[62] One of the problems with this text is the alternation between persons in the verbs used, as most commentators have observed. Levine and de Tarragon are probably correct in suggesting that *qritm* and *qbitm* are second plural perfects.

nether[world][63]	qritm.rpi.a[rṣ
3) You have commanded the council of Di[dani],[64]	qbitm.qbṣ.d[dn
4) Call[65] Ulkn,[66] the Raph[a],	qra.ulkn.rp[a
5) Call Trmn[67] the Raph[a],	qra.trmn.rp[a
6) Call Sdn-wa-Rd[n],[68]	qra.Sdn.w.Rd[n
7) Call the Bull of ʿllmn[[69]	qra.ṯr.ʿllmn[
8) You all call the ancient Rephaim,	qru.rpim.qdmym

---

[63] All commentators read *rpi* as a plural, the "Rapha-beings," in line with 2 Sam 21:16. *arṣ* here must refer to the netherworld, the realm of the dead, not the surface of the earth or the world in general. See lines 21–26.

[64] Pope, "Notes on the Rephaim Texts," 179. *ddn* here is identical to *dtn*, the eponymous ancestor or ancestral tribe of West-Semitic kings, to which the Ugaritic dynasty looks as its founding patron and, as Pope puts it, *primus inter pares* among the Rephaim. See also John Gray, "*DTN* and *RP'UM* in Ancient Ugarit," *PEQ* 84 (1952): 39–41 and the *Keret* text, 15 iii 4 and 15.

[65] Healey and Pitard read *qra* as 3ms perfects; Taylor reads it and *qru* in line 8 as passives. Levine and de Tarragon and Pope read them as imperatives. Healey says, "*qra* could be singular imperative, but this is all but ruled out by the resumptive *qritm* in 1.9." Rather than switch between "you" and "he" throughout the text, it is much simpler and the text flows better if one reads "you call" (imperative, note *qru* in line 8!), followed by "you all have called" (perfect). Read *qra* as a second masculine singular imperative.

[66] Pope read *blkn*. Read *ulkn* with Bordreuil and Pardee and Pitard. Pitard informs us that the "*u*" is clear in his examination of the tablet.

[67] The reading *Trmn* would appear to be confirmed by Bordreuil and Pardee. Pitard suggested that the name is formed with √ *rwm*, either a second feminine singular ("the goddess DN is exalted") or a second masculine singular ("may you be exalted, O DN").

[68] *sdn w rdn* would appear to be the correct reading of the text, according to the analyses of Bordreuil, Pardee, and Pitard. de Moor reads *sdn k rdn*, suggesting that two names are in view here and that the *k* means "as well as." See J. de Moor, "Rapiʾūma—Rephaim," ZAW 88 (1979): 333. Most other commentators read *w* instead of *k* and see this as a single, compound name like *kṯr-w-ḫss*. The translation and vocalization of the name, on the other hand, are difficult to determine at the present with any degree of certainty.

[69] The *ṯr* element is almost certainly "bull." Theodore Lewis, "Toward a Literary Translation of the Rapiʾūma Texts," in *Ugarit: Religion and Culture, Proceedings of the Edinburgh International Conference 20–23 July 1994, Studies in Honor of John Gibson* (UBL 12; Münster: Ugarit-Verlag, 1996), 115–149, translates *ʿllmn*, also found in *KTU* 1.22 as *ʿllmny*, as "eternal." This term is probably related to Hebrew עוֹלָם, but with duplication of the *lamed* and the addition of adjectival *an*. If this is the case, then the name would mean something like, "bull of eternity," or "everlasting bull."

9) You all have called the Rephaim of the netherworld,	qritm.rpi.arṣ
10) You all have commanded the Council of Didani,	qbitm.qbṣ.ddn
11) Call Ammishtamru the king,	qra.ʿmṯtmr.mlk
12) Call also Niqmaddu the king.	qra.u.nqmd.mlk
13) Cry,[70] O throne[71] of Niqmaddu,	ksi.nqmd.ibky
14) And let the stool of his feet [72] weep!	wydmʿ.hdm.pʿnh
15) The table of the kin[g] [73]	

---

[70] For a parallel to *ksu*, *hdm*, and *tlḥn*, see *KTU* 1.3 ii 35–36. According to Bordreuil and Pardee's reading, enough is visible of the signs to read *ibky*, parallel to *ydmʿ* in the following line. It may be a misspelling for *ybky*, "it will cry." It is also possible that *ibky* is a D imperfect 1st common sing., "I will cause the throne of Niqmaddu to cry." If so, one would also expect something of the sort in the following lines: "I will cause to weep . . .," etc., but such is not the case. Although it is difficult in any case to be certain relative to the analysis of *ibky* here and *išḫn* in line 18, it seems to me most likely that these are imperatives with anaptyctic *i* vowels. See Stanislav Segert, *A Grammar of the Ugaritic Language* (Berkeley: University of California Press, 1984), 63.

[71] Taylor suggests that we have attested for the first time a vocative singular noun, *ksi*, "O throne," which works if *ibky* is an imperative with anaptyctic *i* vowel. See G. Taylor, "A Long-awaited Vocative Singular Noun with Final *Aleph* in Ugaritic (KTU 1.161.13)?" *UF* 17 (1985): 315–318.

[72] Since Bordreuil, Pardee, and Pitard's analysis, *hdm pʿnh*, "the footstool of his feet," has become more clear, parallel to the "throne of Niqmaddu" in the preceding line. de Moor read, "and shed tears. His eyes did not cease" and Pope read, "Then let him weep, let his eye flow before him."

[73] Pope, Pitard, de Moor, and Healey all read, "the table was full," or the like, reading *ml[a] for ml[k]*. Pitard, in his more recent analysis, reminds us that the final letter is completely broken away and any restoration is conjectural. In his earlier article, Pitard suggested that *mla*, along with *ksh* "his cup" in line 20, refer to a ritual feeding of the dead similar to the *kispu* rituals mentioned in Babylonian texts. Pitard even finds that the structure of the ritual follows that of the *kispu* texts. Healey goes so far as to say, "The idea behind the rite is, without a doubt, a meal shared with the dead ancestors and Niqmaddu is spiritually present." While not denying connections with such rituals or the cult of dead kings in Mesopotamia, Ugarit, or elsewhere, I suggest that the prevalent motif here is as I have mentioned earlier, that of the expediting of the dead king to his home in the underworld. Furthermore, there is no eating or drinking or providing the dead with food or drink in this text, unless the sevenfold sacrifice at the end of the text serves this function (by no means obvious! See the seventy sacrifices after Baʿal's death in *KTU* 1.6 i, not apparently intended to feed anyone). This understanding is underscored by the newer readings provided by Bordreuil, Pardee and

shall cry[74] before him,	lpnh.ybky.ṯlḥn.ml[k]
16) And it shall swallow its tears!	w.yblʿ.udmaʿth
17) Desolation and desolation of desolations! [75]	ʿdmt.w.ʿdmt.ʿdmt
18) Be bright,[76] O Šapšu!	išḫn.špš
And be bright, (19) O Great Light!	w.išḫn.nyr.rbt
On high Šapšu shouts:	ʿln.špš.tṣḥ
20) After your [lo]rd, to his throne,[77]	ʾaṯr.bʿlk.l.ks<i>h
After (21) your lord, to the netherworld go down,	ʾaṯr.bʿlk.arṣ.rd

---

Pitard, where the throne of Niqmaddu and his footstool weep.

[74] Note the difference in spelling here from *ibky* in line 15. I suggest that the easiest way to understand the text is by reading the verbs in lines 13–14 as an imperative and a jussive, followed by imperfects in lines 15–16. It is also possible that *ybky* and *yblʿ* in lines 15–16 are jussives of the "long type," suggested by Segert (Segert, *A Grammar of the Ugaritic Language*, 62), in which case the *y* of the jussive would be written. Since the long ending of the jussive has yet to be identified with certainty in Ugaritic, it is best to read these as imperfects.

[75] *ʿdmt* is apparently clear in the tablet. The third repetition of the word caused some problems earlier (Pope and de Moor read *tdmt*, Pitard was unsure whether to read a *ṯ* or an ʿ). Bordreuil and Pardee read a clear ʿ. Levine and de Tarragon suggest that the term *ʿdmt* may be 1) a faulty attempt on the part of the scribe to read a prothetic *aleph* and therefore continue the "tears" theme from the previous line; or 2) a cognate form for Arabic *ʿadima*, suggesting desolation. We lack enough data at this point to make a clear determination, but the latter option would appear more likely in light of the clear reading *udmʿth* in the previous line.

[76] *išḫn* has the same difficulty as *ibky*, above. If it is an N imperfect, it would be "I shall be bright," which yields little sense in the context. It is more likely that this, also, is an imperative with anaptyctic *i* vowel (see Segert, *A Grammar of the Ugaritic Language*, 63).

[77] The reading *ksh*, "his cup," prompted Pitard to think of this text as a ritual feeding of dead kings. Levine and de Tarragon suggest that the scribe made an error, "*h*" for "*i*," as these signs are almost identical. Another possibility is that the "*i*" was actually written, but there is a crack in the text exactly where the downward stroke of the "*i*" would go. What would appear definite is that Pitard's understanding that the ritual feeding of dead kings (*tlḥn ml[a]* "full table") is indicated in this text is erroneous. Furthermore, the throne is not being exhorted to descend to the netherworld, but rather the spirit of the dead king Niqmaddu is probably being expedited to the netherworld by Šapšu, who conveys the spirits of the dead there on her nightly course. The mourners, including ʿAmmurapi the new king, are being exhorted to "go down" to Niqmaddu in the underworld, "to his throne," which he possesses as a recently deceased king and where he and the other departed kings sit on thrones, as in Isa 14. *lksh* should therefore read, "to his throne," not "from the throne" as Levine and de Tarragon suggest. See chapter four below for a more complete discussion of this issue.

To the netherworld (22) go down,	arṣ.rd
Even (go) down to the dust!	w.špl.ʿpr
Below is (23) Sdn-wa-Rdn,	tḥt.sdn.w.rdn
Below is the bull of (24) ʿllmn,	tḥt.ṯr.ʿllmn
Below are the ancient Rephaim;	tḥt.rpim.qdmym
25) Below is Ammishtamru, the king,	tḥt.ʿmṯtmr.mlk
26) Below[78] is also Niqmaddu the king!	tḥm(!).u.nq[md].mlk
27) One,[79] and an offering,[80]	ʿšty.w.ṯ[ʿy
Two, and an offering,	ṯn.]w.ṯʿ[y
28) Three, and an offering,	ṯlṯ.w.ṯʿy

---

[78] The text reads *tḥm* on line 26, which most commentators correct to *tḥt*, consistent with lines 22, 23, 24, and 25. L'Heureux reads here and in all other occurrences of *tḥt* "at the foot of," consistent with his desire not to read this as a funeral ritual involving the descent of the king to the infernal Rephaim. Healey reads "seat," consistent with his desire to see the throne of Niqmaddu ritually descend to the underworld. *tḥt*, however, simply means "below" or "under." Taylor reads all occurrences of *tḥt* as "under," meaning the throne is set under the various Rephaim or dead kings. Although this would be an unusual case for *tḥt* so far attested in the Ugaritic language, it appears that the best understanding of the term here is that of the adverbial accusative, "below." If one takes this position, then it is unnecessary to speculate regarding the location of the Rephaim in the poem. They are not called to the surface, nor does the king descend "beneath them." As an adverbial accusative, the Rephaim are "below" and Niqmaddu also descends "below." Further evidence in support of this is line 26, where one would not expect the object of a preposition to be separated from it, but such is the case, suggesting it may be an adverbial usage. This raises the possibility that all of the occurrences of *tḥt* here are also adverbial accusatives. *tḥt* as an adverb or adverbial accusative is also found in Isa 14:11: "Sheol below (מתחת) is stirred up." Similarly, it is this use of *tḥt*, signifying the location of the Rephaim relative to the funeral celebrants on the surface of the earth, which we find also represented in the Niqmaddu text.

[79] There follow a series of seven sacrifices. These are clearly listed by cardinal, and not ordinal, numbers. Apparently, de Moor, Levine and de Tarragon, and Pitard all translate these as ordinals due to the analogy with how such a list might function in English. L'Heureux insists they are cardinals, but offers no explanation for this understanding. Taylor reads them correctly as cardinals. In a spot where the text is clear, I would point out ṯṯ in line 29, rather than *ṯdṯ*, which one would expect if these numbers were ordinals.

[80] L'Heureux and de Moor understood the term *ṯʿy* to be a noun ("offering") rather than a verb, with Caquot ("make an offering"). del Olmo Lete suggests the form is participial and allows both "active" and "objective" meanings: "offerer," "offering." See G. del Olmo Lete, "Ug. *ṯʿ*, *ṯʿy*, *ṯʿt*: Nombre Divino y Acción Cultual," *UF* 20 (1988): 30.

Four, and an offering,	a[rbʿ].w.ṯʿ[y
29) Five, and an offering,	ḫmš.w.ṯʿy
Six, and an offering,	ṯṯ.[w].ṯʿy
30) Seven, and an offering!	šbʿ.w.ṯʿy
You shall present [81] a bird, 31) a peace offering [82]	tqdm.ʿṣr.šlm
A peace offering for ʿAmmurapi	šlm.ʿmr[pi]
32) And a peace offering for his house! [83]	w.šlm.ba(! read n/t)h.
A peace offering for Ṯaryelli,[84]	šlm.ṯryl
33) A peace offering for her house!	šlm.bth.

---

[81] Pitard reads here *tq[dš]*, following the suggestion in *KTU*. Bordreuil and Pardee include both *qdm* and *qdš* as possibilities. Levine, de Tarragon, and Pitard suggest the better reading is *tqdm*, because a sacrifice is almost certainly in view here and also the word *qdš* does not otherwise occur in Ugaritic as a finite verb. To corroborate this reading further, note "Keret," *KTU* 1.15 iv 21–28 (in Dietrich, et al., *Cuneiform Alphabetic Texts*, 42):

bt.krt.tbun	they entered the house of Keret
lm.mṯb.[ ]	to the throne-room [ ]
wlḫmmr.tqdm	and to the audience-chamber they approached
yd.bṣʿ.tšlḥ	she stretched out a hand (to) the dish
ḥrb.bbšr.tštn	a knife she put to the flesh
[w]tʿn.mṯt.ḫry	[and] the maiden Ḫry [ans]wered
[llḥ]m.lšty.ṣḥtkm	[to ea]t and to drink I have ordered you
[wdbḥ.l]krt.bʿlkm	[and to sacrifice for] Keret your lord

tqdm occurs obviously as a finite verb in Hebrew and Ugaritic and in both may have the connotation of "to approach to worship."

[82] Taylor makes the interesting suggestion that the first *šlm* on line 31 really goes with line 30: "present a bird as a peace offering." I have followed this suggestion throughout the closing lines of the text. The word *šlm* then refers to the offerings which are presented, and not a cry, "Peace." Furthermore, if one counts the first in the series, the "bird (as a) peace offering," you end up with exactly seven, the number of offerings listed in lines 27–30.

[83] Dietrich, et al., *Cuneiform Alphabetic Texts*, 151 have *bah*, but suggest reading *bnh*. Some commentators have suggested reading *bth*, which occurs clearly in the following line. Other commentators, such as Healey, L'Heureux, and Pitard, read *bnh*, "his son," with the editors of *KTU*. Pitard suggests either an "*n*" or a "*t*" is possible here. Read *bth* also due to the strict parallelism provided by the series.

[84] Most commentators restore the *ṯ* before *-ryl* on line 32. We know of Ṯaryelli as the name or title of a queen of Ugarit from RS 15.08. Pitard is reluctant to make a restoration, but suggests the last letter could be an "*l*."

A peace offering for Ugarit,	šlm.ugrt
34) A peace offering for its gates!	šlm.ṯǵrh

The structure of the liturgy is simple: 1) It begins with a scribal incipit (line 1). 2) Next come eleven lines in which the various dignitaries of the underworld, the ancient and more recent Rephaim or dead kings, are summoned to appear on the occasion of the descent of Niqmaddu III to the realm of the dead as well as the accession of the new king. 3) The next section is the actual ritual lament, in which the throne, footstool, and royal table are called upon to weep (lines 13–17). 4) Lines 18–26 describe the invoking of the sun, Šapšu, and her command to Niqmaddu to follow her on her nightly journey through the underworld. There, Niqmaddu will meet the ancient Rephaim (*rpim qdmym*) as well as the more recent arrival, Ammishtamru. There is some question whether the Niqmaddu mentioned in the text in line 26 is Niqmaddu II or Niqmaddu III himself, recently arrived in the underworld.[85] 5) Lines 27–30 describe a series of seven sacrifices, presumably on behalf of the new king and queen. 6) Lines 31–34 proclaim the accession of the new king, the son of Niqmaddu (as in the announcement in more modern times, "The king is dead! Long live the king!").

In comparing the structure of *KTU* 1.161 to Isa 14, one should remember that the latter is a parody of, and not a true, funeral dirge. One ought not to expect complete formal agreement between the two texts for this reason and also because of the distance in time and culture. There are, however, formal similarities between the two which need to be underscored. First, there is no summoning of the Rephaim on the part of the assembled congregation (presuming such is intended by the writer) to begin the dirge, but there is the Israelite exclamation "how!", followed by a description of the ruthlessness of the king. The first true point of similarity in form is vv. 7–8, which indicate that inanimate objects, in this case "the world," the cypresses, and the cedars of Lebanon, rejoice rather than "weep" as in the Ugaritic text (*ibky*). Second, the personification of the netherworld, Sheol, rouses the dead kings to greet (*liqraʾt* in Isa 14, *qritm* in the Ugaritic text) the newly deceased king upon his arrival. No mention is made of following the sun god (Šamaš; *Špš* in the Ugaritic text) to the underworld, nor would such be expected in a late pre-exilic composition such as this. Nevertheless, Sheol in this text has a similar function as *Špš* in the Ugaritic text, in that he prepares the way for the coming of the king of Babylon and introduces the new king to the underworld "council" of kings. Third, *Špš* twice utters the

[85] Most commentators think it is Niqmaddu III who is meant here, as ʿAmmurapi was his grandson, the only ʿAmmurapi following a Niqmaddu on the king list from Ugarit. By means of the reconstruction of lost lines, K. A. Kitchen even hypothesizes that this is a theoretical Niqmaddu IV. See Kitchen, "The King List of Ugarit," *UF* 9 (1977): 131–142.

command to "go down" (*rd*) to the underworld. Such commands are not present in Isaiah, but in 14:11 and 15 the Rephaim exclaim, "Your majesty is brought down" and "But you are brought down," reflecting an accomplished fact. Fourth, rather than offer a sevenfold sacrifice, the Isaiah text commands, "Establish for his sons a slaughtering-place," suggesting that the sons of the king will be the sacrifice. Finally, rather than proclaiming the name of the new king as in the Ugaritic text (lines 31–32), Isa 14:20 says, "Let the offspring who do evil not be called out forever" and "Prepare sacrifice for his sons." I might add to this analysis that the actual ordering of the major sections of the Ugaritic dirge are reflected in broad terms in Isa 14 as well.

There are some comparisons which can be made between the texts of *KTU* 1.161 and Ezek 32:16–32 also. A major difference is that Ezek 32:16–32 is a "mass dirge": Pharaoh of Egypt follows the kings and armies of various nations to Sheol. No attempt is made to deliver a "complete" funeral dirge in the same sense as 2 Sam 1 or Isa 14, although it is referred to as a dirge (*qînāh*, 32:2, 16) and Ezekiel is commanded to wail over Egypt (*nĕhēh*, v. 18). The purpose of the dirge is to "bring down" Pharaoh and his helpers. Such a purpose, observable in *KTU* 1.161, is a primary feature of dirges for dead kings, as examples of these dirges extant from the ancient Near East and the Hebrew Bible contain a command to go down or an allusion to being brought down (in the case of Isa 14), except for 2 Sam 1. Among the structural similarities between these texts are the following: first, there is the command, "Go down!" (v. 19b), parallel to lines 20–21. Second, the *ʾêlê gibbôrîm* (reading *ʾêl*, ram, rather than *ʾēlê*, gods, parallel to *ʿattūḏê* in Isa 14), presumably the dead kings or Rephaim, greet Pharaoh and his armies upon their arrival in Sheol, much as in Isa 14 and *KTU* 1.161.

As a preliminary statement, the function of the royal dirge was to 1) hasten and bless the journey of the dead king to join his predecessors in the underworld, and 2) to proclaim the accession of the new king. These observations will be discussed in greater detail in chapters four and five. It is noteworthy that this royal funeral ideology only occurs in the Hebrew Bible in the parodies of the funeral dirges for foreign kings in Isa 14 and Ezek 32.

iii. *The Death of Ur-Nammu*

Samuel N. Kramer said about the *Death of Ur-Nammu* in his translation and analysis of this Sumerian literary piece that "it is rather difficult to categorize—it is neither myth nor epic, neither hymn nor lamentation." [86] The

---

[86] Samuel N. Kramer, "The Death of Ur-Nammu and his Descent to the Netherworld," *JCS* 21 (1967): 104.

occasion for the inscribing of the tablet appears to be the premature death of the great Sumerian king Ur-Nammu. He was a powerful, pious king who built temples throughout his land. The poet questions, in Kramer's words, "why then did the gods see fit to decree his early death and bring him prematurely to his grave?" [87] The poet, according to Kramer, seeks to answer this question by having the goddess Inanna make amends for divine complicity in ending his life, possibly on the field of battle.[88] Kramer believes that the poem is a piece of "Job-like" wisdom literature,[89] an *apologia* for the death of a good, pious king and the ways of the gods.

While the text is intended to address the issue of the righteous sufferer and the inscrutability of the gods as Kramer suggests, he discounts the closing lines of the poem to understand its genre and function.[90] These lines read,

> . . . -am$_3$ i-lu-am$_3$
> ir$_2$-am$_3$ a-nir-am$_3$
>
> "it is . . ., it is a wail,
> it is a weeping, it is a lament." [91]

Clearly, whether the tablet was intended to be read at the king's funeral or sometime later, or whether the closing lines were added at another time, at some time, those who either wrote or read the *Death of Ur-Nammu* considered it to be a lament for the dead.

There are also internal indications which suggest that this is so. While the poem intends to narrate a story, it is also intended as a lament for the death of the king. But is it actually a dirge, or does it contain a dirge? Clearly, the entire poem does not describe the intoning of a dirge. Ur-Nammu, however, voices a lament for his own death from the netherworld, as described by the Sumerian author (lines 154–195) and the people of Ur and its countryside also lament.

The importance of the *Death of Ur-Nammu* to this analysis is in the fact that the story itself narrates a series of events which closely resemble the structure of *KTU* 1.161 surveyed above and the activities described in it. First, there is

---

[87] Kramer, "Death of Ur-Nammu," 104.

[88] See 2 Chr 35:20–25.

[89] Kramer, "Death of Ur-Nammu," 104.

[90] Kramer, "Death of Ur-Nammu," 120. He says, "Just why the last two lines reading '. . . it is . . . it is a wail; . . . it is weeping, it is a lament' were added, is not clear."

[91] See Ezek 32, which begins by identifying what the prophet is to intone over the king of Egypt; that is, a lament for the dead. It is not, however, until v. 17 that the dirge per se begins. In the *Death of Ur-Nammu*, we have the reverse: it is a narrative the ritual usage of which we do not fully appreciate until the colophon at the end.

the lament proper, parallel to the lament in lines 13–17 of *KTU* 1.161:

> Because the righteous shepherd was carried off,
> The . . . weep in their . . .
> The people . . . sleep not,
> Spend (their) days [in mourning(?)] for their righteous shepherd in his "captivity,"
> Their irrigation canals have been silted (?) up by their *kugal*,
> Their *gunu*-grain, grown on their acres, the life of the land, has been uprooted . . . (lines 18–23)

Second, the command to, or the statement about, the "going down" of the king is reflected in this text as in *KTU* 1.161 and Isa 14:

> In . . . (her?) unknown place, their boat sank (?) . . .
> He arrived in the netherworld, the desolate (?)
> The chariot was covered with . . ., the road turned and twisted (?), it could not go further (?) . . . (lines 66, 73–74)

Third, there is the invoking of the underworld inhabitants and dead notables, similar to the calling of the Rephaim in *KTU* 1.161 and Isa 14:

> Ur-Nammu, (his) coming, they announced to the people, a tumult arose in the netherworld. (line 79)

Fourth, the "gods of the netherworld, the seven, the *išib*, the *lumaḫ*, the *gutug* who had died," greet Ur-Nammu on his coming, similar to the Rephaim in Isa 14:4b–21 and *KTU* 1.161:

> My king presented gifts to the gods of the netherworld, the seven,
> The *išib*, the *lumaḫ*, and the *gutug* who had died,
> The king, (his) coming, the dead *nindingir* chosen by oracle. (lines 76–78)

Fifth, Ur-Nammu sacrifices to the gods of the netherworld, as in *KTU* 1.161:[92]

> The righteous king, his heart "knew" the gods of the netherworld!
> The king offers the gifts of the netherworld as sacrifices,
> Ur-Nammu offers the gifts of the netherworld as sacrifices. (lines 83–85)

There is, therefore, a close structural connection between the presence and ordering of the events in the *Death of Ur-Nammu* and the dirge in *KTU*

---

[92] Nine underworld deities are mentioned, and nine sacrifices offered to them—Nergal, Gilgamesh, Ereshkigal, Dumuzi, Namtar, Hushbishag, Ningišzida, Dimpiku, and Ninazimua—although only seven are mentioned in line 76. If one does not count the wives of some of the deities, and so indicated in the text (Hushbishag and Ninazimua) then there are precisely seven, the number of sacrifices performed in the Niqmaddu text.

1.161. As we have seen above, this order also roughly corresponds to the structure of Isa 14:4b–21.

b. Old Testament Dirges

The following is a list of dirges in the Old Testament with an analysis of their formal structure. I have not included laments for cities in my analysis, even though they share many of the themes of the common dirge. Their purpose and structure diverges from that of the common dirge, as noted above. It is my purpose here to note important features of dirges and how they cohere with or diverge from common dirges in the ancient Near East surveyed above. The following is not intended to be a comprehensive list of dirges or dirge-like literature in the Old Testament (excluding those which Dobbs-Allsopp has identified as city laments). It is intended rather to demonstrate that there are two kinds of dirges with differing ideologies, structures, and themes in the Bible and the ancient Near East.

a) 2 Samuel 1:19–27 (lament for Saul and Jonathan).
- Introduction: v. 19a.
- Exclamation: ("How the mighty are fallen!"): v. 19b.
- Admonition for silence and mourning/affect on bystanders: vv. 20–21a.
- Reason for mourning/present reality: v. 21b.
- Memory of past glory: vv. 22–23.
- Summons to mourn/memory of past (Saul): v. 24.
- Exclamation: v. 25.
- Present reality (Jonathan): v. 25b.
- Memory of past glory (Jonathan): v. 26.
- Exclamation: v. 27.

b) 2 Samuel 3:33: dirge for Abner.
- Introduction ("Shall Abner die as a fool?"): v. 33b.
- Memory of past state ("he was not bound"): v. 34a.
- Present reality: v. 34b.

c) Isaiah 14:4b–21 (dirge for the king of Babylon).
- Exclamation/Introduction: v. 4b.
- Memory of past affliction: vv. 5–6.
- Present reality (in the royal dirge, the weeping of inanimate objects; but in Isa 14, their rejoicing; also the rousing of the Rephaim to greet the deceased):
  - on earth (singing, rather than weeping): vv. 7–8.
  - in Sheol (the Rephaim are incredulous): vv. 9–11.
- Exclamation: v. 12.
- Memory of past glory ("you said in your heart, 'I will ascend'"): vv. 13–14.
- Present reality: v. 15.
- Affect on bystanders/bewilderment about the death: vv. 16–17.
- Present reality: vv. 18–20a.

Summons to sacrifice ("Prepare slaughter for his sons," rather than weep for him or prepare coronation for his son): v. 20b–21.

d) Jeremiah 22:18: Lament for Jehoiakim.

Exclamation ("Alas, brother, alas, sister; alas, lord, alas, his majesty"): v. 18.

e) Ezekiel 32:18–32: Royal dirge for Pharaoh of Egypt.

Memory of past glory (reversed—"Whom do you surpass in beauty," rather than "Who surpasses you in beauty?"): v. 19a.
Admonition ("Go down!"): v. 19b.
The "greeting committee"/rousing of the dead kings/Rephaim ("The king of Asshur/Edom/etc. are there"): vv. 21.
Description of the dead kings/Rephaim: vv. 22–30.
Arrival in the underworld: v. 31.

It is apparent from this analysis that Old Testament dirges generally follow a similar structural pattern, which I will call the "common dirge pattern." Dirges for commoners contain similar themes and follow a roughly similar pattern. True city laments, including the five Sumerian exemplars and the biblical book of Lamentations, bear some structural resemblance to the common dirge, but differ in terms of form and overall purpose. *KTU* 1.161 departs significantly from this pattern, as does Ezek 32. Isaiah 14:4b–21 resembles the common dirge in terms of structure (see above), but also resembles the royal dirge in terms of imagery and thematic content, exemplified by *KTU* 1.161. Note the diagram below for a comparison of the various "royal dirges" in this analysis:

Comparison of "Royal Dirges" in the Old Testament and the Ancient Near East

	Command to go down	**Lament**	**Rousing Underworld Dwellers**	**Rephaim/ Dead Kings**	**Sacrifice For/ By King**	**New King Proclaimed**
***KTU* 1.161**	√	√ (objects-footstool, table- cry)	√	√	√	√
Death of Ur-Nammu	√	√ (performed by king)	√	√ (7, *ishib, lumah, gutug* who had died greet king)	√	(lacking)
Isa. 14:4b-21	√ (past tense)[1]	√ (trees of Lebanon rejoice; parody of dirge)	√	√	√ (slaughter - place [מַטְבֵּחַ] for his sons)	√ (offspring *not* called out)
Ezek. 32:18-32	√	√ (a קִינָה, command to wail [נְהֵה])	√	√	(no sacrifice; kings and armies are slain)	(lacking)

1 Vv. 11 and 15.

III. Conclusion

The foregoing analysis suggests that there were two types of dirges extant in the ancient Near East: one characterized by memory of the deceased and intended to eulogize him or her; and another, a liturgical dirge intended to ensure the safe and proper descent of the deceased king to the underworld and legitimate the new king on his throne. Isaiah 14:4b–21 resembles to some degree the common dirge in terms of structure, but also resembles the royal dirge in terms of thematic content and even the ordering of those themes. It is possible that the writer borrowed the themes and ideology from the ancient Near Eastern royal dirge and inserted them into the structure of the more typically Israelite common dirge. I may perhaps go further and suggest that of the dirges for dead kings found in the Old Testament (2 Sam 1, Isa 14, Ezek 32),[93] the one which refers to an Israelite king (2 Sam 1, Saul), is most similar to the common dirge and bears little resemblance to Isa 14, Ezek 32, or *KTU* 1.161. The other two refer to the deaths of foreign kings (Babylon and Egypt) and are parodies of, and not true, royal dirges. The evidence surveyed seems to indicate the following: 1) Elegies for private individuals (the "common dirge") were widespread in and outside of Israel. 2) The common dirge in the Old Testament is intended to bemoan, memorialize, and eulogize the deceased. 3) Most dirges in the Old Testament are actually "personified city dirges," which Dobbs-Allsopp classifies as city laments, dirge-like literature in prophetic judgment speeches resembling the common dirge in form. 4) The royal dirges preserved for us for Israelite kings (2 Sam 1 and possibly Jer 22:18) resemble the common rather than the royal dirge, suggesting that the royal dirge was not used in Israel (at least not in the Old Testament), except when borrowed in order to parody foreign kings. Finally, 5) the two dirges which resemble the Niqmaddu dirge (Isa 14 and Ezek 32) are parodies and refer to foreign kings. While the evidence is not extensive enough to make categorical statements, one is perhaps justified in suggesting first that the royal dirge was a pattern known outside of Israel and served the ideological function of legitimating the dynasty and reflecting the privileged status of the king in the netherworld. Second, it functioned to legitimate dynastic succession. Third, it incidentally informs us of widespread understandings of cosmology, mythology, and the relationship of the king to the realm of the dead in the ancient Near Eastern world. It is these understandings (the "mythological elements" in Isa 14) to which we turn in chapters 3–4.

---

[93] Jer 22:18 is a dirge-like fragment within a prophetic oracle pertaining to Jehoiakim. This "dirge allusion," such as it is, seems to connect more readily with the common, rather than the royal, dirge pattern (the common dirge exclamation "how!"), although there is not enough of it to make categorical statements.

Chapter 3
Hêlēl ben Šaḥar

I. Introduction

One of the most enigmatic references in Isa 14 is to Hêlēl ben Šaḥar, usually translated "Day Star, son of Dawn."[1] Early in the century it was understood to be a reference to a celestial body. Sigmund Mowinckel, in his "Die Sternnamen im Alten Testament," suggested it was a reference to the planet Venus.[2] Most scholars would agree today that Šaḥar is to be associated in some manner with the gods Šaḥar and Šalim in *KTU* 1.23. Hêlēl is another matter entirely.

There are few references to Hêlēl ben Šaḥar or Hêlēl outside of the Old Testament and the sole occurrence of it there is in Isa 14. It is possible that the Ḫu-le-e-lu and Šaḫru mentioned in a ritual text from Emar refer to the same deities as Hêlēl and Šaḥar in Isa 14.[3] At least, the deity Šaḫru would appear to

---

[1] See the textual discussion on these terms in chapter 5.

[2] Sigmund Mowinckel, "Die Sternnamen im Alten Testament," NedTT 29 (1928): 65.

[3] The *ḫ* of Akkadian becoming *h* in Hebrew is unusual. There are at least two considerations here: 1) Šaḥar and Hêlēl are West-, and not East-, Semitic DNN. On the other hand, one would expect Šaḥar to be rendered *šēru* in an Akkadian text, but rather it is rendered by a close approximation to its Northwest-Semitic form. 2) This at least raises the possibility that Hêlēl also is rendered by an approximation to Northwest-Semitic pronunciation and not its East-Semitic analogy (probably related to √ *elēlu*). As Akkadian has no other h sound than the *ḫ*, if the writer were attempting to approximate the pronunciation of Northwest-Semitic words, it is reasonable to suggest he would have used the Akkadian *ḫ*. 3) Emar was a "crossroads" city, with both East- and West-Semitic influences. One might expect to find at Emar dialectal differences reflecting the cultures and languages which converged there. I suggest that is what we find here with both DNN *Ša-ḫa-ri* and *Ḫu-le-e-li*.

be related to Šaḥar.[4] *hll*, a deity mentioned in the Ugaritic texts *KTU* 1.24 (*Nikkal and the Kotharat*) and *KTU* 1.23 (*Šaḥar and Šalim and the Gracious Gods*), may be a reference to Hêlēl. Because of scant references, most scholars have looked for analogies in Near Eastern or Greek mythology for the fall of a god characterized by hubris, as we have seen in chapter one. Most often, Phaethon of the Greek myth and ʿAṯtar of the Ugaritic cycle of Baʿal are cited.[5] As I have suggested in previous chapters, it is dubious whether such an approach will bear fruit, if the form of the poem is that of the royal dirge.

I cannot here survey all of the various interpretations or do justice to the secondary literature, given the amount which has been written about the interpretation of Hêlēl ben Šaḥar, Venus and Venus deities in the ancient Near East, and associated astral phenomena and deities. I will attempt merely to cite some important works on Venus and Venus deities, proceed to a discussion of celestial omen literature from Mesopotamia, and end with an analysis of the Ugaritic evidence and the inscription from Emar.

II. Venus and Venus Deities in the Ancient Near East

At least from the late third millennium B.C.E., the Sumerian Inanna and the Akkadian Ištar were identified. Inanna was apparently originally a peaceful deity who later acquired the warlike attributes of the Semitic Ištar.[6] Inanna was associated clearly with the planet Venus and with the constellation Annunītu.[7] Ištar, likewise, was so identified, probably by identification with Inanna.

There existed several deities with names similar to Ištar which have been identified with this deity. The problem with such identification, as Heimpel has pointed out, is that 1) they are male deities, while Ištar was female, and 2) their planetary association cannot be ascertained.[8] The deity Aštar occurs at Ebla ca. 2500 B.C.E. In Ugarit, around the year 1300, occurs *ʿṯtr*, well known for his role in the Baʿal/Môt myth. The Moabites of the ninth century knew an *ʿštr*. Finally, the southern Arabs of Yemen of the late first millennium B.C.E. and the early

---

[4] Daniel Arnaud, *Recherches au pays d'Aštata: Emar 6.3 and 6.4, textes Sumériens et Accadiens* (Synthèse 18; Paris: Editions Recherche sur les Civilisations, 1986).

[5] In recent articles, the Arabic moon god Hilāl and the Akkadian Illil (EN.LIL) have also been cited as candidates for Hêlēl ben Šaḥar. See below and textual notes in chapter 5.

[6] Wolfgang Heimpel, "A Catalog of Near Eastern Venus Deities," *Syro-Mesopotamian Studies* 4 (1982): 13.

[7] For Annunītu, see comments below. For Inanna as Venus, see Heimpel, "Near Eastern Venus Deities," 9–13.

[8] Heimpel, "Near Eastern Venus Deities," 13.

first millennium C.E. knew an *ʿṯtr*. Heimpel points out that only in the case of the South Arabic *ʿṯtr* is there proof of a planetary aspect to the deity[9]—in fact, *ʿṯtr* was the head of the South Arabic pantheon.[10] While the names listed above seem to reflect an original identification of the deities with a common root, the attributes and gender of that deity and subsequent transformations are not clear.

Heimpel suggests that Ištar, originally a Semitic male deity, and Inanna, originally a Sumerian female deity, became fused in Mesopotamian religion and Ištar became the Sumero/Babylonian female Venus deity. This transformation did not occur everywhere. There is substantial evidence that outside of Mesopotamia Ištar was venerated as a male deity under the name Aštar, *ʿṯtr*, or the like.[11] The likelihood is that outside of Mesopotamia, Ištar (and derivative deities) developed into two deities, one male and one female. Evidence from Ugarit suggests that only one of the pair (*ʿṯtr*/*ʿṯtrt*) was associated with Venus, and even this evidence is ambiguous. Heimpel goes on to say that at Mari, halfway between Ebla and Babylon, both deities, Ištar and Aštar, were venerated side by side. In Assyria and Babylonia, the female goddess Ištar was venerated in both female and male aspects, representing her appearances as evening and morning star. This can be clearly seen in *Enūma Anu Enlil* text IV, lines 6–7:

> [MUL.UŠ.A.KE$_x$ a-na] NAM.BAD ME$_3$ ŠUB.BA
> [................ ^{d}Dil-b]at ina ^{d}UTU.ŠU$_2$.A IGI.ma zik-[rat]
> [MUL.SAL.A.KE$_x$ a-na] NAM.SAL TUK [......... ana UŠ.MEŠ u]l-lu-di
> ^{d}Dil-bat ina ^{d}UTU.E$_3$ [IGI-ma sin-ni-šat]
>
> [The star of men is for] pestilence...
> Ven[us is seen in the west, she is ma]le.
> The star of women is for taking a wife [...for g]iving birth [to males]
> Venus is seen in the east, [she is female.][12]

Heimpel cites other examples of the androgyny of Ištar, suggesting that such androgyny was widespread in Mesopotamia, while the bifurcation of male *ʿṯtr*/female *ʿṯtrt* (Astarte, later Aphrodite) was prominent in the West.

---

[9] Heimpel, "Near Eastern Venus Deities," 13–14; he suggests that *ʿṯtr* as *srkn wgrbn*, the "eastern and western one," provides proof of *ʿṯtr*'s planetary aspect among the Arabs.

[10] See Ulf Oldenburg, "Above the Stars of El."

[11] Heimpel, "Near Eastern Venus Deities," 14, suggests that at Ebla Aštar and Ištar are clearly related as Venus deities.

[12] Erica Reiner, in collaboration with David Pingree, *Babylonian Planetary Omens, Part 2: Enūma Anu Enlil, Tablets 50–51* (Bibliotheca Mesopotamica 2, Fascicle 2; Malibu: Undena, 1981), 46–47. The transcription and transliteration are Reiner and Pingree's.

Venus, as Ištar or *ʿṯtr*, was clearly associated with the king and the quality and length of his reign. Note the following from *Enūma Anu Enlil:*

> Venus (Dil-bat) rises heliacally in its month; if this star rises early: the king of that land will have a long life; if this star rises late: the king of that land will die soon.[13]

Note also this astrological omen to an Assyrian king:

mi-i-nu ra-ʾ-a-mu an-ni-u
ša ^{d}15 a-na LUGAL En-ia
[t]a-ra-ʾa-a-mu-u-ni
[SI]G$_5$ ša a-dan-niš a-na LUGAL En-ia$_2$
[taš-pu]-ra-an-ni
[^{d}dil-bat man-z]a-sa tu-sa-lim
[....] ar$_2$-ḫiš ta-at-ta-mar
[SIG$_5$ ša LUGAL u BALA-šu$_2$
[1 ^{d}dil-b]at man-za-sa ur-ri-ik
[UD.M]EŠ LUGAL GID$_2$.DA.MEŠ
[1 ^{d}dil-bat] MUL-ša$_2$ iḫ-ru-um-ma IGI-ir
LUGAL KUR TI.LA ur-rak
ša ^{m}15-MU-KAM

What is this love which Ištar has loved the king my lord!
She has sent the greatest good to the king my lord.
Venus made her position perfect...
...She became clear quickly,
Very good for the king and his reign.
Venus prolongs her position:
The days of the king will be prolonged.
Dilbat (Venus), her star is seen early:
The king of the land will prolong life.
From Issar-šumu-ereš.[14]

Other stars are said also to affect the reign and livelihood of the king himself, although not with the same frequency as Venus. These include EN.TE.NA.BAR.ḪUM and the "lion stars":

---

[13] Reiner and Pingree, *Enūma Anu Enlil*, 56–57.

[14] Hermann Hunger, *Astrological Reports to Assyrian Kings* (SAA 7; Helsinki: Helsinki University Press, 1992), 16. The transcription is Hunger's and the translation is my own. Venus omens also may affect the king adversely:

> "If at Venus' rising the Red star enters into it: the king's son will seize the throne. . . ." (Reiner and Pingree, *Enūma Anu Enlil*, 49).

> If in month VII EN.TE.NA.BAR.ḪUM (Ḫaṣirānu? Ḫabaṣīrānu?)[15] rises heliacally: the king's days will be long.[16]

Certainly the most prevalent of celestial omens involving the life and livelihood of the king concern Šamaš, the sun:

> If a sun disk stands above the moon and below the moon: the foundation of the throne will become stable; the king of the land will stay in his truth . . . . Tonight Saturn approached the moon. Saturn is the star of the sun, and the relevant interpretation is as follows: it is good for the king. The sun is the star of the king.[17]

In the second case, the close association of the king with Šamaš/Šapšu in the ancient Near East has long been known, although identifying the sun as a star is surprising. In the first case, it is unclear why the star Centaurus has a positive effect on the king. Besides these omens, reflecting the effect of other celestial bodies on the king besides Venus, lunar eclipses were also understood to have a generally malevolent effect on him.[18] It would appear that at least in the Neo-Assyrian period, when the *Astrological Omens* and the *Enūma Anu Enlil* cited above should be dated, solar and lunar eclipses and unusual behaviors associated with Venus commonly affected the king, possibly more so than any other celestial phenomena.[19] The importance of Ištar/Inanna and various derivative deities mentioned above cannot be overemphasized relative to common Semitic religious

---

[15] There is some confusion about how to transcribe the Sumerian name of this star, as well as its exact identity. R. Labat, *Manuel d'epigraphie Akkadienne* (6th ed.; Paris: Guethner, 1988), 303 gives the name of the star as EN.TE.NA.BAR.LUM/SIG and identifies it as Ḫaṣirānu, although on page 83 he also gives the star name as Ḫabaṣīrānu. *CAD* 6:8 lists it as Ḫabaṣīrānu, often written mul EN.TE.NA.BAR.GUZ. Reiner and Pingree, *Enūma Anu Enlil*, 81 identify the star as Ḫabaṣīrānu, or Centaurus.

[16] Reiner and Pingree, *Enūma Anu Enlil*, 67.

[17] Hunger, Astrological Reports, 55. The translation is Hunger's. Note also H. Hunger and D. Pingree's translation of MUL.APIN in *MUL.APIN: An Astronomical Compendium in Cuneiform* (BAfO 24; Horn: Ferdinand Berger & Söhne, 1989), 114: "If the sun sets in a *nīdu* cloud: the king will die."

[18] See Francesca Rochberg-Halton, *Aspects of Babylonian Celestial Divination: The Lunar Eclipse Tablets of Enūma Anu Enlil* (BAfO 22; Horn: Ferdinand Berger & Söhne, 1988), 84: "If an eclipse occurs and the weather becomes dark: hard times will beset the king."

[19] Note that in Hunger and Pingree, *MUL.APIN*, 112, the "stars of the lion" are said to make the king victorious. At least one of the extant editions of *MUL.APIN* dates from the time of Sennacherib. Venus is not said to have direct effect on the king in this compendium, but it also contains very few planetary omens.

beliefs.[20] We have seen that in many instances, Ištar or ʿAṯtar is identified with Venus, the morning and evening star.

III. Hêlēl and Šaḥar in Extra-Biblical Writings

There are few occurrences of the divine names Hêlēl or Šaḥar within or without the Bible. Among these occurrences note Isa 14 (Hêlēl ben Šaḥar), *KTU* 1.23 (Šaḥar; *Šaḥar and Šalim and the Gracious Gods*), the possible mention of Hêlēl (*hll*) in *KTU* 1.24 (*Nikkal and the Kotharat*) and *KTU* 1.17 (*Aqhat*), RS 24.251 (*KTU* 1.107 43) and RS 24.271 (*KTU* 1.123 11; Šaḥar), the ritual of the installation of the *entu* priestess at Emar (Ḫu-le-e-lu might be Hêlēl [??] and Šaḥar), as well as several occurrences of the term *šēru* in Akkadian literature with clear connections to Ištar. In addition, it is difficult to know if several occurrences of the word Šaḥar in the Hebrew Bible are actually reflexes of an older Šaḥar mythology (see, for example, Pss 57:8, 108:2, 139:9, Job 3:9, 38:12, 41:18; these may, on the other hand, simply be poetic personifications unrelated to an original deity Šaḥar). Šaḥar, "dark," "black," also clearly means "dawn" in some contexts. Hêlēl is much more difficult. In chapters one and five I relate it to *ellu*, "bright," but this really does not take us far in terms of its association with a particular star. I would like to suggest that, like the star Amaušumgalanna (Dumuzi, the "Hired Man," see chapter four below) in Mesopotamia, Hêlēl is a star closely associated with the Venus star in Syria and Canaan, but not identified with it. The Venus star would be none other than Šaḥar as the morning star or dawn aspect of Venus and Šalim as its evening star or dusk aspect. The king in the ancient Semitic world, though not identified with the Venus star as he was in Egypt, nevertheless had a close association with it.

Recently, Daniel Arnaud has published a two volume critical edition of inscriptions from ancient Emar. Among the inscriptions discovered at this Syrian "crossroads" city of the second millennium B.C.E. (including Hurrian, Anatolian, Mesopotamian, and Syrian elements) were several texts describing religious rituals in detail. Among the rituals described was one in which the *entu* priestess, a major cult functionary, was "married" to a god and thus installed as high priestess. In his analysis of these texts, Daniel Fleming has suggested that the reason for the installation of a new high priestess was because of the death of

---

[20] In Neo-Assyrian seals, for example, the Ištar star is a prominent motif. Many of these seals contain the sun, moon, and a star, certainly Ištar, together. Others contain a group of seven stars ("the seven") along with a much larger star, probably also Ištar. See Suzanne Herbordt, *Neuassyrische Glyptik des 8.–7. Jh. v. Chr* (SAAS 1; Helsinki: Helsinki University Press, 1992), especially Tafeln 10–12, but also see 14–16.

the old one, so the ritual is a kind of funerary eulogy for the old and the exaltation of the new priestess.[21]

The god Šaḫru is mentioned three times in this *entu* installation text: lines 24, 52, and 96 and a god ^{d}Ḫu-le-e-li occurs on line 73:[22]

4 GIŠ.BANŠUR a-na pa-ni DINGIR.MEŠ GAR-nu 1 GIŠ.BANŠUR a-na ^{d}IŠKUR 1 GIŠ.BANŠUR a-na ^{d}S[a-a]h-ri (line 24)

4 tables before the gods they shall set; 1 table for Adad (and) 1 table for Š[a]ḫru [23]

1 GIN$_3$ KI.LA$_2$.BI a-na ^{d}IŠKUR u$_3$ ^{d}He$_2$-bat u$_2$-še-el-la 1 UDU a-na ^{d}Sa-ah-ri SISKUR-u (line 52)

1 shekel its weight for Adad and Hebat, he shall offer up 1 sheep to Šaḫru (as) a sacrifice (*nīqu*)

TUG$_2$.NIG$_2$.URI ša E$_2$ ur-ši-ša KU$_2$.GA u$_2$ ma-aṣ-ṣu-u GIŠ.BANŠUR ša ^{d}Ḫu-le-e-li (line 73, Fleming 71–72)

an Akkadian garment of her pure bedroom; they will set up the table of Hulēlu

1 UDU 1 DUG za-du I$_3$.GIS hi-zi-bu 2 me-[at GIŠ.HAŠHUR.KUR.]RA a-na ^{d}Ša-ah-ri SISKUR (line 96, 92 in Fleming)

1 sheep, 1 clay (?) pot of oil, *ḫizzibu*[24] of 2 [hundred armannu-trees] (?)[25] for Šaḫru (as) a sacrifice

All occurrences have to do with various sacrifices to be performed on the days of the feast, so this text along with the installation ceremony text for the *maš᾿artu* priestess and the *zikru* festival comprise some of the few religious ritual texts we possess from Syria or Canaan.

As we have seen above, Aštar/Ištar was venerated in Syria from the third millennium on, but the god's/goddess's relationship to the planet Venus is ambiguous in those texts. Neither Aštar nor Aštart is mentioned in the three ritual texts mentioned above, but Ištar does appear in the installation of the

---

[21] Daniel E. Fleming, *The Installation of Baʿal's High Priestess at Emar: A Window on Ancient Syrian Religion* (Atlanta: Scholars Press, 1992), 291.

[22] Arnaud, *Emar 6.3*, 326–329.

[23] Fleming inexplicably reads "Hebat" here; I have followed Arnaud's reconstruction of the text (Arnaud, *Emar 6.3*, 326).

[24] Fleming, *The Installation of Baʿal's High Priestess at Emar*, 59, attempts no translation, but normalizes the text here as *ḫizzibu*.

[25] Fleming, *The Installation of Baʿal's High Priestess at Emar*, 59, attempts no reading after "2." I follow here Arnaud's reconstruction of the text.

maš'artu priestess text.[26] Šaḫru, on the other hand, is prominent in the *entu* text. I shall explore below the identity of Šaḫru, but for now I will simply suggest that the identification of Šaḫru and Aštar/Ištar is not out of the question.

The name Ḫu-le-e-li is also problematical. Could this be an occurrence of the same deity or entity mentioned as Hêlēl ben Šaḥar in Isa 14? The vocalization is inconclusive. The double "e" vowel could be the sign of vowel contraction, or it could simply be a long "ē", as in the second vowel of the Hebrew Hêlēl.

The "u" vowel is more difficult. If this were the same entity, one would expect a "u" or an "o" vowel in the Hebrew, not an "ê". S. Moscati and W. von Soden have noted the existence of "graphic interchanges" between "i" and "u" in the Akkadian language, suggesting this may be "evidence for the existence of vowel qualities of the type [y], [ɔ]."[27] Most of the examples von Soden gives of this interchange are verbs, but it occurs in nouns and proper names as well.[28] This rendering may differ from *ellu* or *ellilîtu* in other Akkadian texts, terms applied to Ištar, because Emar, as a north Syrian town, would have pronounced the names of deities in its own distinctive ways. Likewise, one does not expect the "h" of *hll* in an Akkadian text. One can see at a glance, however, that DNN have been influenced in this Syrian inscription by local pronunciation. Rather than Akkadian *šēru* or *šērētu* ("dawn," "morning"), we read Ša-ḫa-ri, influenced more by Syrian than Akkadian pronunciation. It is possible that Hulēl is the pronunciation at Emar in Syria for *hll* in the second millennium. Therefore, though written in Akkadian script, Ḫu-le-e-li is not otherwise attested as a divine name in Mesopotamia and may reflect current and local pronunciation.

In terms of the ritual setting of both Ḫu-le-e-li and Šaḫru, it is of more than passing interest that of the three ritual texts from Emar surveyed by Fleming only the installation of the *entu* priestess text mentions these two deities. If Fleming is correct in his analysis and text 369 from Emar describes rituals to be performed at the death of the old *entu* priestess and the installation of the new, then the connection between Ḫu-le-e-li, Šaḫru, and Hêlēl ben Šaḥar with funerary and installation rituals ("the king is dead; long live the king," except in this case a high-priestess is in view) is at least a provocative possibility. If this is at all

---

[26] Arnaud, Emar 6.3, 340, lines 71'–73'.

[27] *An Introduction to the Comparative Grammar of the Semitic Languages: Phonology and Morphology* (ed. Sabatino Moscati; Wiesbaden: Otto Harrassowitz, 1964), 48 and Wolfram von Soden, "Vokal Färbungen im Akkadischen," *JCS* 2 (1948): 291–303.

[28] So von Soden, "Vokal Färbungen im Akkadischen," 299, "ferner Sa-ar-da-ur-ri neben Sa-ar-du-ur-ri bei Tiglatpilesar III" and 300, "so etwa die Schreibung ku-ri-il-li für sonstiges kurulli." Other examples of the i/u interchange in Akkadian are cited in Richard Hess, *Amarna Personal Names* (Winona Lake: Eisenbrauns, 1993), 240 and Herbert Huffmon, *Amorite Personal Names in the Mari Texts* (Baltimore: Johns Hopkins University Press, 1965), 97.

the case, then we are justified in suggesting that this funerary/installation ritual mentioning Šaḫru and Ḫu-le-e-li may be analogous to *eršemma* and *tigi* laments (see chapter four). More than this it is not possible to say at present.

There are a few other occurrences of Hêlēl or Šaḥar in Near Eastern inscriptions. There are two possible occurrences of Hêlēl in *KTU* 1.24.[29] Lines 40–42 have the following to say regarding the Kotharat, the daughters of *hll*:

> [bn]t hll.snnt
> bnt hll bʿl gml
>
> the daughters of *hll*, the Swallow
> the daughters of *hll*, lord of the staff.[30]

Gibson suggests that the *hll* in this text is "not to be confused with the *hll* in the title of the Kotharat."[31] He gives no explanation for this assertion, but simply says that Hêlēl ben Šaḥar is the morning star,[32] and that *hll* is the "crescent moon."[33] It is mysterious to me how he can deny out of hand any connection with Hêlēl ben Šaḥar in an un-vocalized text.

In his recent article, William Gallagher suggested that the identification of Hêlēl with the Arabic *hilālu* is based upon faulty assumptions. Nowhere is Hilāl, an Arabic lunar deity, unequivocally present at Ugarit,[34] nor is there any reason to assume Arabic influence. Rather, the moon god, Yariḫ, is ubiquitous. I would add to his analysis that the one text which places Yariḫ in the same context with *hll* (*KTU* 1.24) does not imply any genealogical relationship between

---

[29] "Nikkal and the Kotharat," *KTU* 1.24 41–42 (in Gibson, *Canaanite Myths and Legends*, 129).

[30] "Nikkal and the Kotharat," *KTU* 1.24 41–42 (in Gibson, *Canaanite Myths and Legends*, 129). The transcription is his; see below for my understanding of *snnt* as the constellation "Swallow" as opposed to a possible adjective "swallow-like."

[31] Gibson, *Canaanite Myths and Legends*, 29.

[32] Gibson, *Canaanite Myths and Legends*, 29n.

[33] Gibson, *Canaanite Myths and Legends*, 129.

[34] This is true even of the single statement in *KTU* 1.24 41–42, which says, *bnt hll bʿl gml*, "the daughters of *hll* the lord of the sickle," which Gibson, *Canaanite Myths and Legends*, 129 presumes to be the "emblem of the new moon." Gallagher suggests that *gml* here is the Akkadian constellation Gamlu, the Crook or "curved staff" (see, for example, *MUL.APIN* I.ii.37, iii.28.43, iv.5.14.34; see also William R. Gallagher, "On the Identity of Helel ben Sahar of Is. 14:12–15," *UF* 26 [1995]: 133). In *KTU* 1.24, *gml* is parallel to *snnt*, almost certainly the constellation Šinūnūtu. Alternatively, *bʿl gml* may simply be here the "lord of the (royal) staff," as *gamlu* in Akkadian can also be a symbol of divine or human sovereignty, thought to have powers of exorcism and cleansing. See *Šurpu* VIII.41, in Erica Reiner, *Šurpu: A Collection of Sumerian and Akkadian Incantations* (BAfO 11; Osnabrück: Biblio-Verlag, 1970), 41. If *gml* is the constellation, it is unclear how *hll* is its lord.

or the equation of Yariḫ and *hll*, but rather implies that the daughters of *hll*, the Kotharat, were needed to ensure the fertility of Nikkal's union with Yariḫ.[35] The equation of *hll* with a lunar deity has no evidence in support of it from Ugaritic literature. Gallagher's alternative suggestion, that Hêlēl is the same as Akkadian Illil, seems initially promising but poses several problems. First, never is *hll* unequivocally associated with Illil at Ugarit. That Illil is equated with ʾEl at Ugarit has been established, but Gallagher does not convincingly demonstrate that ʾEl is *hll*, only that Illil *could* be written *hll* at Ugarit. Second, Gallagher admits that nowhere is ʾEl referred to as "son of the Dawn." He rather refers to a first millennium text which "denotes the rising sun as Illil."[36] Finally, he acknowledges that the Kotharat, the daughters of *hll*, are not mentioned as ʾEl's daughters—Ištar, rather, is ʾEl's daughter. If Ištar is to be equated with Šaḥar, and Hêlēl is in some manner Šaḥar's son, either through proximity or genealogy, then according to Gallagher, ʾEl would be Ištar's son, an impossibility.

I have suggested above that Ištar is clearly related to Venus and the dawn in Mesopotamian and Syrian inscriptions. Ištar is equated with the dawn/morning star in several inscriptions in Akkadian (*šēru*, *šerētu*, etc.).[37] Note the following:

> Ištar ilat šimētān anāku, Ištar ilat še-re-e-ti anāku
> I am Ištar goddess of the evening (šimētān), I am Ištar, goddess of the morning (šērēti).[38]
>
> še-e-ru ša urḫāti upattû kīma AŠ.ME
> šēru (Ištar) who opens paths like the sun.[39]

If I am correct, then the children born to ʾEl and his union with Athirat and Anat, Šaḥar and Šalim, would be the dusk and dawn aspect of ʿAṯtart in *Šaḥar and Šalim and the Gracious Gods*.[40] Note that after the birth is announced, the next thing said has to do with the stars and "Lady Šapšu:"

> yldy.šḥr.wšl[m]
> šuʾ.ʿdb.lšpš.rbt
> wlkbkbm.kn[m]

---

[35] Both Ugaritic texts which mention *hll* and the Kotharat (*Aqhat* and *Nikkal and the Kotharat*) ascribe this function to the daughters of *hll*.

[36] Gallagher, "On the Identity of Helel ben Sahar," 143.

[37] Gallagher, "On the Identity of Helel ben Sahar," 143, alerted me to this connection.

[38] John Brinkman et al., "šērētu/i," *CAD* 17/2: 313.

[39] Brinkman et al., "šēru A (šīru)," *CAD* 17/2: 331.

[40] Gibson, *Canaanite Myths and Legends*, 30. He suggests that the two women are his sometime consorts, Anat and Athirat. This suggestion may be evidenced in the mention of Athirat and Rahmay (Gibson identifies her as Anat) in line 13.

Two have been born, *Šḥr* and *Šlm*
Raise (and) prepare (an offering) for Lady *Špš*
and the fixed stars.[41]

If *hll* is not to be identified with Illil or Hilāl, what is his identity and where is he to be found? A clue is given to us in both the name Hêlēl ben Šaḥar in Isa 14 and in *bnt hll snnt* in the Ugaritic texts. In the first title, Hêlēl is the son of, and not equivalent to, Šaḥar. It is possible that, if Šaḥar is to be equated with ʿAṯtart/Venus, Hêlēl may also be an astral body not far removed from the Venus star. Second, *bnt hll snnt* has been translated by Gibson as "the swallow-like daughters of *hll*." Following Gallagher, I would like to suggest that a better translation would be, "the daughters of *hll*, the (constellation) Swallow." Gallagher has alerted us that *snnt*, Akkadian Šinūnūtu/Sinūnūtu, is a constellation among the "stars of Anu" [42] and can be translated "the Swallow." Evidence that Hêlēl is a star in close proximity to Venus or the Ištar constellation, Annunītu (see under "Venus deities" above and "Hymns to Inanna and Dumuzi" in chapter four) comes from the astronomical compendium *MUL.APIN*:

The Field, the seat of Ea, which goes at the front of the stars of Anu.
The star which stands opposite the Field: the Swallow (Šinūnūtu).
The star which stands behind the Field, Annunītu.
The star which stands behind it, the Hired Man, Dumuzi.[43]

Out of the 23 stars of Anu, which follow the 33 stars of Enlil in the compendium, the first three, following the primordial god of heaven Anu, are stars of importance to this study. First, the Swallow, associated with *hll* in *Aqhat* (*KTU* 1.17 ii 27) and *Nikkal and the Kotharat* (*KTU* 1.24, 6, 15, 41); second, Annunītu, the constellation of Inanna/Ištar; and third, the Hired Man, Dumuzi, associated with Amaušumgalanna king of Sumer and his ascent to heaven in ritual texts. One also should note that the Venus star, Dilibat in *MUL.APIN*, is the first planet recorded in the series "stars of Anu," wherein we find the three constellations above, and Dilibat is associated with Ištar and Venus.[44] Finally, the last three

---

[41] "Schahar and Shalim and the Gracious Gods," *KTU* 1.23 53–54 (in Gibson, *Canaanite Myths and Legends*, 126).

[42] Not among the stars of Illil, problematical for Gallagher's thesis, as he admits.

[43] Hunger and Pingree, *MUL.APIN*, 29–30.

[44] Hunger and Pingree, *MUL.APIN*, 33. For Dilibat/d, see Labat, *Manuel d'epigraphie Akkadienne*, 43. See also Rochberg-Halton, *Enūma Anu Enlil*, 219. Apparently, these stars virtually always appear grouped together. Note the following:

If Sîn is in the land (and) ^{mul}Annunītu is obscured, the prediction is (of) the River Idigna and the land of Agade.

stars listed on tablet one of *MUL.APIN* are the Swallow, Annunītu, and the Hired Man, listed together once again, with the following comment:

> All these are the gods who stand in the path of the Moon, through whose regions the Moon in the course of a month passes and whom he touches.[45]

One other bit of evidence for this theory may be gleaned from *KTU* 1.24 and the Akkadian *Šurpu* incantations. *hll* is also referred to as *bʿl gml*, "lord of the *gamlu*." The first possibility, that Gamlu is the constellation "the Crook/Staff," is appealing, in light of the parallel with Š/Sinūnūtu, the Swallow. This is unlikely, however, for never is the constellation Gamlu associated with the Swallow in the astronomical compendia and it is difficult to ascertain in what sense *hll* is its lord. The more likely explanation is provided by the line in *KTU* 1.24 above: *bnt hll bʿl gml*. As I state above, *gamlu* is a crook or staff used by kings and divinities, but also used in exorcisms and rites of purification. Note *Šurpu* VIII.41:

> ᵈMar-tu ᵈMar-tu na-aš$_2$ gam-li BA.AN.DU$_8$.DU$_8$-e *mul-li-lu* muš-ši-pu
> ᵈMartu, ᵈMartu who carries the Crook and the drawing bucket, the "*purifier*" and the "conjuror." [46]

Note the association of *gamlu* and *elēlu*/*hll* here, as in *KTU* 24: the *gamlu* is said to purify. Note also VIII.78: "May the great gods who dwell in the heavens of Anu (including precisely the Swallow, Hired Man, and Annunītu! See *MUL.APIN* and my analysis above) release [you], absolve you in their assembly,"[47] and in line 83 the subject of the incantation is "purified" (*utallil*). In VIII.90, the function of the *gamlu* is to purify from sin: "May the Crook release your sin."[48] *hll* is *bʿl gml* because he is the "pure, bright one" (*ellu*), wielder of the purifying *gamlu*. In terms of cosmology, he traverses the heavens as a star in the constellation *snnt*, Šinūnūtu/Sinūnūtu, in immediate proximity to the Ištar constellation Annunītu and the Venus star, Šēru/Šaḥar.

It is unclear exactly what role the Swallow plays in Akkadian cosmology. It may be that in the West, *hll*/Šinūnūtu fulfilled a similar function as Agru/Dumuzi/Amaušumgalanna in Mesopotamia in terms of the ideology of the

---

If Sîn is in the land (and) ᵐᵘˡŠinūnūtu is obscured, the prediction is (of) the River Euphrates and the Sea.
If Sîn is in the land (and) ᵐᵘˡAgru is obscured, the prediction is (of) the land of Uruk and Kullaba.

[45] Hunger and Pingree, *MUL.APIN*, 68–69.

[46] Reiner, *Šurpu*, 41.

[47] Reiner, *Šurpu*, 43.

[48] Reiner, *Šurpu*, 44.

death of the king. A further possibility is that this grouping of three constellations, almost invariably found together in the astronomical texts, implies a genealogical relationship in which Ištar (Venus and the constellation Annunītu) and her consort in Mesopotamian literature Dumuzi (Agru), perhaps gave birth to *hll* (Šinūnūtu). Yet a third possibility is that "son of" in the text of Isa 14 simply implies proximity; in that case, *hll* (a star in or equivalent to the constellation Šinūnūtu) is near to Annunītu/Ištar, as the astronomical compendia attest.

IV. Summary

To summarize, *hll snnt* may be 1) a star in the constellation Šinūnūtu, in visual proximity to the constellation Annunītu, associated with Ištar and through which passes Venus/Dilibat, likewise the star of Ištar or 2) a star associated in some manner with kingship in close proximity to ("son of"), or in a genealogical affiliation with, the Ištar star Dilibat and the constellation Annunītu, immortalized in ritual hymns about the death and ascent of the king through the first century B.C.E.

Chapter 4
Ascent, Descent, and Other Mythological Motifs in Isaiah 14

I. Introduction

In chapters one and two I argued that commentators on Isa 14 have largely overlooked one of the most fundamental features of the chapter: that the poem is a dirge, specifically a "royal dirge," parodied with consummate skill. I also suggested that the concept of "myth" is exceedingly complex and ought not to be understood *only* in terms of a story about the gods. The word μύθος, to be sure, means "story," but a story with continuing political and ritual importance. As Mircea Eliade has suggested, myth is the bringing of the primordium into the present primarily by means of ritual and the cult. If this is the case, then the intense search for a narrative myth about the gods as the background for the chapter is not necessarily the most fruitful approach one could take. It is equally possible that the chapter reflects myth in the sense of cultic or ritual reenactment, or, in Eliade's terms, a bringing near of the primordium.

In this chapter we will begin by looking in general at the concept of the descent and ascent of the king in the ancient Near East and then at several ritual and mythological texts which reflect imagery similar to the ascent and descent motifs in Isa 14. We will also survey two other images prevalent in the poem: those of the Rephaim and the Cedar Forest of Lebanon.

II. The Ascent and Descent of the King: "Reach" or "Travel"?

Before looking at possible analogies to the heavenly ascent and netherworld descent imagery in Isa 14, a preliminary question must be addressed: that of the nature of the heavenly and netherworld imagery as they relate to the king. Specifically, does this imagery relate to the king's arrogant reach (his ability to make his presence and power felt universally), or to his identification with deified stars and their ability to travel to the heavens and the underworld?

The first thing to keep in mind is that Isa 14 is dirge literature, albeit a mock dirge, relating to the death of the king. As we saw in previous chapters, imagery found in Near Eastern royal dirges should then provide us with the most illuminating analogies. Many other texts exist, however, which also provide us with insight into the nature of this imagery, but a few examples each from Mesopotamian and Egyptian literature will suffice to show the complexity of the ideology and imagery surrounding the death of the king and his relationship to the heavens and the underworld.

Perhaps the most startling example of the ambiguity relating to understanding whether the metaphor of the *postmortem* existence of the king is one of reach or travel is that of the *Maqlû* incantation series. The *Maqlû* incantations include imagery which suggests the reach of the king or other ritual actor, performing the incantation:

> Enlil is my head, the Arrow is my body.
> The forehead is the Crescent Moon.
> My arms are the Crook (*gamlu*) of the gate of Marduk.
> My ears (?) are the Bull, my feet are the *laḫmu* gods which tread upon the body of the *laḫme* (?).
> You are the great gods, which are bright in the heavens.[1]

This passage suggests that the ritual actor becomes thoroughly identified with the stars of the heavens in order to ward off witchcraft. His body becomes one with various stars and constellations, while he himself remains standing on the rooftop where the ritual transpired, suggesting that the metaphor is one of reach. On the other hand, Tzvi Abusch suggests that the reason for the identification with astral bodies is to possess their wakefulness and ability to travel to both the underworld and the heavens, in order to prevent evil witches from escaping to the realm of the living.[2] Note tablet one, lines 42–45:

> An incantation. My city is Zabban, my city is Zabban,
> My city Zabban has two gates:

---

[1] Compare with *Die assyrische Beschwörungssammlung Maqlû* (Gerhard Meier, BAfO 2; Osnabrück: Biblio-Verlag, 1967), 48. I follow here Meier's transcription of the Akkadian, but the translation is my own. See below for details on the Maqlû incantations.

[2] Tzvi Abusch, "Ascent to the Stars in a Mesopotamian Ritual: Social Metaphor and Religious Experience," in *Death, Ecstasy, and Other Worldly Journeys* (ed. John J. Collins and Michael Fishbane; Albany: State University of New York Press, 1995), 20–21, 24–25.

The first for the going out of the sun, the second for the setting of the sun,
The first for the going out of the sun, the second for the setting of the sun.[3]

"Zabban," according to Abusch, is probably the same as Saphon, the holy mountain of the Canaanites in the West. Here it is not intended to connote a specific geographical location, but rather to designate the gate of the heavens and the underworld through which the heavenly bodies pass.[4] By identifying himself with Zabban, an *axis mundi*, the ritual actor qualifies himself to possess the same attributes as the stars which pass through its gates. The reason for the identification with the stars in these incantations is at least partially to access their ability to travel to the heavens and the underworld.

The ancient Egyptian *Pyramid Texts* also provide evidence for the ambiguity of the imagery relating to the king's *postmortem* existence. With reference to the king, utterance 415 says

Your head is Horus of the netherworld, O Imperishable.
Your face is Mḫnt-irty, O Imperishable.
Your ears are the Twin Children of Atum, O Imperishable.
Your eyes are the Twin Children of Atum, O Imperishable.
Your nose is the Jackal, O Imperishable.
Your teeth are Sopd, O Imperishable.
Your hands are Ḥapy and Duamūtef.[5]

This utterance is similar to the description of the ritual actor's identification with the heavens in the *Maqlû* incantation series, suggesting the king's cosmic reach and personal identification with the heavens and the underworld. The very next lines of this utterance, however, broaden and complicate the imagery:

You demand that you ascend to the sky and you shall ascend—
Your feet are imsety and ḳebḥsenuf—
You demand that you descend to the Lower Sky and you shall descend—
Your members are the Twin Children of Atum, O Imperishable.
You shall not perish and your double shall not perish,
For *you* are a double.[6]

Utterance 210 is unambiguous that the dead king traverses the heavens:

O you two Companions who cross the sky, who are Rēʿ and Thoth, take me with you, that I may eat of what you eat, that I may drink of what you drink, that I may live on

---

[3] Meier, *Maqlû*, 8. The translation is my own.

[4] Abusch, "Ascent to the Stars," 20–21.

[5] Raymond Faulkner, *The Ancient Egyptian Pyramid Texts* (Oxford: Oxford University Press, 1969), 42.

[6] Faulkner, *Pyramid Texts*, 42–43.

> what you live on, that I may sit on what you sit on, that I may be strong through that whereby you are strong, that I may sail in that in which you sail. My booth is plaited with rushes, my drink supply is in the Field of Offerings, my food-offerings are among you, you gods, my water is wine like that of Rēʿ, and I go round the sky like Rēʿ, I traverse the sky like Thoth.[7]

Apparently, there was room in the Egyptian royal ideology to accommodate views which seem contradictory to us.

What is true of kings is also true of gods, relative to terminology of ascent, descent, and reach. An example from Mesopotamian literature will illustrate that the complexity of the imagery of travel and effective power and reach are also found with respect to deities: the *Poem of Erra.* In this poem, the god Erra determines to destroy Babylon and Akkad against Išum's advice and with Marduk's misgivings. In tablet three, Išum extols Erra's power and reach:

> Hero Erra, you are holding the nose-rope of heaven.
> You dominate the whole earth. You lord it over the country.
> You convulse the sea, you destroy the mountains.
> You govern men, you shepherd the herds.
> Ešarra is at your disposal, E'engurra is in your hands.
> You control Šuanna, you give orders to Esagila.
> You gather all the divine powers to yourself. The gods fear you.
> The Igigi shy away from you. The Anunnaki are in dread of you.
> (If) you make a decision, Anum listens to you.
> Enlil gives you his favor. Without you, is there (any) hostility?[8]

Erra is shown here to have effective power and control in the realm of the heavens, humanity, and the underworld, suggesting the metaphor of reach. One of the ways this power is made manifest, is through the metaphor of travel:

> As soon as Erra heard such words, he opened his mouth and spoke to prince Marduk:
> "Until you enter that house, prince Marduk, and Girra purifies your garment, and you return to your place,
> Till then I shall rule in your stead and keep strong the government of heaven and earth.
> Up to the sky I shall go and give orders to the Igigi.
> Down into the Apsû I shall descend and keep the Anunnaki under control."[9]

Note the use of both images, travel and reach, in Isa 14:

> The one who smote peoples with fury, a never-ceasing blow,
> The one who ruled the nations with anger, persecuting without restraint. (v. 6)

---

[7] Faulkner, *Pyramid Texts*, 39.

[8] Luigi Cagni, *The Poem of Erra* (SANE 1/3; Malibu: Undena, 1977), 48.

[9] Cagni, *The Poem of Erra*, 34.

> You have said in your heart, "I will ascend to heaven, above the stars of ʾEl I will
> raise my throne,
> And I will sit down in the mount of assembly, in the heights of Saphon,
> I will ascend above the heights of the cloud, I will become like ʿElyôn." (vv. 13–14)

The metaphor of ascent ("I will ascend," v. 14), descent ("How you are fallen," v. 12), and reach ("smote peoples," "ruled the nations," v. 6) are all used in the poem. As with *Erra*, *Maqlû*, and the *Pyramid Texts*, these images are not mutually exclusive at all, but are both ways of expressing effective power and presence in the heavens, on earth, and in the underworld.

III. The Ascent and Descent of the King in the Ancient Near East

There are some texts which suggest that dead kings throughout the ancient Near East were understood to enjoy royal and occasionally divine status in the realm of the dead.[10] Several texts describe the ascent of certain kings to the heavens as deified stars or as possessing status in the underworld. The two aspects of the king's *postmortem* life as a star in heaven and as king, enthroned in the underworld, will therefore be surveyed in the ancient Near Eastern literature. Without minimizing the differences which existed between different cultures and their conceptions, we are perhaps justified in pursuing a synchronic approach in order to ascertain the nature of their understanding of the dead king's state in the underworld, their similarities and dissimilarities, and extent of congruence with Isa 14.

A. EGYPTIAN EVIDENCE

The ancient Egyptian *Pyramid Texts* provide a great deal of evidence for the king's *postmortem* ascent to the heavens and descent to the underworld. The Egyptian king was considered the son of Rēʿ and therefore capable, at least after death, of following his father on his course through the heavens and the

---

[10] See the description by Lowell Handy, *Among the Host of Heaven: The Syro-Palestinian Pantheon as a Bureaucracy* (Winona Lake: Eisenbrauns, 1994), 142: "The king, after his death, became a god (*il*) who retained the title *mlk*, while joining a collective group known as the *mlkm* or *rpʾm*." William Hallo makes a strong case for the veneration of dead kings in his article "Royal Ancestor Worship in the Biblical World," in *"Shaʿarei Talmon": Studies in the Bible, Qumran, and the Ancient Near East Presented to Shemaryahu Talmon* (ed. Michael Fishbane and Emmanuel Tov; Winona Lake: Eisenbrauns, 1992), 399.

underworld. The first utterance in the *Pyramid Texts* which refers to the close association of the deceased king with Rēᶜ is utterance 50:[11]

> O Rēᶜ, if you dawn in the sky, you dawn for the king, lord of all things.

Throughout much of Egyptian history the king is called the son of Rēᶜ, or some other term for the sun god.[12] This understanding of the king as the son of the sun god is also inextricably bound up with the myth of Isis, Horus, and Osiris. Throughout Egyptian history the living king is identified with Horus, son of Osiris. The deceased king becomes Osiris and goes to the underworld where he holds court.[13] It is sufficient here to note that Utterance 49, immediately preceding the utterance quoted above, refers to the recently deceased king as Osiris.

Utterance 215 refers to the ascension of the king as a star in a rather oblique way:

> O King, your messengers go, your heralds run to your father, to Atum. O Atum, raise him up to you, enclose him within your arms. There is no star-god who has no companion, have you your companion? [14]

Line 149 of utterance 215 captures the notion of ascent and descent of the king well:

> You demand that you ascend to the sky and you shall ascend . . ., you demand that you descend to the Lower Sky and you shall descend.[15]

Utterance 216 furthers this concept of ascent as a star, from the perspective of the king actually in the heavens:

> I have come to you, O Nepthys;
> I have come to you, O Night-bark;
> I have come to you O Mꜣᶜ-ḥr-ṯrwt;
> I have come to you, my father, I have come to you, O Sharp of Teeth.

---

[11] Faulkner, *Pyramid Texts*, 10.

[12] In the pre-historic period in particular, there were a number of different deities with solar aspects. Among these were Amun, Rēᶜ, Atum, and several others. Even into the dynastic period several conflicting theologies with their corresponding pantheons existed, in particular the Memphite and Theban. Eventually, Amun and Rēᶜ became associated in the DN Amun-Rēᶜ; in the Pyramid Texts, Rēᶜ had already become associated with Atum in the DN Rēᶜ-Atum. See Adolf Erman, *Life in Ancient Egypt* (London: MacMillan, 1894), 260–261.

[13] Many differing and contradictory accounts of the myth of Isis and Osiris exist. It is beyond the scope of this analysis to go into detail relative to these accounts.

[14] Faulkner, *Pyramid Texts*, 42.

[15] Faulkner, *Pyramid Texts*, 42.

> Grant that I may seize the sky and take possession of the horizon.
> Grant that I may rule the Nine and provide for the Ennead.

Nowhere is the ascent/descent motif more clearly enunciated than in lines 209–210 of Utterance 216:

> Ascend and descend; descend with Rēᶜ, sink into darkness with Ndi.
> Ascend and descend; ascend with Rēᶜ, rise with the great Float-user.
> Ascend and descend; descend with Nepthys, sink into darkness with the Night-bark.
> Ascend and descend; ascend with Isis, rise with the Day-bark.

Lines 207 and 208 of this utterance also explicitly refer to both the ascent and descent of the king:

> Cast off your impurity for Atum in On and go down with him; assign the needs of the Lower Sky and succeed to the thrones of the Abyss. May you come into being with your father Atum, may you go up on high with your father Atum, may you rise with your father Atum. . . . Go up, open your way by means of the bones of Shu, the embrace of your mother Nūt will enfold you. Be pure in the horizon and get rid of your impurity in the Lakes of Shu.

Of special note here is the graphic way in which the daily course of the king as a star in the heavens is described. He ascends with the night-bark and descends during the day in the day-bark, presumably through the underworld. Of particular interest is the descent with the sun god (here Atum, line 207) to the thrones of the Abyss. In some manner, the king of Egypt may retain a throne in the netherworld not unlike Niqmaddu of Ugarit or Ur-Nammu in the preceding chapter.[16] Finally, note the connection with the pictorial representations described above: the king ascends to the sky by means of the night-bark, climbing in some manner the bones of Shu,[17] and then is received into the body of Nūt.

In the *Pyramid Texts* the king's identification with a star is often stated or implied. Indeed, In one utterance he is called the Lone Star (*sbꜣ wᶜti*).[18] In several others, the star he is equated with is *nṯr dwꜣ(w)*, Venus or the morning star.[19] In Utterance 320, the star is Babi, lord of the night skies. Faulkner cites

---

[16] Faulkner, *Pyramid Texts*, 42. All other quotes are from the corresponding utterance in Faulkner, *Pyramid Texts*.

[17] See Utterance 246, lines 255–256, where a reference to ruling over the Ennead is made explicit. What is not explicit is where such ruling occurs, whether in the sky or in the netherworld.

[18] Utterance 257; Faulkner, *Pyramid Texts*, 67.

[19] Utterance 245; Faulkner, *Pyramid Texts*, 58. Faulkner equates this star as well with Venus, in its evening star aspect. See Faulkner, "The King and the Star Religion in the Pyramid Texts," *JNES* 25 (1966): 160.

K. Sethe's hypothesis that Orion might be intended here and then suggests his own opinion, that it "may be a description of Canopus, which is yellowish in color and which, as the second brightest star in the sky, might well be called lord of the night skies."[20] One might well ask, "Why not the brightest star in the sky?" This would certainly be Venus, *nṯr dwꜣ(w),* in its dual role as the evening and morning star. Contra Neugebauer and Parker, Venus was not known as *nṯr dwꜣ(w)* only in the late period, but was already known by this appellation in the Old Kingdom and is mentioned repeatedly in the *Pyramid Texts* of the Old Kingdom and the *Coffin Texts* of the Middle Kingdom.[21]

Further evidence that the king was occasionally identified with Venus may be found in the early designation of the planet as *Wsir*, Osiris.[22] As the dead king became Osiris *par excellence*, he was identified with the Osiris star.[23]

The earlier designation for Venus in the Senmut, Seti I, and Hermopolis (2nd millennium) groups of decanal stars, according to Neugebauer and Parker, was *ḏꜣ* (the Crosser) or *sbꜣ ḏꜣ* (the star which crosses).[24] It is possible that this name signifies Venus's movement back and forth about the sun.[25] If this is correct, it may be that references in the *Pyramid Texts* to the king as one who goes to and fro with Rēʿ (Utterances 258 and 259), one who travels the air and traverses the earth (Utterance 261), and the one who crosses on the [reed floats] to the horizon (Utterance 264) may be oblique references to Venus, the Crosser.[26]

B. MESOPOTAMIAN EVIDENCE

Some evidence exists for the descent of the deceased king into a privileged and ruling position in the netherworld and for the ascent of at least some dead

---

[20] Faulkner, *Pyramid Texts*, Utterances 132, 804–805, 871, 1295, 1366, 2014, 2015, etc. These occurrences are listed and categorized by Faulkner, "Star Religion," 153–161. Faulkner has missed one occurrence: Utterance 306, p. 94, where the king is called *Dwꜣw*, which might mean daytime, dawn, or morning star. The hieroglyphs are written, however, in the usual way for depicting the morning star, Venus, and not dawn, even though the forms *sbꜣ* (star) or *nṯr* (god) do not precede *Dwꜣ(w)*.

[21] Faulkner, *Pyramid Texts*, 102.

[22] O. Neugebauer and Richard Parker, *Egyptian Astronomical Texts, Vol. 1: The Early Decans* (London: Lund Humphries, 1960), 180. Faulkner, *Coffin Texts*, 59 and 67.

[23] Neugebauer and Parker, *Egyptian Astronomical Texts*, 180–181. Note also that the king is addressed in the *Pyramid Texts*, utterances 47–49, as Osiris the king (Faulkner, *Pyramid Texts*, 10).

[24] Osiris was also associated with Orion. See Faulkner, "Star Religion," 158.

[25] Neugebauer and Parker, *Egyptian Astronomical Texts*, 180.

[26] Neugebauer and Parker, *Egyptian Astronomical Texts*, 182. They think this interpretation is possible, but not compelling.

kings into the heavens as a star. Most of the direct evidence for such ideology comes from Sumerian Ur III texts, where the king was apparently worshipped as divine. We shall first survey Babylonian cosmology as it relates to the course of the heavenly bodies through the skies and the netherworld and then turn to specific texts dealing with deceased kings.

1. The Course of the Heavenly Bodies

Wolfgang Heimpel has surveyed passages in Babylonian and Sumerian literature which allude to the movement of the sun and other heavenly bodies.[27] He assumes that the sun traveled through the netherworld at night, as was the case with Egyptian cosmology. His analysis confirms this assumption and he goes on to make a number of other interesting assertions. According to Heimpel, the sun, Šamaš or UTU, traveled across the heavens during the day and entered the gates of "heaven's interior" or lap (*utlu*) at night. In the lap of heaven, the sun rested in his abode, known as the "white house,"[28] met his wife and vizier,[29] and fulfilled there some of his duties as judge.[30] While the sun god had some official functions in the realm of the dead, his course, according to Heimpel, was not actually a part of it, but was the "road of Šamaš," through "Twin Mountain" to the gates of the sunrise as explained in *Gilgamesh* tablet 9.[31] Some texts, however, do have the sun entering and judging in the netherworld and finding no time for rest at all.[32] Other deities also followed the sun on the daily course through the heavens and the underworld, or lap of heaven; Nanna or Sîn, the moon god,[33] Ištar,[34] one passage each for Ninurta and Aššur,[35] and star gods.[36] Heimpel posits numerous gateways out of the lap of heaven to the Heavens proper, as a single gateway would not be possible for all the stars in

---

[27] Wolfgang Heimpel, "The Sun at Night and the Doors of Heaven in Babylonian Texts," *JCS* 38 (1986): 127.

[28] Heimpel, "The Sun at Night," 128.

[29] Heimpel, "The Sun at Night," 128–129.

[30] Heimpel, "The Sun at Night," 130. The sun might have fulfilled these duties at the "level place," an obscure reference Heimpel thinks might relate to such activities.

[31] Heimpel, "The Sun at Night," 140.

[32] Heimpel, "The Sun at Night," 146–147. See also Kramer, *Two Elegies*.

[33] Heimpel, "The Sun at Night," 134.

[34] Heimpel, "The Sun at Night," 135.

[35] Heimpel, "The Sun at Night," 135–137.

[36] Heimpel, "The Sun at Night," 139–140.

their diverse ecliptics and thinks this is confirmed by the plural form "gateways of heaven." [37]

Finally, an important aspect of this "heavenly highway" is the mountains of sunrise and sunset. The first is often called the "Cedar Mountain," usually designating the mountains to the west, which cannot be mountains of sunrise for Mesopotamia. Heimpel takes the description figuratively. The sunset mountain, according to Heimpel, is mentioned only once in extant literature, called the "dark mountain" alongside the "light mountain" of sunrise. The dark mountain, according to Heimpel, was inhabited by demons who ran about and played.[38]

Generally speaking, there are points of contact between the Egyptian and the Babylonian cosmologies. Both have courses which the sun, moon, and stars run on a daily basis which encompass the heavens and the underworld. At least some Babylonian and Egyptian formulations contain mountains of sunrise and sunset. The day-bark and the night-bark figure largely in the Egyptian cosmology. There is also in some Babylonian conceptions a "bark" of the heavenly bodies:

> When An, Enlil, Enki, the great gods, set up among themselves the great powers through their true counsel, they established the gondola of Suen. They established the waxing of the new moon, the giving birth to the month. . . . For the gondola to appear brightly in heaven, it emerged from heaven's interior.[39]

Interestingly, deified stars in Sumer travel in a gondola, or night-bark, as was also the case in Egypt. Note this description of king Šulgi's *magur*-boat:

> His shining royal *magur*-boat, which he had caulked—which was adorned with pure "horns," whose golden "ram" was shining in the midst of the sky. . . He decorated it with stars like the sky.[40]

This idealized picture depicts him in a god-like stance with his heavenly gondola and divine oarsmen.[41] Šulgi later becomes a deified star upon his death.

---

[37] Heimpel, "The Sun at Night," 139. See also the section above on the metaphors of reach and travel for discussion of the Akkadian *Maqlû* incantations and their references to the *axis mundi* of "Zabban" and the gateways of the sun from the netherworld to the heavens.

[38] Heimpel, "The Sun at Night," 145; tablet 12 of *Utukku Lemnutu.*

[39] From the *Enūma Anu Enlil*, quoted in Heimpel, "The Sun at Night," 131.

[40] Jacob Klein, *Three Šulgi Hymns: Sumerian Royal Hymns Glorifying King Šulgi of Ur* (Ramat-Gan: Bar-Ilan University Press, 1981), 86–87.

[41] The *magur*-boat is clearly the heavenly gondola or bark in other texts. See Jacob Klein, *Three Šulgi Hymns,* 75: "The king, the [pure] *magur*-boat [which traverses the sky]." For the restoration see Klein, *Three Šulgi Hymns*, 95. For another recent study of the *magur* boat, see Jacob Klein, "Šulgi and Išme-Dagan: Originality and Dependence in Sumerian Royal Hymnology" (*Bar-Ilan University Studies in Assyriology*; Ramat-Gan: Bar-Ilan University Press, 1990), 65-136. Klein says, "The *magur*-boat served as a ceremonial

Nevertheless, at several points the Egyptian and Babylonian conceptions do not converge. Not least of these divergences is the preoccupation of the Egyptians with an afterlife in the netherworld and the heavens. Mesopotamians seem never to have had the same kind of preoccupation. Indeed, the *arallu*, or realm of the dead, is almost uniformly a dismal and unhappy place and speculation about life in the heavens is minimal at best.[42] Mesopotamian literature is not nearly as graphic in its imagery about the possibility for deceased humans to survive and thrive in the underworld, nor is it so pictorial in its depiction of various modes of ascent to the heavens (falcon, boat, ferry, etc.). One might say that to the Sumerian and Babylonian mind, life in the netherworld is best characterized as death, while to the Egyptians the afterlife could be life indeed.

On the other hand, one must not be too quick to characterize the afterlife among the Sumerians, Babylonians, and other inhabitants of Mesopotamia as uniformly hostile and evil. In the *Death of Ur-Nammu*, Ur-Nammu was greeted warmly and afforded a royal place in the realm of the dead. Obviously, some dead people were more equal than others, to misuse a phrase from George Orwell. It is my hypothesis that deceased kings throughout the ancient Near East were, as a rule, conceived as having the right and the position of rule in the netherworld and for some, the possibility of life among the gods of the heavens as a star. Let us now move on to a discussion of specific texts which deal with the *postmortem* ascent and descent of kings in Mesopotamia.

2. The Ascent and Descent of the Deceased King[43]

a. The Sumerian King List

We will survey now possible evidence from the *Sumerian King List* in order to determine which Sumerian kings a later author or authors felt may have

procession-boat for gods and kings alike, in their religious as well as military journeys" (Klein, *Three Šulgi Hymns*, 96). Of all of the Sumerian "boat texts" mentioned by Klein in his survey, it is interesting that Šulgi is the only human king who constructs and utilizes a *magur*-boat; otherwise, only deities are said to have these kinds of boats (Nanshe, Enki, Nanna). For a further cosmological description of the *magur*-boat see Klein, "Šulgi and Išme-Dagan," 105–107.

[42] See, for example, the depictions of the netherworld in tablet 12 of the *Epic of Gilgamesh* and the *Descent of Ištar*. We shall see below that speculation about divine kingship was not entirely lacking in Mesopotamia.

[43] Donald Gowan, *When Man becomes God*, 54–58, has also presented a brief survey of the "ascent/descent" motif in the ancient Near East in his analysis of Isa 14. His analysis, however, is of the ascent and descent of deities in the ancient Near East and Greece. Little work has been done in the analysis of texts in the ancient Near East which relate to the ascent and descent of the king.

been deified.[44] While the *King List* has been collated over many years from a number of sources and there are many lacunae in the text relative to names and regnal years,[45] there is ample evidence that some, at least, of the Sumerian kings were considered later to have been deified, ascended to heaven, or both. We look first at explicit statements to this effect and then at name formulae.

Etana, of the first dynasty of Kish, according to Thorkild Jacobsen is the first king with any real claim to historicity in the *King List*. *King List* ii 16 says

> e-ta-na sipa lu_2 $an-se_3$
> $ba-e_{11}-de_3$
> lu_2 kur-kur mu-un-gi-na
> $lugal-am_3$ mu 1,560 i_3-a_5
>
> Etana, a shepherd, the one who to heaven
> ascended,
> the one who consolidated all lands,
> became king and reigned 1,560 years.[46]

More will be said about Etana below, but for now it is sufficient to say that his "ascent" to heaven may be no more than a reference to his aborted attempt to ascend to the "highest heaven" with the eagle in the *Legend of Etana*.

The only other unusual feature relative to our topic is the note given about Gilgamesh (iii 18):

> ab-ba-ni li_2-la_2
> his father was a lillû demon.

---

[44] Thorkild Jacobsen, *The Sumerian King List* (AS 11; Chicago: University of Chicago Press, 1939). Jacobsen suggests on linguistic and thematic grounds that the list was first compiled from ancient sources during the reign of Utu-Hegal, after the defeat of the Gutian invaders during the late third millennium B.C.E. (Jacobsen, *King List*, 140–141). It goes on to include the rulers of the Ur III dynasty and several of the kings of Isin, however, so a later updating of the king list in the period of Isin (if Jacobsen is correct) must be posited. This supposition is further bolstered by the lack of any narrative or descriptive lines after Utu-Hegal (Jacobsen's "notes"), but simple reporting of names and regnal years.

[45] The date of the *King List* continues to be a thorny issue. Suggestions have ranged between Jacobsen's early date (Utu-Hegal), along with the theory that several of the dynasties were coterminous, to Krause's late date in the Isin period. A recent discovery of a fragment of the *King List* suggests that there was an edition of the list which dates to Utu-Hegal (due to a variant note that Dumuzi, and not Gilgamesh, defeated Enmebaregesi), but was subsequently updated and edited during the reign of Šulgi, who thought of Gilgamesh as the "divine brother and patron of the Ur III kings" (see Klein, "A New Nippur Duplicate of the Sumerian King List in the Brockman Collection, University of Haifa," *AuOr* 9 [1991]: 128–129).

[46] The translation and transliteration are from Jacobsen, *King List*, 80–81.

Jacobsen suggests that this note may be read in conjunction with the description of Gilgamesh in the *Epic of Gilgamesh* (I ii 1: "Two-thirds of him is god, [one-third of him is human]" [47]), that his parentage was not exclusively human. This statement does not necessarily imply divine status for Gilgamesh himself.[48]

Other possible evidence from the *Sumerian King List* may be in king names preceded by the divine determinative DINGIR (^{d}). Kings with the divine determinative *before* their names in the *List* include the following:[49]

Name	Place of Rule/Dynasty	Citation in King List
^{d}dumu-zi	Bad-tibira	i 15
^{d}lugal-ban$_3$-da[50]	1st dynasty of Uruk	iii 12
^{d}dumu-zi	1st dynasty of Uruk	iii 14
^{d}giš-bil-ga-mes (Gilgamesh)	1st dynasty of Uruk	iii 17
^{d}utu-he$_2$-g[al$_2$][51]	2nd dynasty of Uruk	viii 3
^{d}ur-^{d}nammu[52]	3rd dynasty of Ur	viii 9,11
^{d}šul-gi	3rd dynasty of Ur	viii 11
^{d}bur-^{d}sin$_2$	3rd dynasty of Ur	viii 13
^{d}šu-i$_3$-lī-šu	1st dynasty of Isin	viii 25
^{d}li-pi$_2$-it-eš$_4$-tar$_2$	1st dynasty of Isin	viii 31
^{d}ur-^{d}ninurta	1st dynasty of Isin	viii 33
^{d}bur-^{d}sin$_2$	1st dynasty of Isin	viii 34
^{d}li-pi$_2$-it-^{d}en-lil$_2$	1st dynasty of Isin	viii 36
^{d}ir$_3$-ra-i-mi-ti[53]	1st dynasty of Isin	viii 38
^{d}en-līl-ba-ni[54]	1st dynasty of Isin	viii 39
^{d}za-am-bi-ia	1st dynasty of Isin	viii 40
^{d}i-te-er-pi$_4$-ša	1st dynasty of Isin	viii 41

---

[47] "The Epic of Gilgamesh," translated by E. A. Speiser (*ANET*, 73).

[48] See Jacobsen, *King List*, 90–91.

[49] One expects the divine determinative before a god name as part of a PN. The bulk of these names do not begin with a DN, but some other element. In a few cases, where the PN does begin with a DN, the evidence is ambiguous and I have indicated it as such below.

[50] Lugalbanda was clearly worshipped as deified in the Ur III period. He was married to the goddess Ninsun; both were the parents of Gilgamesh, himself understood to be part divine. See Jeremy Black and Anthony Green, *Gods, Demons and Symbols of Ancient Mesopotamia: An Illustrated Dictionary* (Austin: University of Texas Press, 1992), 123.

[51] As most king names in the *King List* do not begin with a DN, it is impossible to determine here whether the DINGIR sign has to do strictly with DN UTU or if it does "double-duty" for Utu-hegal as a deified monarch.

[52] Ur-Nammu is written as both ^{d}ur-^{d}nammu and ur-^{d}nammu here. Jacobsen did not recognize this and did not translate as he usually does, "divine PN."

[53] Irra here begins the PN with DN and is therefore ambiguous.

[54] As with Utu-Hegal, the use of the divine determinative here could be ambiguous; it is taken here by Jacobsen as a reflection of divine kingship.

^{d}ur-du$_6$-ku$_3$-ga	1st dynasty of Isin	viii 42
^{d}sin$_2$-ma-gir	1st dynasty of Isin	viii 43

One must be cautious, of course, in the use of divine determinatives in the reconstruction of royal ideology. Note, however, that several of the PN's above do not have the divine name as the first element, suggesting that it is the king himself, and not the title of the god, which is being referred to by DINGIR. In the majority of these cases, Jacobsen has translated the king's names with this in view: "the divine PN." When one compares this list with the inscriptions cited below, there are some interesting correspondences. Those said to ascend to heaven, descend to the netherworld with royal prerogatives, or both, are Etana (although Etana does not have the divine determinative in this text), Dumuzi, Ur-Nammu, Šulgi, and Šu-Ilišu. It is also interesting that kings' names with the divine determinative become much more prevalent in the Ur III and Isin periods than in any prior period, at least according to the *King List*. It is possible that the use of the divine determinative partially reflects the Sumerian ideology of divine kingship/ascent to heaven upon death. If this is at all correct, then William Hallo's position that only legendary and antediluvian kings could be deified and ascend to heaven must be questioned.[55]

b. Dumuzi

There are two Dumuzis who were kings in Sumer, one antediluvian (king of Bad-tibira) and one postdiluvian (king of Uruk). While either, or neither, may be an historical (?) figure behind the myth of Dumuzi and Inanna,[56] what is important for this analysis is that kings, in the Ur III period at least, were identified with him and there is at least one text which may allude to his own ascent to heaven as a star. This is BM 88318, transcribed in CT 58, no. 13. This is a Dumuzi-Inanna hymn, analyzed by S. N. Kramer in 1984. According to Kramer, it depicts Dumuzi's ascent to heaven in an appeal to "station him against the sky." Kramer suggests that this stationing may well have been identification with one of the stars or planets not far from the Venus star.[57]

---

[55] See William Hallo, "The Death of Kings: Traditional Historiography in Contextual Perspective," in *Ah, Assyria: Studies in Assyrian History and Ancient Near Eastern Historiography Presented to Hayim Tadmor* (ed. Mordecai Cogan and Israel Eph'al, Scripta Hierosolymitana 33; Jerusalem: Magnes, 1991), 148–165.

[56] Samuel N. Kramer assumes an historical personage behind the Dumuzi myth in *The Sacred Marriage Rite* (Bloomington: Indiana University Press, 1969), 57.

[57] Samuel N. Kramer, "BM 88318: The Ascension of Dumuzi to Heaven," CEPOA 2 (1984): 5–9. Unfortunately, this article has been unavailable to me. The analysis and quotes herein come from Daniel Foxvog, "Astral Dumuzi," in *The Tablet and the Scroll: Near*

c. Gilgamesh

Gilgamesh does not ascend to heaven in the Neo-Assyrian version of the epic. According to Heimpel, he may well travel through at least a portion of the netherworld, the "road of Šamaš," on his way to see Utnapishtim. Tablet IX of the Neo-Assyrian version of the *Gilgamesh Epic* says the following relative to his entry into this subterranean road whose gate was at the mountains of sunrise and sunset, the mountain range Mashu:

> When [he arrived] at the mountain range of Mashu,
> Which daily keeps watch over sun[rise and sunset]—
> Whose peaks [reach to] the vault of heaven
> (And) whose breasts reach to the netherworld below—
> Scorpion-men guard its gate,
> Whose terror is awesome and whose glance was death.
> Their shimmering halo sweeps the mountains
> That at sunrise and sunset keep watch over the sun.[58]

After an exchange with the scorpion-men, Gilgamesh is sent on his way, through the gate of the underworld on the road of the sun:

> "Go, Gilga[mesh...].
> The mountains of Mashu [...].
> The mountains (and) ranges [...].
> In safety may [...].
> The gate of the mountain [is open to thee]!"
> When Gilga[mesh heard this],
> To the word [of the Scorpion-man he gave heed].
> Along the road of the sun [he went].[59]

After twelve long leagues of total darkness, Gilgamesh emerges into the light of a jewel forest. While the Neo-Assyrian version is here broken, the beginning of the Old Babylonian version at tablet X gives a brief discussion between Šamaš, the sun god, and Gilgamesh. The importance of this analysis is simply to underscore 1) that it was possible for human kings (although Gilgamesh was "two-thirds god")[60] in Mesopotamian tradition to have access to the underworld,

---

Eastern Studies in Honor of William W. Hallo (ed. Mark Cohen et al.; Bethesda: CDL, 1993), 103–108. On the Venus star, see my analysis below.

[58] "The Epic of Gilgamesh" (*ANET*, 88).

[59] "The Epic of Gilgamesh" (*ANET*, 89).

[60] Everyone in the Neo-Assyrian version seems to be aware of this, even the scorpion-men: "His wife answers the scorpion-man: "two-thirds of him is god, one-third of him is human" ("The Epic of Gilgamesh" [*ANET*, 88]).

or at least that part which the sun god traveled, and 2) that the picture of the sun god's course described by Heimpel is essentially correct.

In many later texts it is clear that Gilgamesh was identified as a major deity, especially as king and judge in the netherworld.[61] Many of these texts come from the first millennium B.C.E. At least in the case of Gilgamesh, his descent to the netherworld, retention of royal status, and even exaltation as a deity are clear.

d. Etana

Etana was one of the earliest antediluvian kings of Sumer, according to the *Etana* epic and the *Sumerian King List*. In a recent article, Bendt Alster has identified a new fragment of a bi-lingual text long known (RS 25.130, published in *Ugaritica V* by J. Nougayrol), in part a duplicate of BM 80184.[62] Alster translates this "new composition," beginning in line 4, as follows:

> [Etana?] the king, the man who ascended to heaven,
> ...Like Ziusudra sought for life.
> .....
> Where are they, the early kings, those of early days?
> They are not engendered, they are not born (anymore).
> As heaven is far away, my hand can [not] reach them.
> As earth is broad, no man knows (them)...
> Having been given [life] by the gods,
> It was sought for [Ziusudra],[63]
> [But] death is the share of mankind.

There are a number of interesting features in this text. Etana is clearly the prime candidate for restoration in line four, as Alster suggests. In the *Legend of Etana*, he is the king who ascended to heaven, but attempted to rise higher than his station allowed (see my analysis of *Etana* below). Kinnier Wilson suggests from the recent collation of fragmentary texts that Etana in fact fell with the eagle he rode upon, resulting in his death. Also, although Etana is said to ascend to heaven, it is a "pessimistic" text; that is, it deals with the finality of death, the shortness of life, and the impossibility of communication between the living and the dead. The text clearly deals with death. Also, if Etana should be restored in line four with Alster, it is not a text which celebrates his attempt to reach the

---

[61] Jeffrey Tigay, *The Evolution of the Gilgamesh Epic* (Philadelphia: University of Pennsylvania Press, 1982), 13–14 and Thorkild Jacobsen, *The Treasures of Darkness: A History of Mesopotamian Religion* (New Haven: Yale University Press, 1976), 86, 210–211.

[62] Bendt Alster, "A Sumerian Poem about Early Rulers," ASJ 8 (1986): 7.

[63] Alster assumes the restoration should be Ziusudra, but see my analysis below.

heights of heaven. He fails in his attempt and falls. Rather than ascent to heaven and eternal life, the lot of humans, even that of the "early kings," is dismal:

> Instead of a single day of joy, there will be days of silence for 36,000 bad(?) years. (line 15)

It is possible that the text does not suggest that normal mortals, whose whole life "is like the twinkling of an eye" (line 12), are compared with deified kings who did not die. If Etana is in view, he reigned 36,000 years and "like Ziusudra sought life" (line 5). Immediately after he "sought life," the poet asks where he (and the other ancient kings) are. The answer: they are not born anymore and are far away. Also, it is possible that Etana or another king is in view at the end of the composition due to the mention once again of a search for eternal life:

> Having been given [life] by the gods,
> It was sought for [Ziusudra? Etana?],[64]
> Death is the share of mankind.

While Ziusudra is a possible restoration in line 18, it is possible that Etana or another king mentioned in line 4 should be restored due to the mention of "seeking," in both lines 5 and 18. In other words, the king is being compared with Ziusudra, who sought eternal life on earth, when death is the ultimate lot for all human beings (line 19). The ascent into heaven is not necessarily incompatible with the state of death. As we have seen with Mesopotamian cosmology, the netherworld and the heavens had a good deal of "traffic" between them (divine traffic, to be sure, but several of the Sumerian kings were deified mortals). It is possible that ascent to the heavens is a metaphor for the death of Sumerian kings. In this sense, to desire eternal life on the earth, like Ziusudra, is vain, because death has been ordained for humans. This state, however, must be understood not generally as obliteration of consciousness, but as the continuation of conscious existence in a realm and in a state known as "death." This approach might also explain how Gilgamesh may be said to be utterly foiled in his attempt to achieve "life" like Utnapishtim, yet to be remembered as "2/3 god and 1/3 man" and revered as a deity of the underworld for many centuries.

The *Legend of Etana* itself may provide some startling parallels to the text of Isa 14 and mythopoeic imagery from which Isaiah or one of his disciples could have drawn, parallels which have gone largely unnoticed. J. V. Kinnier Wilson has recently produced a new edition of the *Etana* legend, a new collation of several fragments and new translation with notes.[65] While the text is fragmentary

---

[64] Alster, "A Sumerian Poem," 8 restores Ziusudra in the broken text.

[65] J. V. Kinnier Wilson, *The Legend of Etana: A New Edition* (Warminster: Aris &

and therefore much said about the story must, of necessity, be hypothetical, the story line is now more coherent thanks to Wilson's work.

Etana is extant in three known versions: the "Old Version," which nomenclature Wilson prefers over "Old Babylonian," the "Middle Assyrian Version," and the "Late Version." The Old Version may have roots in the Ur III period during the time of Šulgi or even earlier, according to Wilson,[66] although "most of the known sources of the Version seem undoubtedly to belong to the Old Babylonian period." [67] The Middle Assyrian Version has been reconstructed from 5 fragmentary texts, one of them recently collated, and Wilson dates it to the late second millennium B.C.E.[68] The Late Version was discovered in the Küyünjuk (Nineveh) library and, according to Wilson, may have existed there in seven or eight editions. Also according to Wilson,

> So far as one may judge from those portions of the Old and Late Versions where there is a text in common, the Late Version of Etana is a conscious rewriting of the earlier version, rendered into the language of its own time with alterations and additions.[69]

While Wilson suggests that restoration of one version from another "is neither proposed without risk nor should be accepted without reserve,"[70] he more or less restores the story of Etana by means of such cross-version reconstruction in his "reconstruction of the story." [71]

There are two or three elements of the story, especially highlighted in the Late Version (which also happens to be the longest extant version), which are especially pertinent to our subject. The first is that the legend of Etana in both Old and Late Versions is a mythological etiology for the institution of kingship. Whereas the *Sumerian King List* puts Etana 13th in the line of kings and first after the flood, *Etana* says that the gods declared Etana as the first king in Sumer, over the city of Kish:

> šar-ra-am la iš-ku-nu ka-lu ni-ši e-pi$_2$-a-tim
> i-na ši-a$_3$-tim la ka-aṣ-ra-at ku-ub-šum me-a-nu

Phillips, 1985). Of earlier translations which did not have access to the fragments currently available, see especially S. Langdon, *The Legend of Etana and the Eagle, or the Epical Poem "The City They Hated"* (Paris: Paul Guethner, 1932).

[66] He cites Edith Porada's publication of a cylinder seal with Etana riding on the eagle, dated as far back as the Old Akkadian period, as an example of the possible antiquity of the legend. Wilson, *Etana*, 27.

[67] Wilson, *Etana*, 27. The Old Version has been reconstructed from four tablets.

[68] Wilson, *Etana*, 51.

[69] Wilson, *Etana*, 81.

[70] Wilson, *Etana*, 81.

[71] Wilson, *Etana*, 5–16.

u_3 ha-aṭ-ṭu_3-um uq-ni-a-am la ṣa-ap-ra-at
la ba-nu-u_3 iš-ti-ni-iš pa-ra-ak-ku

A king they had not established (over) all the peoples (and) the teeming humanity
At this (time), headgear (and) royal crown had not been bound (on)
And a scepter was not decorated with lapis lazuli
A throne had not been built anywhere.[72]

The text goes on to say,

[ša]r-[r]u-tum i-na ša-ma-i ur-da-am
[ ] X [Iš]tar šar-r[a-am] i-ši-i

Kingship came down from heaven,
[ ] [Iš]tar sought a ki[ng].

The Late Version, tablet 5, lines 8 and 25 says that it is Etana who is chosen as king and all versions confirm by their later contexts that this is indeed what occurs. Jacobsen suggests also that it is only with Etana that we are dealing with anything like a human king who might be considered an historical figure.[73] We appear, therefore, to have in the *Legend of Etana* a story which at least partially treats the subject of the origin and ideology of kingship. A story which was passed down in numerous editions and versions over a period of 1000 years and deals with the first human king and his foibles ought to have something to say about the relationship between the human king and the divine realm. Such is indeed the case.

Wilson suggests further that the specific problem addressed in the epic is the problem of the succession, as Etana and his wife have no children. Childlessness is a familiar motif in several epics from the ancient Near East such as *Keret* and *Aqhat.* Etana's wife's dream about the "plant of birth" sets up the plot in the Late Version, while all three versions allude to the problem of childlessness early on. The Middle Assyrian version records that Etana prays to Šamaš, who directs him to an eagle he had cast into a pit to die. It was by means of the eagle that Etana was to procure the plant of birth.

The eagle had been cast into the pit because he had broken a solemn oath before Šamaš with the serpent, that they would hunt together and not eat one another's offspring. After some time, the eagle "plotted evil" and decided to eat the offspring of the serpent. His comments in this regard bear closer scrutiny:

---

[72] Old Version, tablet I, I/A, 5–8; the transliteration is in Wilson, *Etana*, 30. The translation is my own.

[73] Jacobsen, *King List*, 152 and 167.

erû [mušen] lib_3-ba-šu le-mu-tu ik-pu-du-m[a]
ik-pu-du-ma lib_3-ba-šu le-mu-tu
a-na ad-mi ša lib_2 ru-u_2ʾ-a-šu a-ka-li p[a-n]i?-$šu_2$ iš-kun
eruḫ [mušen] pâ-šu i-pu-uš-ma i-zak-kar a-[na mārī-šu(?)]
mārū ṣerrim-mi lu-ku-lu a-na-ku
ṣerru [l]ib_3-b[a-šu?] [ ]
e-li-ma i-na $ša_2$-ma-mi uš-[šab]
ur-rad i-na ap-pi iṣ-ṣi ma-a dan šarrum-ma

The eagle, his heart planned evil,
His heart planned evil;
He set his face to eat the young of his friend.
The eagle opened his mouth and says t[o his young]:
The young of the serpent I will indeed eat!
The serpent [his wr]ath.
I will ascend and in the heavens I will dwell;
(If)[74] I descend to the top of the trees—the king alone is strong![75]

Compare this with Isa 14:13:

וְאַתָּה אָמַרְתָּ בִלְבָבְךָ הַשָּׁמַיִם אֶעֱלֶה
מִמַּעַל לְכוֹכְבֵי־אֵל אָרִים כִּסְאִי
וְאֵשֵׁב בְּהַר־מוֹעֵד בְּיַרְכְּתֵי צָפוֹן׃

You have said in your heart, "I will ascend to the heavens,
Above the stars of ʾEl I will set my throne
and I will sit in the mountain of assembly, in the heights of Saphon."

While there are, of course, numerous differences between these texts, nevertheless there are a few interesting parallels. First, the heart of the eagle "plans evil" (*ikpudma libbāšu lemuttu*), parallel to the king of Babylon's planning in his heart, וְאַתָּה אָמַרְתָּ בִלְבָבְךָ. Second, there is the desire to ascend to the heavens and dwell or be enthroned there (Akkadian *uššab* corresponds to Hebrew אֵשֵׁב). Finally, not included in the citation given above is the serpent's revenge (lines 85, 118, Late Version), where he cuts off the eagle's wings and casts him into a pit (Akkadian *šuttātu* corresponds to Hebrew בּוֹר, Isa 14:15). If there is a "myth" which may be said to lie behind Isa 14:11–14, one should look more toward such an etiology of kingship in Mesopotamia and the ideology of kingship

---

[74] The Old Version includes here *tu-uš-šā-am-ma*, an adverb which denotes a situation contrary to actual fact. Wilson assumes that the eagle is afraid to descend once he has devoured the offspring of the serpent and translates, "If I come down from the tree-top, the king alone could save me!" Wilson, *Etana*, 93.

[75] Late Version, tablet II, lines 37–44. The transliteration is in Wilson, *Etana*, 90 and 92. The translation is my own.

and associated imagery, rather than restrict oneself to "stories about the gods." In any event, this legend is clearly "mythological" in the sense that it deals with an ongoing social reality with its inception in the primordium. However, if Isa 14:12–15 is directly or indirectly dependent upon the *Legend of Etana*, it is neither more nor less "mythological" than the rest of the poem.[76]

There are a couple of other points from the *Legend of Etana* which, if 's reconstruction of the story is correct, may allow us to find parallels in Isa 14. First, Wilson suggests that Etana makes at least two trips to the "heaven of Anu." He has no difficulty in doing this with the eagle and goes through various gates (gates of Šamaš, Ea, Enlil, etc.). In one of these trips, he meets with a terrifying appearance of Ištar. Apparently, in neither of these trips is the plant of birth procured. In Wilson's view, there is a third trip where Etana attempts to ascend with the eagle to the *ellāti*, the heights of heaven, in search of the plant. He seems to lose nerve at their extreme height and the eagle and Etana fall and are saved from certain death at the last second. The location of the plant of birth, according to the Middle Assyrian Version, is possibly in these *ellāti.* This at least raises the question of the ability of human kings to have access to (at least) the heaven of Anu, apparently not located as high up as the "heights of heaven." This in turn raises the question of what the king of Babylon is doing when he wishes to ascend "above the stars of ʾEl" in Isa 14. Secondly, the question of motivation comes up. Wilson suggests that Etana goes beyond the prescribed instructions and seeks with the aid of the eagle to reach the highest heaven, which appears inaccessible to him. The resulting fall may be attributable to what Wilson calls the "spirit of adventure taking over."

Secondly, in Wilson's last fragment he allows as part of the epic, Etana's wife may have yet another dream in which she sees the "ghost-body" (*eṭemmu*) of Etana. Wilson suggests that this indicates the death of Etana and his subsequent lack of burial, causing his ghost to roam about the earth.[77] Isaiah 14 also describes the fate of the king of Babylon: his maggot-eaten body would lie unburied on the ground.

---

[76] Donald Gowan recognized the "ascent" and "descent" motifs in the Legend of Etana several years ago without, however, recognizing either Etana's or the eagle's arrogant presumption or the verbal affinities with Isa 14. At the time he wrote, Gowan did not have access to the more complete critical text we now possess. See Gowan, *When Man becomes God*, 54 and 57.

[77] See *Gilgamesh* tablet 12 for a description of the fate of those without proper burial:

> "Him whose corpse was cast out upon the steppe hast thou seen?"
> "I have seen:
> His spirit finds no rest in the netherworld" ("The Epic of Gilgamesh," [*ANET*, 99]).

Direct literary dependence is probably not in view between *Etana* and Isa 14. It is also possible, on the other hand, given the long history of the legend, its many versions and editions, and widespread geographical distribution, that aspects of the imagery could have influenced the choice of terminology in Isa 14. At least, there are several striking parallels which deal with a king and an eagle who overstep their prerogatives and are cast down.

Finally, much as Gilgamesh becomes an underworld deity in later Sumerian and Old Babylonian tradition and ritual, so Etana becomes "doorkeeper" for the underworld after his death.[78]

e. Ur-Nammu

Of all the civilizations of Mesopotamia, the one which is best documented relative to the notion of divine kingship and the ascent/descent motif is that of Ur III Sumer. Apparently, the kings of the Ur III civilization—Ur-Nammu, Šulgi, Amar-Sin, Šu-Sin, and Ibbi-Sin—were accorded some kind of divine status after (and in the case of Šulgi, before) their deaths.[79] To be sure, most of them met with a less than ideal or suspicious demise: Ur-Nammu died in battle, Šulgi, after a 48 year reign, may have been done in by his son Amar-Sin, Amar-Sin may have died of a "foot disease,"[80] and Ibbi-Sin died of "disaster" and "annihilation" (or was exiled?).[81] These suspicious circumstances, at least in the cases of Ur-Nammu and Šulgi, provoked literary *apologia* in order to explain how a divine king could die as they did.[82]

There is little to add here to what was said about Ur-Nammu in chapter two. That he descended to the netherworld and retained a throne and the rights and privileges of kingship is clear. It is interesting, as was noted above, that his name is once written with the divine determinative in the *Sumerian King List*. This at least raises the possibility that he was not only a kind of first among

---

[78] See the Pushkin Museum elegies quoted in chapter 2 above for further discussion on Etana and his *postmortem* role in the underworld.

[79] See comments above on the *Sumerian King List*. The Sumerians had a long history of venerating at least some of their deceased kings as gods. See above on Dumuzi, Gilgamesh, and below on Šu-Ilišu. The Sumerian king Lugalbanda also was deified: see Šulgi D line 42: "Your (personal) god Lugal[banda] fashioned [you," Jacob Klein, *Three Šulgi Hymns*, 75.

[80] The "bite of a shoe." See Hallo, "The Death of Kings," 159.

[81] Hallo, "The Death of Kings," 157–160.

[82] See Kramer, "The Death of Ur-Nammu" and for Šulgi, see P. Michalowski, "The Death of Šulgi," *Or* 2/46 (1977): 220–225 and D. J. Wiseman, *Chronicles of Chaldean Kings (626–556 B. C.) in the British Museum* (London: The Trustees of the British Museum, 1956), 40f; quoted in Hallo, "The Death of Kings," 158.

equals in the netherworld, but could also ascend to the heavens, at least upon occasion.

f. Šulgi[83]

ᵈŠulgi, son of Ur-Nammu of Ur, is the best documented Mesopotamian king in terms of the "ascent to heaven" motif. He was deified and worshipped even before his death, according to Jacob Klein:

> Although the great Sumerian kings and rulers preceding Šulgi were deified as a rule only posthumously, we know from his royal inscriptions that toward the middle of his reign, Šulgi assumed divinity on his own initiative.[84]

Šulgi was prolific in literary output. According to the words of one of his own hymns, he had numerous hymns and prayers commissioned to be written down, so that future generations might continue to worship him. Of those hymns and prayers we are in possession of more than 20.[85] Furthermore, the brilliance of his long reign inspired other writings about him, of which those which deal with his death and ascent to heaven are of most interest to this study.[86]

Two or three Šulgi texts are important in this regard. The first text, recently published, is BCT 1, 132, an economic text from Drehem dating from Šulgi's 48th (and last) year.[87] In this text the king is said to have ascended to heaven:

> 19 female full-time slaves, (and) 2 female slaves at 2/3 wage, for seven days. Their work of 142 1/3 female slave days, on the day when Šulgi ascended to heaven and

---

[83] I use Šulgi and ᵈŠulgi interchangeably, although properly speaking ᵈŠulgi would apply only after his death, or at least from the middle of his reign on.

[84] Jacob Klein, *The Royal Hymns of Shulgi King of Ur: Man's Quest for Immortal Fame* (Transactions of the American Philosophical Society 71/7; Philadelphia: American Philosophical Society, 1981), 7.

[85] See especially G. R. Castellino, *Two Šulgi Hymns (BC)* (Studi Semitici 42; Rome: Istituto di Studi del Vicino Oriente, 1972); Jacob Klein, *Three Shulgi Hymns*, and Jacob Klein, "The Coronation and Consecration of Šulgi in the Ekur (Šulgi G)," in *Ah, Assyria*, 292–313.

[86] Šulgi has recently been compared to Solomon: the second in a dynasty, prolific in literary output, brilliant in administration, and ushering in a "golden age." See in this regard Samuel N. Kramer, "Solomon and Šulgi: A Comparative Portrait," in *Ah, Assyria*, 189–195.

[87] P. J. Watson and W. B. Horowitz, *Catalogue of Cuneiform Tablets in Birmingham City Museum, vol. 1: Neo-Sumerian Texts from Drehem* (Warminster: Aris & Phillips, 1986). This text has been reviewed with notes by Horowitz and Watson, "Further Notes on Birmingham Cuneiform Tablets, Volume 1," ASJ 13 (1991): 409–417.

> was released, was withdrawn against Ananna. The month of the festival *me.ki.ĝal*$_2$, the year that Harshi and Kimash were destroyed.[88]

Horowitz and Watson raise the question of whether this simply means Šulgi died violently, as in a fire, so that his smoke "went up to heaven."[89] There is evidence, as mentioned above, that Šulgi died violently.[90] Dying violently and being burned alive are not necessarily synonymous, however. William Hallo suggests that Šulgi did ascend to heaven, but that it was a temporary position.[91] Horowitz and Watson go on to suggest that there is other evidence for Šulgi's divine ascension. The first of these is a reference to $^{mul\ d}$Šulgi in MSL XI 133 viii 41 138 rev. ii 2' (a list of star names where MUL is the determinative for "star"). ^{d}ŠUL.GI.AN.NA, "Šulgi of heaven" also occurs in the Sumerian temple hymn, TCS 3 24:132.[92] N. Schneider included 6 or 7 pages of occurrences of the divine name ^{d}Šulgi in *Die Götternamen von Ur III*.[93] Finally, in Šulgi C, probably during his own lifetime Šulgi encouraged prayer to him as to a star:

> I am the brave one, let the people trustingly invoke my name.
> I am the shepherd, let them honor me in prayer like a star.[94]

Clearly, ^{d}Šulgi was understood to have been deified and the evidence suggests that he also became a star.[95]

---

[88] The translation is that of Horowitz and Watson, *Catalogue of Cuneiform Tablets*, 410–411.

[89] Horowitz and Watson, "Further Notes," 412. They describe a scene in "Gilgamesh and the Ḫullupu Tree": "Individuals belonging to all categories, save one, are to be found in the underworld:

'Did you see the man who was burned by fire?'
'I did not see him there. His spirit was not present.
His smoke went up to heaven.'"

[90] See P. Michalowski, "The Death of Šulgi," 223–224, where foul play on the part of Amar-Sin is suggested, but not immolation of the aged king.

[91] Hallo, "The Death of Kings," 159. Hallo states reasonably that ascent to heaven was reserved for gods, such as Dumuzi, "antediluvian counselors such as Adapa and Utu-Abzu, and legendary early kings such as Etana." The point is that at least certain Sumerian kings *were* deified and thus could "ascend." Hallo gives no evidence whatever for his suggestion that Šulgi ascended to heaven as "heaven's gate-keeper" for a seven day temporary stay.

[92] Horowitz and Watson, "Further Notes," 413.

[93] N. Schneider, *Die Götternamen von Ur III* (Rome: Pontifical Biblical Institute, 1939), 79–85.

[94] Castellino, *Two Šulgi Hymns*, lines 18–19, 249.

[95] Šulgi G also contains a reference to the king's divine birth. See Jacob Klein, "Coronation," 233.

g. Šu-Ilišu

In the tablet BIN X 190:12, Šu-Ilišu is also said to ascend to heaven, but without mention of descent to the underworld. Mamoru Yoshikawa transliterates and translates as follows:

> [e]r_2-gu-la u_4 lugal an-$še_3$ ba-a-da
>
> A great mourning at the time when the king went up toward the heaven, that is, when the king died.[96]

Šu-Ilišu is probably the king in view, mentioned in line 5 of the text.

h. *Maqlû*: The Ritual and Incantation Series

In several recent articles, T. Abusch has analyzed the ritual series *Maqlû*.[97] These are a series of magical incantations to be performed in three sections[98] on the last night of the month Abu, a sort of "all soul's night" when the dead could ascend from the netherworld and wreak havoc on the living.[99] Abusch suggests that the spirits of the dead are always potentially dangerous in ancient Mesopotamian thought, but the spirits of dead witches especially so. If they were not checked, dead witches could once again enter into the land of the living and cast evil spells. On this night, the king or other ritual participant would stand on a rooftop facing the stars of the heavens and become, through the ritual, one of the stars. The reason for this ritual was, according to Abusch, so that the ritual participant might be able to stop the spirits of dead witches

---

[96] Mamoru Yoshikawa, "an–šè–a (= è/e_{11}) 'to die'," ASJ 11 (1989): 353.

[97] Among these are, "Ascent to the Stars," "The Ritual Tablet and Rubrics of *Maqlû*: Towards the History of the Series," in *Ah, Assyria*, 233–253; "Mesopotamian Anti-Witchcraft Literature: Texts and Studies, Part I: The Nature of the *Maqlû*: Its Character, Divisions, and Calendrical Setting," *JNES* 33 (1974): 251–262; "Ritual and Incantation: Interpretation: Interpretation and Textual History: A Consideration of *Maqlû* VII:58–105, IX:152–59," in *Sha'arei Talmon*, 367–380; "An Early Form of the Witchcraft Ritual *Maqlû* and the Origin of a Babylonian Magical Ceremony," in *Lingering Over Words: Studies in Ancient Near Eastern Literature in Honor of William L. Moran* (ed. Tzvi Abusch, John Huehnergard, and Piotr Steinkeller, HSM 37; Atlanta: Scholars Press, 1990), 1–57; and "The Demonic Image of the Witch in Standard Babylonian Literature: The Reworking of Popular Conceptions by Learned Exorcists," in *Religion, Science, and Magic: In Concert and in Conflict* (ed. Jacob Neusner, Ernest Frerichs, and Paul V. M. Flesher; New York: Oxford University Press, 1989), 27–58.

[98] Abusch, "An Early Form of the Witchcraft Ritual *Maqlû*," 2.

[99] Abusch, "Mesopotamian Anti-Witchcraft Literature," 260.

from ascending from the netherworld.[100] The only way this could be accomplished was by identification with the stars, as they were capable of ascending to the heavens as well as descending into the netherworld.[101] As a star, the participant could stop the upward progress of witches and contain them in the netherworld so they could do no evil in the realm of the living. While close analysis of most of these texts would take us too far afield from the subject at hand, the reason for including *Maqlû* here is that the king was at least one of the possible participants in the ritual.[102] He was enabled, through the ritual, to become a star, capable of travel or reach to the heavens and the netherworld, in order to negate the effects of evil witchcraft.

There are many passages in the *Maqlû* series which refer to (ritual) travel or reach to the heavens and the underworld as a star, but perhaps two or three suffice for our purposes.[103] Tablet VII contains some of the most explicit references to the ritual actor becoming a star:

(Tablet VII, 1–11)
EN$_2$ rit-ti ^{d}man-za-ad$_2$ zu-qa-qi-pi-(?)
[....] ši-i kaššaptu u$_2$-nak-ka-ma kiš-pi-ša$_2$
[u$_2$-sa]-(ap?)-paḫ-kim-ma ki-ma marrati ina šamê
[u$_2$-za]-qa-kim-ma kîma iltâni amurrî.
[u$_2$]-sa-ap-paḫ urpata-ki u$_2$-ḫal-laq ûm-ki
u$_2$-sap-paḫ kiš-pi-ki ša$_2$ tak-ki-mi mu-ša u ur-ra
u$_3$ na-aš$_2$-pa-rat zitarruṭâ ša$_2$ tal-tap-pa-ri ia-a-ši
ṣa-lil nêbiru ṣa-lil ka-a-ru
mârê^{meš} ^{amēl}malâḫi ka-li-šu$_2$-nu ṣal-lu
elî ^{iṣ}dalti u$_3$ ^{iṣ}sikkuri na-du-u ḫur-gul-lu
na-da-at ši-pat-su-un ša$_2$ ^{d}siris u ^{d}nin-giš-zi-da

An incantation. My hand is the Rainbow,[104] the Scorpion (?)[105]
[...] she (?) the witch, piles up her enchantment,
I [scat]ter you like the rainbow in the heavens,
I blow you like the North Wind (and) the West Wind.
[I] scatter your cloud, I make your storm vanish.

---

[100] Abusch, "The Demonic Image of the Witch," 49.

[101] Abusch, "Ascent to the Stars," 29.

[102] Abusch, "Ascent to the Stars," 18.

[103] The transliteration of the Akkadian is from Meier, *Maqlû*, 46 and 48. The translation is my own.

[104] See Hunger and Pingree, *MUL.APIN*, 112. *Manzât* is the "Rainbow," in Sumerian the constellation ^{d}TIR.AN.NA.

[105] Zuqaqīpu, the Scorpion, is a constellation in the "stars of Ea." See Hunger and Pingree, *MUL.APIN*, 38. The *Maqlû* text says "my Scorpion," *zu-qa-qi-pi*, perhaps an error for *Irat Zuqaqīpi*, "the Breast of the Scorpion," a portion of the Scorpion constellation. *MUL.APIN*, 38 describes the various parts of the constellation ("Breast" and "Sting").

I scatter your enchantment, which you pile up day and night,
and the messenger of your evil spells, which you send to me.
The Ferry is asleep,[106] the quay is asleep.
The sailors, all of them are asleep.
On the door and the bolt a lock is cast,
Their incantation of Siriš and Ningišzida is cast.

In this incantation, the ritual actor so identifies himself with the heavenly bodies (Manzât, Scorpio) that he is able to utilize their power and various capacities to stop the witches and their evil spells from ascending. Note especially that the ritual actor, as a heavenly body, pronounces the ferry (ferryman?) and the harbor at the gate of the netherworld asleep, so there is none to ferry the witches across. Also, the gate itself is shut and barred with a lock upon it (lines 8–10).

(Tablet VII, 50–57)
EN$_{2}$ ^{d}en-lil qaqqadi-ia$_{5}$ ^{mul}KAK.SI.SA$_{2}$ la-an-ni
pûtu ^{d}azqaru
[idâ]-ai ^{iš}gamlu ša$_{2}$ bâb ^{d}marduk
uznâ(?)-ai li-'-u$_{2}$ šêpâ^{II}-ai laḫ(?)-mu mu-kab-bi-sa šîr laḫ(?)-me
at-tu-nu ilâni^{meš} rabûti^{meš} ša$_{2}$ (?) ina šamê nap-ḫa-tu-nu
kîma an-na ku an [............] ip-šu bar-tum ka-ar-tum
la iṭeḫḫû^{meš}-ku-nu-ši [la i-sa-ni]-qu$_{2}$-ku-nu-ši
ip-šû bar-tu$_{2}$ ka-ar-[tu la iṭeḫḫû]-ni la isanniqû-ni iaši EN$_{2}$

An incantation. Enlil[107] is my head, the Arrow[108] is my body.
The forehead is the Crescent Moon.
My arms are the Crook (*gamlu*)[109] of the gate of Marduk.
My ears (?) are the Bull,[110]

---

[106] *nēberu* can be a simple ferry, a ferry-man, or the star Nēberu (the "Ford" or "Ferry," equated with the planet Jupiter). *MUL.APIN* I i 37 says:

> One big star—although its light is dim—divides the sky in half and stands there: that is, the star of Marduk, the Ford (translation of Hunger and Pingree, 28).

In this case, the *nēberu* does not refer to a star, but is probably the ferry at the gate to the underworld. The harbor and the ferry are pronounced "asleep," so that the witches cannot pass from the underworld to the realm of the living.

[107] See Hunger and Pingree, *MUL.APIN*, 18. Enlil is the first star mentioned in the compendium and the "Field of Enlil" is the first constellation or quadrant of stars mentioned.

[108] See Hunger and Pingree, *MUL.APIN*, 32.

[109] See Hunger and Pingree, *MUL.APIN*, 19.

[110] See Hunger and Pingree, *MUL.APIN*, 30. Meier suggested "tablet," but was unsure. See Miguel Civil et al., "lû," *CAD* 9:227-228. "Bull" (or Lion?) can be written either *lu-u* (*ú*), *le-e*, or *liu*. The constellation Bull is normally "*is le-e*" (Jaw of the Bull) or in Sumerian ^{mul}GUD.AN.NA or ^{mul}AGA.AN.NA (see Ignace J. Gelb et. al., "is lê," *CAD* 7:188-189). If the proper translation is "tablet," it is uncertain how it fits into the context. There is no determinative for the term in Meier's transcription. *le'u* "tablet," would normally be written

> my feet are the *laḫmu*[111] which tread upon the body of the *laḫme* (?).
> You are the great gods, which are bright in the heavens.
> As now .... the witchcraft, rebellion, (and) hardship
> do not draw near to you, do not reach you,
> (So) the witchcraft, rebellion (and) hardsh[ip do not draw near to] me, do not reach me. An incantation.

This is perhaps the most graphic portrayal in the *Maqlû* series of the identification of the ritual actor with stars. His entire body takes on the characteristics of the stars: head, torso, forehead, arms, ears, feet. As the stars (identified here as "great gods") cannot be touched by witches and their evil incantations, so the ritual actor, in his identification with the stars, cannot be touched.

i. Hymns to Dumuzi and Inanna

There is further evidence in support of Sumerian kings ascending to heaven as a star. A text which has been known for many years,[112] recently re-edited by Daniel Foxvog, almost certainly relates to the Sumerian divine kingship and its astral connotations.[113] The final line of the tablet says it is a *tigi* hymn of Inanna. The text seems to relate to the death of a king, who has been "born over the mountains" after the "night had passed in the land and the rulers and gods had come to stand before you at daylight." Inanna, the Venus deity of Sumer, makes the king into her own husband, who now possesses the divine consort name Amaušumgalanna, an aspect of Dumuzi, according to Foxvog.[114] Inanna makes him come before her in royal splendor (section 6), he appears over the distant mountains and rebel lands, and he appears "like the sun come forth from the Mountains of Aromatic Cedar" (section 7, an interesting comment

---

with the GIŠ determinative (see *Enūma Anu Enlil,* 145) and *lê, lû,* or *liu* one would expect to be written with the star determinative MUL.

[111] Meier was unsure of his transcription of this word. See "laḫmu," *CAD* 9:42, which translates this passage from *Maqlû* without hesitation as "my feet are *laḫmu* monsters standing on *laḫmu* monsters." The *laḫmu* were a group of deities or divine monsters.

[112] A. Falkenstein, "Untersuchungen zur sumerischen Grammatik (Fortsetzung)," *ZA* 48 (1944): 105–118.

[113] Daniel A. Foxvog, "Astral Dumuzi." All quotes in this analysis are from Foxvog. Kramer had earlier made similar suggestions as Foxvog in "CT XXXVI: Corrigenda et Addenda," *Iraq* 36 (1974): 98–99.

[114] Foxvog, "Astral Dumuzi," 103. For a graphic depiction of the living king's relationship to the priestess of Inanna in the temple Eanna of Kullab and allusion to the *hieros gamos* see Šulgi X, lines 4–73, in Jacob Klein, *Three Šulgi Hymns*, 137–140. There are many synthetic treatments of the Inanna/Dumuzi myth(s) and the *hieros gamos* rite in the ancient Near East. Among the most insightful and helpful is Samuel N. Kramer, *The Sacred Marriage Rite.*

in light of Isa 14 with its mention of cedars of Lebanon and an ascent to heaven of the king of Babylon). Finally, because the deceased king in his role of Amaušumgalanna has "relied upon" Inanna and she has "cloaked him as with your (own) mantle of divine power," Heaven will then "beget him (anew) each month on the day of the new moon, like the Moon (himself), and king Amaušumgalanna, the beloved of your heart, they shall praise like the risen sun" (sections 12–13).

Foxvog suggests that Dumuzi/Amaušumgalanna was not identified with the planet Venus, as was Inanna,[115] but had his own constellation.[116] These constellations, according to Foxvog, are "contiguous in many Babylonian descriptions":

> The star which stands behind the field, Annunītu.
> The star which stands behind it, the Hired Man, Dumuzi.[117]

Foxvog goes on to suggest that to the ancient Sumerian astronomer, who had no conception of a heliocentric solar system, the moon would appear to return each month to its starting point in the zodiac (Aries): "The sky could indeed be said to give birth every month to both Suen and Amaušumgalanna/Aries on the day of the new moon."[118] Dumuzi/Amaušumgalanna, then, was not identified with Venus, as was Osiris/the king in Egypt, but rather with a star which appeared in close proximity to Venus.

No king is mentioned by name in this tablet. Foxvog suggests that in light of the recent discovery of BCT 1, 132, and the other evidence in support of Šulgi's divine ascension as a star, he is the likeliest candidate.[119] While it is tempting to attach an historical figure to this specific tablet, it seems to me much more likely that what we have is a text celebrating the ascent of any Ur III, or possibly OB, king into heaven as a star in close association with the Dumuzi star and in visual proximity to Annunītu. This is, of course, somewhat analogous to the death of the Egyptian king and his association with another dying god, Osiris, and his star (in this case) *nṯr dwꜣ(w)*, Venus. As with the

---

[115] ^{d}Si-pa-zi-a-na, Annunītu or Pisces.

[116] LU$_2$.ḪUN.ĜA$_2$, Agru or the Hired Man, the later Aries. See Foxvog, "Astral Dumuzi," 106.

[117] Foxvog, "Astral Dumuzi," 106. See also the star catalogue BM 82923, which seems to equate ^{mul}Annunītu with Inanna (the text is broken), in C. B. F. Walker and H. Hunger, "Zwölfmaldrei," *MDOG* 109 (1977): 30. Dumuzi is not mentioned. See also Hunger and Pingree, 144, who place Annunītu (Pisces) and Hired Man (Aries) together in table VII.

[118] Foxvog, "Astral Dumuzi," 106.

[119] Foxvog, "Astral Dumuzi," 105.

Egyptian texts, no specific king is named, nor should we expect to attach a *specific* historical setting to it.

There is another, briefer, Inanna/Dumuzi text which possibly alludes to the ascent of the king as a star: BM 98396.[120] It is an *eršemma* of Ninḫursag (Inanna portrayed as a mother goddess, weeping for her son Dumuzi, according to Kramer).[121] This composition is in three parts, as are all *eršemmas*. The first part (lines 1–13), deals with Ninḫursag searching for her son, like a ewe for its lamb. The second part (lines 14–25) suggests in a soliloquy that once she has found her son she will give him "something like a heavenly star." In the third section (lines 26–31), the truth is revealed to her: there is no point in searching for her son, because he is in the *arallu*, the underworld.

Of special interest to this analysis is the second section, which states she would give her son "something like a star" (lines 16–18). After telling her absent son she would give it (line 16), she says it is ominous (line 17) and that it has been brought to her son (line 18), after which she "feared it and paid homage to it." Once again, as in the "Astral Dumuzi" text, the aromatic cedar forest figures in connection with the death of a god/king:

> It (the star?) turned moon into dusk against me—something ominous—
> As for me—it acted (?) treacherously towards me—it is true! it is true!
> Me, the birth-giving mother—it sets the earth atremble against me like a forest fragrant with cedars.[122]

Kramer suggests that the Dumuzi in view here is "no doubt to be identified metaphorically with the unfortunate ruler of her ravaged city."[123] Again, no specific king is mentioned. Kramer surmised that the destruction of a city and its ruler is in view, but nowhere in the text is such destruction mentioned or even alluded to. It is also possible a ruler's death and ascension into the heaven as a star is meant. This text, unlike the previous one, does mention the descent of the king into the underworld: he has gone to the *arallu* (line 31). Admittedly, the text is obscure and difficult, but may well allude to both the ascent of the king as a star (the star had already been presented to him!) and his abode in the underworld.

An important point to underscore with respect to these ancient poems in Sumerian is that many of them may not at all have been a product of a period in which Sumerian was a "living" language. Sumerian continued to be used for

---

[120] Samuel N. Kramer, "BM 98396: A Sumerian Prototype of the *Mater Dolorosa*," *ErIsr* 16 (1982): 141*–146*.

[121] Kramer, "BM 98396," 141*.

[122] Kramer, "BM 98396," 142*–143*.

[123] Kramer, "BM 98396," 141*.

religious and cultic writings, as well as for "shorthand" in historical annals and even administrative records,[124] well into the Neo-Assyrian and -Babylonian periods.[125] Certain types of cultic lamentations, including the *balag*, the *eršemma*, and possibly the *eršaḫunga* and the *šuilla* (religious compositions which may not have blossomed until the first millennium, according to M. Cohen) continued to be copied, performed, and even composed in Sumerian well into the Seleucid period.[126] At least with regard to the second of the two texts mentioned above, as an *eršemma* it, or a text very similar to it, may well have continued in circulation and influenced the imagery and ideology pertaining to the death of kings in the first millennium.

C. UGARITIC EVIDENCE

There is little evidence from Ugaritic sources for the ascent and descent of the king or the ideology of divine kingship. We have looked previously in chapter two at *KTU* 1.161 as a funerary ritual expediting the dead king Niqmaddu to the underworld (see below on dead kings). Other possible evidence includes the Ugaritic king list[127] which may shed some light on the ideology of the royal

---

[124] See, for example, the administrative records of the Neo-Assyrian period, written mostly in Sumerian: F. M. Fales and J. N. Postgate, *Imperial Administrative Records Part 1: Palace and Temple Administration* (SAA 7; Helsinki: Helsinki University Press, 1992).

[125] See, for example, Bendt Alster, "A Dumuzi Lament in Late Copies," ASJ 7 (1985): 1–9. According to Alster, this "Dumuzi Lament" is a "Neo-Babylonian tablet . . . imitating an older text." Alster implies by this that the tablet is not really a copy of an older text, but rather a Neo-Babylonian composition, imitating an old Sumerian Dumuzi lament. He suggests the reason might be that Dumuzi was supposed in the late period to carry diseases with him to the underworld and that the three fragmentary incantations on the reverse of the tablet may be addressed to Dumuzi towards this end (p. 3).

[126] See Mark Cohen, *Sumerian Hymnology: The Eršemma* (HUCAS 2; Cincinnati: Hebrew Union College, 1981), 1–2. Cohen suggests that Sumerian continued to be the literary and religious language of choice throughout the OB period, but that the Kassite invasion forced changes in literary production. After this, according to Cohen, Akkadian became the literary language of choice, but that religious compositions and lamentations, inherently conservative and written in the EMESAL dialect, were preserved. In the first millennium there was a revival of interest in Sumerian literary and religious texts and subsequent copying and transmitting of such texts in bilingual editions. That these *balags* and *eršemmas* were considered "canonical" in some sense seems a reasonable hypothesis; they were used for well over a millennium and were copied and expanded, mainly as a ritual for the rebuilding of temples. For the various editions of the "canonical" lamentations in Sumerian from the OB to the first millennium, see especially the *eršemma* ELUM GUSUN and the *balag* A ABBA HULUHA in Mark Cohen, *The Canonical Lamentations of Ancient Mesopotamia*, 272–318, 374–400.

[127] Kitchen, "The King List of Ugarit," 131–142.

dead. The kings listed are each preceded by the designation, "the god." This would seem to indicate that down to the end of the second millennium dead kings were assumed to be deified at Ugarit. J. N. Ford, however, takes a different view: that *all* the dead are said to be gods, and the difference between the royal and common dead would be only in the degree to which they possessed divinity, manifested in their power and authority.[128]

IV. The Cedar Forest of Lebanon

I have already surveyed in chapter one several texts which mention the cedars of Lebanon, "aromatic cedars," or "Cedar Mountains" in a mythological or ritual context. These were the *Epic of Gilgamesh,*[129] BM 96739 (*tigi* hymn of Inanna), and BM 98396 (*eršemma* of Ninḫursag). Also, cedars from Lebanon were highly prized by Mesopotamian monarchs whose cedar collecting expeditions are chronicled in inscriptions from the third to the first millennium B.C.E. In any event, cedars from Lebanon and the Anti-Lebanon areas were apparently considered to have divine properties and may figure in the *tigi* and the *eršemma* hymns mentioned above.[130]

Another possible reference to cedar trees in a mythological context comes from the cylinder inscriptions of Gudea, *ensi* of Lagash. The god Ningirsu appears to Gudea in a dream and provides a blessing and promise of prosperity to him. Part of this prosperity includes

> From below, the *halub* and *bihan* (?) wood
> I will have come to you,
> From above, cedar, cypress, and *zabalum* wood
> I will have brought to you freely (?)[131]

Gilgamesh is also said to deal with the *halub* tree from below; the other trees may be the heavenly counterpart.[132]

---

[128] J. N. Ford, "The Living Rephaim of Ugarit: Quick or Defunct?" *UF* 24 (1993): 90–91.

[129] See also the parallel Sumerian text, "Gilgamesh and the Land of the Living" and a discussion about it in Tigay, *The Evolution of the Gilgamesh Epic*, 23–38 and Kramer, *The Sacred Marriage Rite*, 37–38.

[130] See, for example, Aaron Shaffer, "Gilgamesh, the Cedar Forest, and Mesopotamian History," *JAOS* 103 (1983): 307, note 3.

[131] "The Cylinders of Gudea," translated by Richard E. Averbeck (*COS* 2.155:424).

[132] For the consequences of the misuse of trees or their products, which come from divine precincts, see Aase Koefoed, "Gilgames, Enkidu, and the Netherworld," ASJ 5 (1983): 17–18.

It will be helpful to look a bit more closely at tablets III–V of the *Gilgamesh Epic*, the incident of Gilgamesh and Enkidu in the Cedar Forest. It is clear in the Epic that the Cedar Forest/Mountain is not a normal woodland. First of all, it is called in tablet V i the "dwelling-place of gods." [133] Irnini (Ištar) is said to be enthroned on this mountain and, after Huwawa (Humbaba) is killed, Gilgamesh is said to have "opened up the secret dwelling of the Anunnaki."[134] At the slaying of Huwawa and the cutting down of the trees, the cedars themselves reacted, for the monster was their master, "at whose word Saria and Lebanon [trembled]." Secondly, it is at a distance from Uruk,[135] requiring much preparation and a lengthy journey. It is unclear exactly where the Cedar Mountain is located, but Enkidu knows the way. He is himself a creation of the gods and wandered close to the Forest when he was living as a savage with the animals (III iii).[136] Thirdly, Enlil, Adad, Ištar, and Šamaš are involved with the disposition and well-being of the Forest. Enlil himself has appointed the monster Huwawa as its guardian in order to keep it safe from and be a "terror to people" (II vi).[137] There is apparently bad blood between Šamaš and Huwawa (and possibly by extension, his lord Enlil), for Gilgamesh requests, and receives, help from Šamaš, resulting in Huwawa's death just when it seems that Enkidu and Gilgamesh will fall to the monster (Standard Babylonian Version V i).[138] Fourth, Huwawa himself is clearly not mortal:

> We hear that Huwawa's looks are alien:
> Who could face his weapons?
> The forest extends (?) for sixty (?) leagues in each direction.
> Who can penetrate to its depths?
> Huwawa's shout is the flood-weapon,
> His utterance is fire, his breath is Death! [139]

---

[133] "Gilgamesh," tablet V i 6 (Stephanie Dalley, *Myths from Mesopotamia* [Oxford: Oxford University, 1989], 71).

[134] "The Gilgamesh Epic—Additions to Tablets V–VIII and X," translated by Albert Kirk Grayson (*ANET*, 504).

[135] The journey took them from the "new moon to the full moon, then three days more" (see "Gilgamesh," tablet IV i 1–4 [Dalley, *Myths from Mesopotamia*, 67]).

[136] "Gilgamesh," Old Babylonian Version, tablet III iii (Dalley, *Myths from Mesopotamia*, 143).

[137] "Gilgamesh," tablet II vi (Dalley, *Myths from Mesopotamia*, 63).

[138] According to Dalley, *Myths from Mesopotamia*, 72. *ANET* includes this account as tablet 5, column iv in "The Epic of Gilgamesh" (*ANET*, 83).

[139] "Gilgamesh," Old Babylonian Version, tablet III v (Dalley, *Myths from Mesopotamia*, 145).

Huwawa is a frightful servant of the gods, guarding the divine precincts against human encroachers. Lastly, the Cedar Mountain is not simply an innocuous place which the gods wish to keep from humankind. Upon approaching the Cedar Forest, Enkidu's arms become limp and paralyzed, from terror of Huwawa and the divine forest. Only Gilgamesh's encouragement and clasping Enkidu's hand enables him to go on.[140] Entering the divine precinct itself is dangerous and to encounter its guardian doubly so. Only the intervention of Šamaš saves the heroes.[141] Whatever else the Cedar Forest might be, it is an abode for deities only. It is the height of hubris and presumption which leads Gilgamesh and Enkidu to this precinct of the gods and only divine intervention allows them to be successful. Gilgamesh, being mostly deity, has apparently less difficulty entering than Enkidu. His desire is to destroy the guardian and make a name for himself:

> Let me conquer him [Huwawa] in the Pine Forest!
> And give the country cause to hear
> How powerful Uruk's scion is!
> Let me set to work and cut down pines,
> Ensure fame that will last forever![142]

Only gods may enter the abode of the gods. For mortals to do so means death. The Cedar Forest is the abode of the Anunnaki and the throne of Ištar. Gilgamesh, in supreme arrogance and presumption, enters the forest, cuts down its trees and slays its guardian, and in so doing claims for himself the right and prerogatives of godhood. He later discovers how wrong he was. His arrogance eventually brings about the death of Enkidu and his long search to escape his own inevitable death.

V. Dead Kings in Sheol

The discussion about the dead kings in Isa 14 has centered upon their identity relative to the Rephaim with which they are mentioned in parallel cola in v. 9 of Isa 14. The identification of the Rephaim has been complicated by two factors: first, the fact that the Old Testament mentions Rephaim as giants of

---

[140] See "The Epic of Gilgamesh" (*ANET*, 82). Speiser insinuates that it is Enkidu's attempt to open the gate to the Forest which paralyzes him, but Gilgamesh, 2/3 god and 1/3 human, is able to bring Enkidu in. Dalley's translation suggests it is Enkidu's fear which brings on the paralysis. See "Gilgamesh," tablet IV iv (Dalley, *Myths from Mesopotamia*, 70).

[141] See "The Epic of Gilgamesh" (*ANET*, 83).

[142] "Gilgamesh," Old Babylonian Version, tablet III v (Dalley, *Myths from Mesopotamia*, 145).

antiquity and/or a pre-Israelite ethnic group,[143] also known as the Emim or Zamzumim, as a valley named for the Rephaim in Judah,[144] and as spirits of the dead.[145] The second factor is that the Ugaritic texts which mention the Rephaim seem to portray them as the spirits of dead nobles or kings[146] and possibly as a living aristocracy.[147] Several attempts have been made to relate these diverse conceptions to a single phenomenon, but after almost one hundred years of research several problems remain.

In order to address pertinent questions, I will first survey representative works since the discovery of the Rephaim texts from Ugarit and then discuss several outstanding issues which relate to the identification of the Rephaim and their meaning in Isa 14. It is not possible to survey all that has been written on this subject since the 1970s, nor will it be possible to explore in detail several matters of tangential interest, such as the identity of the god (?) Rapiʾu.[148] My attention will focus, rather, on the identity of the Rephaim in Isa 14 and the Ugaritic texts and especially the issue of descent and ascent of the dead king.

Since Charles Virolleaud published his critical edition of the Rephaim texts in 1941,[149] arguments have raged concerning the exact nature and identity of the Rephaim. Virolleaud suggested that the Rephaim of these texts are gods, although not on the same level as Baʿal. First, *rpum* occurs throughout these texts parallel to *ilnym* or *ilm.*[150] Virolleaud says, "D'ordinaire, les hémistiches se

---

[143] For example, Gen 14:5, 15:20, Deut 2:11, 20, 3:11, 13, Josh 17:15, etc. See also 1 Chr 20:6, which portrays the descendants of the Rephaim as gigantic in stature.

[144] For example, Josh 15:8, 18:16, 2 Sam 5:18, etc.

[145] For example, Isa 14:9, 26:14, 19, Ps 88:10, etc.

[146] I would say this in regard to *KTU* 1.161 and *KTU* 6.6 44–47.

[147] Several scholars have attempted to make this identification, notably John Gray and Conrad L'Heureux, from *KTU* 1.20–22 in particular, but also *KTU* 1.161. See my analysis below.

[148] Many articles have been written on this subject. See, for example, Simon Parker, "The Ugaritic Deity Rapiʾu," *UF* 4 (1972): 97–104, M. Dietrich and O. Loretz, "Baal *RPU* in KTU 1.108; 1.113 und nach 1.17 VI 25–33," *UF* 12 (1980): 171–182 and M. Dietrich and O. Loretz, "Rapiʾu und Milku aus Ugarit: Neuere historische-geographische Thesen zu *rpu mlk ʿlm* (KTU 1.108:1) und *mt rpi* (KTU 1.17 I 1)," UF 21 (1989): 123–131.

[149] Charles Virolleaud, "Les Rephaîm: Fragments de poèmes de Ras-Shamra," *Syria* 22 (1941): 1–30 and an initial report in *CRAI* (1939): 638–639.

[150] See *KTU* 1.20 ii 1–2 (in Gibson, *Canaanite Myths and Legends*, 135):
[aṯrh.rpum.] tdd
aṯrh.tdd.iln[ym
and also *KTU* 1.21 ii 11–12 (in Gibson, *Canaanite Myths and Legends*, 136):
aṯrh.rpum [ltdd]
[aṯr]h.ltdd.i[lnym]

terminent, l'un par *rpum*, l'autre par *elnym*"[151] and also, "Danel ordonne maintenant aux Rephaim, appelés aussi "les dieux.'"[152] They are not at the same level of divinity as Ba'al or Anat, however:

> Sans doute les boeufs et autres animaux—grands et petits—sont destinés aux Rephaîm . . .; mais dans la légende "de Ras-Shamra," les Rephaîm sont, comme on l'a vu ci-dessus . . ., les serviteurs ou les assistants de Ba'al.[153]

John Gray responded to Virolleaud's identification of the biblical Rephaim with the suggestion that they are clearly referred to in the texts as *ilnym*, "divine beings," but just as clearly do human-like activities. He suggests that they should be identified with the king and his cultic associates:

> Our conclusion is that the *rp'um* of the texts we have examined were human agents, cultic functionaries, probably the king and his immediate associates, who were termed *'elnym* "divine beings" in virtue of their function.[154]

In a follow-up article in 1952, Gray suggested further that these *rp'um* were identical to the *qbṣ dtn*, which he considered to be members of the old royal house of Ugarit, dispensing healing and fertility to the land.[155]

In 1960, Andre Caquot attempted another analysis of the available biblical and extra-biblical texts.[156] Caquot understands these texts in a manner opposite to Gray:

> Quant aux *rp'um*, ce sont peut-être les morts, plus exactement les ancêtres de Dan'el. Ils viennent d'une "ville": ce terme peut designer à Ougarit comme ailleurs le séjour infernal. Ils arrivent à destination à l'aube du troisième jour, c'est le délai rituel pour remonter de la mort au domaine des vivants.[157]

The Rephaim are the dead ancestors of Dan'el brought up from the dead by means of a lengthy journey (three days) in order to participate in a ritual meal. Caquot supposes that by means of this ritual, Ba'al and the dead ancestors, the Rephaim, would be able to revitalize the defunct line of Dan'el:

> La postérité de Dan'el sera donc rétablie par l'intervention de Ba'al mais aussi à l'occasion d'un culte rendu aux morts de la maison. . . . Dans une conception plus

---

[151] Virolleaud, "Les Rephaîm," 4.

[152] Virolleaud, "Les Rephaîm," 6.

[153] Virolleaud, "Les Rephaîm," 24.

[154] John Gray, "The Rephaim," *PEQ* 81 (1949): 138.

[155] John Gray, "*DTN* and *RP'UM* in Ancient Ugarit," *PEQ* 84 (1952): 39–41.

[156] Andre Caquot, "Les Rephaim Ougaritiques," *Syria* 37 (1960): 75–93.

[157] Caquot, "Les Rephaim Ougaritiques," 92–93.

ancienne on aurait attribué aux ancêtres disparus le pouvoir de susciter une descendance aux vivants.[158]

Conrad L'Heureux, in his dissertation *El and the Rephaim: New Light from Ugaritica V*,[159] asserts that the *rapi'u* mentioned in Ugaritic texts is to be equated with ʾEl, while the Rephaim are gods in his retinue. He also believed that there were earthly Rephaim, members of an aristocratic warrior guild, under ʾEl's patronage. He thus mediated in this work between Virolleaud (that the Rephaim are gods) and Gray (Rephaim are human cultic functionaries, although Gray did not think of them as a warrior class). In a later publication,[160] L'Heureux expanded this view and suggested, along with Pope and Caquot, that the Rephaim were deities, but he did not limit that status only to the dead, but rather to all those nobles and kings who took part in the *marzēaḥ* of ʾEl. He feels he has proof of such identification in *KTU* 1.15 iii 3, 14, which refers to the *rpi arṣ*. He understands this term to refer to the Rephaim of the earth as opposed to the Rephaim of the underworld and these would more or less correspond to the heroes of gigantic stature which occur in Old Testament texts. L'Heureux, however, does not account for the fact that *arṣ* in Ugaritic may refer equally to the underworld as to the surface of the earth, as in Akkadian *erṣētu* and even in Hebrew (Ps 139:15; Job 10:21–22; and especially Jonah 2:7).

With the publication of Andre Caquot's transcription of RS 34.126,[161] analyzed in the preceding chapter, numerous articles have appeared in rapid succession. First appeared an article by J. de Moor, "Rapiʾūma—Rephaim," in which he looks at all the available evidence for the Rephaim, within and without the Bible, including RS 34.126 (*KTU* 1.161). He concludes that the Rephaim are basically nobles, heroes, and kings, living or dead, and that the root meaning of *rpʾ*, "to heal," often carries the connotation of "savior." Thus,

> In a number of cases a medical meaning would seem to be out of the question. It rather indicates that YHWH comes to the rescue of harassed nations and restores the *šalôm* on earth.[162]

The Ugaritic dead kings and heroes, therefore, were those considered "saviors" and "healers" of the country, according to de Moor. de Moor also found a way to connect the pre-Israelite race of giants known in the Old Testament as Rephaim

---

[158] Caquot, "Les Rephaim Ougaritiques," 93.

[159] Conrad L'Heureux, "El and the Rephaim: New Light from Ugaritica V," (Ph. D. diss., Harvard University, 1972).

[160] Conrad L'Heureux, "The Ugaritic and Biblical Rephaim," 265–274.

[161] Andre Caquot, "Report," *Annuaire du collège de France* 75 (1975): 427.

[162] de Moor, "Rapi'ūma—Rephaim," 336.

(Deut 2:11, 20, 3:11–13, 1 Chr 20:4–8) by suggesting that these reflect ancient traditions about the greatness of the early heroes of the land and their "presumed supernatural tallness."[163] de Moor concludes,

> So it was a common belief in Canaan that dead kings, the *rp'u 'arṣ* "Saviours of the Country," enjoyed the privilege of sitting at table with Baal/Hadad, the eternal Saviour (*rp'u b'l mlk 'lm*). This took place within the framework of the ancestral cult and reached its culmination during the banquets of the New Year's Festival.[164]

In an article in 1976, M. Dietrich, O. Loretz, and J. Sanmartín suggested that the Rephaim cannot be associated with any ethnic group or living person. They discuss first the Old Testament evidence and arrive at the conclusion that

> Die Existenz eines Volkes mit dem Namen Rephaim kann aus den biblischen Quellen nicht erhoben werden. Sie sind die Totengeister allgemein. . . . Von den biblischen Texten her läßt sich somit keine Hilfe für die These gewinnen, daß die ug. *rp'm* "Totengeister" und zugleich Menschen bezeichnen.[165]

Since the existence of a folk-group called the Rephaim cannot be demonstrated outside of the biblical sources, Dietrich et al. feel that the biblical writings do not constitute proof of their existence. In the second part of their study, the Ugaritic texts which mention the Rephaim or cognate terms are surveyed. The same result is achieved in this section. The Rephaim are the spirits of the dead, especially dead ancestors:

> Die Aussagen der Ugarit-Texte über *rpu* und die *rpum* ergänzen die Mitteilungen der he. und phön. Texte über die "Rephaim." Auch in Ugarit bezeichnen die *rpum* nur die toten Ahnen, die Mannen, keinesfalls irgendeine ethnische, soziale oder religiöse Gruppe.[166]

They therefore deny any connection between the Rephaim and any cultic (Gray) or social (L'Heureux) group.

Beginning with Marvin Pope in 1977, there has been a marked tendency away from associating the Rephaim with living persons, nobles or otherwise. He cites with approval J. Ratosh's article on ancestor worship[167] that

---

[163] de Moor, "Rapi'ūma—Rephaim," 337.

[164] de Moor, "Rapi'ūma—Rephaim," 339.

[165] M. Dietrich, O. Loretz, and J. Sanmartín, "Die ugaritischen Totengeister *Rpu(m)* und die biblischen Rephaim," *UF* 8 (1976): 47.

[166] Dietrich, Loretz, and Sanmartín, "Die ugaritischen Totengeister *Rpu(m)*," 52–53.

[167] J. Ratosh, "'עבר' במקרא או ארץ העברים," *Beth Mikra* 16 (47) (1972): 549–568.

> The connection of OBRM (sic) with the Rephaim and the cult of the dead has already been made by J. Ratosh, who correctly divined that the term means "ancestors passed away."[168]

Pope suggests that the Rephaim are not just any of the dead, but the "deified dead."[169] In connection with *qbṣ ddn* of *KTU* 1.161, he states

> Ditānu/Didānu is thus an early ancestor of the West Semitic kings who has long since joined the infernal heroes, BTK RPI ARṢ. It appears, moreover, that Ditānu, or Didānu, is *primus inter pares* among the assembly of the deified dead who are collectively called PḪR QBṢ DTN, "the plenary gathering of (descendants of) Ditān." As a descendant of the hero Ditān, Krt now has merit among the patrons and dispensers of fertility, his deified progenitors, because he is now blessed with progeny to take the place of his lost family.[170]

To Pope, therefore, the Rephaim are restricted to the dead, but not just any dead: these are the dead with status and nobility in the underworld.

Caquot's and other analyses which preceded and followed his suffered from the extremely fragmentary condition of the three Rephaim texts *KTU* 1.20–22 and the fact that A. Caquot and subsequent analysts had to rely on a mold of the text of RS 34.126/*KTU* 1.161. The Rephaim texts 1.20–22 will regrettably remain in broken condition, although a new reading of these important texts has been prepared by T. Lewis. *KTU* 1.161, on the other hand, was re-read and analyzed in 1982 by P. Bordreuil and D. Pardee, yielding a number of new readings which help clarify both rituals for dead kings in the ancient Near East and the nature and identity of the Rephaim.[171] These new readings I discuss in chapter two above, but I reiterate here that they serve to underscore the nature of the text as a ritual expediting of the dead king to the underworld, where he will meet his fathers the dead kings who preceded him, identified also with the Rephaim. Bordreuil and Pardee end their study of the text by referring to its beginning and end as a means of understanding its contents:

> Le début du texte RS 34.126 se réferait donc au rituel funéraire accompli à l'intention de Niqmaddu III lorsque "le Roi est morte!" et la fin du texte ferait allusion à l'intention de sa veuve ou de sa bru Ṯryl et à l'intention de son fils et successeur ʿAmmourapi pour que "vive le roi!" [172]

---

[168] Pope, "Notes on the Rephaim Texts from Ugarit," 173.

[169] Pope, "Notes on the Rephaim Texts from Ugarit," 170.

[170] Pope, "Notes on the Rephaim Texts from Ugarit," 179.

[171] Bordreuil and Pardee, "Le rituel funéraire Ougaritique RS 34.126," 121–128.

[172] Bordreuil and Pardee, "Le rituel funéraire Ougaritique RS 34.126," 128.

According to this text, the Rephaim would definitely include, but not necessarily be restricted to, the dead kings, ancestors of Niqmaddu III and the reigning monarch ʿAmmurapi.

Following up this article on RS 34.126, B. Levine and J. de Tarragon offered a slightly different translation and interpretation than that of Bordreuil and Pardee the preceding year.[173] Levine and de Tarragon do not in this article associate the dead kings with the Rephaim. They presume, rather, that the dead kings do not immediately become deified, but *may* at a later time become Rephaim. The Rephaim are invoked to the funeral ritual in a similar manner as the witch of Endor raised the ghost of Samuel in 1 Sam 28, by "commanding" or "invoking" his presence.

In 1983, Shemaryahu Talmon responded to the increasing attention given to the Ugaritic texts mentioning Rephaim and the devaluing of the biblical evidence for a pre-Israelite ethnic group by surveying the biblical evidence and suggesting that the biblical evidence should be treated with as much respect as the Ugaritic.[174] He suggests that there are two roots and two separate phenomena called Rephaim in the biblical texts, one the well-known shades of the dead also attested in the Ugaritic texts and a second root denominating an ancient Levantine tribe.

John Healey, in a 1989 *Festschrift* for Dermot Ryan, attempts to evaluate some of Ryan's earlier work on the Rephaim.[175] One of Ryan's conclusions, that the Rephaim were chariot warriors like the Hurrian *maryannu*, he says can no longer be maintained. Another conclusion, that the Rephaim could have been a pre-Israelite tribe in Canaan, Healey suggests may well have been the case and that the Hebrew tradition confuses two originally separate terms.

The final article I will survey is that of J. N. Ford.[176] Throughout the history of the debate concerning the Rephaim one question has remained relatively constant: whether the Rephaim constitute living or dead persons and to what extent they may include one or both categories. Ford forcefully argues that the Rephaim on no account included the living and furthermore that there is not sufficient evidence to conclude that there were different types of Rephaim, divine and non-divine, among the dead.[177]

---

[173] Levine and de Tarragon, "Dead Kings and Rephaim," 649–659.

[174] Shemaryahu Talmon, "Biblical Repha'îm and Ugaritic rpu/i(m)," *HAR* 7 (1983): 235–249.

[175] John F. Healey, "The Last of the Rephaim," in *Back to the Sources: Biblical and Near Eastern Studies* (ed. K. Cathcart and J. Healey; Dublin: Glendale, 1989), 33–44.

[176] Ford, "The Living Rephaim of Ugarit," 73–101.

[177] Ford, "The Living Rephaim of Ugarit," 97.

From the survey above it is readily apparent that the Rephaim continue to pose significant questions to interpreters. Among these questions one must include the following: 1) Do the Rephaim include living persons or are they strictly spirits of the dead? 2) If the latter, were the Rephaim an "aristocracy" among the dead, or all the dead in general? 3) What is the relationship between *KTU* 1.161, *KTU* 1.20–22, and the ritual feeding of the dead in Ugarit and elsewhere? 4) What is the relationship between Šapšu and the dead in Ugaritic literature? 5) Did a pre-Israelite tribal group called the Rephaim ever exist and is there any relationship between this group and the clear attestation in the Bible and Ugaritic literature that the Rephaim were spirits of the dead?[178]

Several of these questions need not detain us here. In response to the first and last of these, most commentators now recognize that the Rephaim are indeed spirits of the dead, as later biblical and Phoenician inscriptions attest. If there was a cultic or military class of living Rephaim, we have no real evidence for it. It is possible, in response to the fifth question, that there existed a pre-Israelite tribal group known as Rephaim, but if so we know about them only through the Old Testament. It is also possible that the Old Testament understanding of Rephaim as an ethnic designation is the application of a misunderstood term to tribal groups known for their outstanding size or military prowess. It is perhaps safest to admit with Healey and Talmon the possibility that such a tribe existed, but our current state of knowledge is not such that we can confirm it.

The second question deals with the identification of the Rephaim as an aristocracy among the dead. As I mentioned earlier, while this is still a possibility, *KTU* 1.161 also raises the possibility that the Rephaim are the ancient deified dead (Pope), while the recently dead kings Ammishtamru and Niqmaddu are not to be counted among their number. In support of this, lines 2–10 and 22–24 mention the "ancient Rephaim" in possible distinction to the more recent dead (Levine and de Tarragon). Levine and de Tarragon leave open the possibility that the recent dead kings may themselves hope to be included among the number of the Rephaim by virtue of tenure in the underworld. It is also possible that the distinction here is not between the Rephaim and non-Rephaim dead kings, but rather between the *rpim qdmym* (*Ulkn, Ṯr ʿllmn, Sdn w Rdn, Trmn*; the "ancient Rephaim") and the more recent Rephaim (Ammishtamru, Niqmaddu), which line of reasoning Ford follows. It seems certain, following Levine and de Tarragon, that at least some of the dead kings achieve Rephaim status.[179]

---

[178] For more questions about the Ugaritic dead in general, see John Healey, "The Ugaritic Dead: Some Live Issues," *UF* 18 (1986): 27–32.

[179] Keret is clearly a king (see *KTU* 1.14 vi 14). In *KTU* 1.15 iii 3–4, 14–15 ("Keret," in Gibson, *Canaanite Myths and Legends*, 91), Keret is blessed:

In response to the third question, as opposed to Pitard, Healey, and Levine and de Tarragon, there does not appear to be any allusion in *KTU* 1.161 to feeding the dead kings or ancient Rephaim in a manner reflective of the Mesopotamian *kispu* ceremony.[180] As I mentioned in chapter 2, Pitard based his analysis on *ksh* as "his cup" and the reconstruction of *ṯlḥn ml[a]*, "full table," rather than "table of the king," reflective of royal furnishings which mourn his departure. The only possible reference to the feeding of the deceased is in lines 27–30, the sevenfold sacrifices. These may not at all have to do with the feeding of the dead, however. In the Ur-Nammu text, Ur-Nammu offers seven (!) sacrifices to the gods of the underworld ("the seven, the *išib*, the *lumaḫ*, the *gutug* who had died"), a possible corollary to sacrifices made to the ancient Rephaim, also at least partially consisting of deceased kings (see Gilgamesh in the Ur-Nammu tablet!).[181] It is unclear in *KTU* 1.161 who does the sacrificing, whether it is the priestly or royal celebrants of the ritual or Niqmaddu himself, being exhorted to perform the required sacrifices in the underworld. If the latter,

---

btk rpi arṣ
bpḫr qbṣ dtn

It is possible that Keret is blessed "in the midst of the Rephaim of the earth" because he is later to become one of them. Likewise, Danʾel in the *Aqhat* legend may also be a king or a dignitary later to be counted among the Rephaim. I therefore translate *mt rpi* in *KTU* 1.17 i 17 as "[Danʾel] the rapha-man." See also the *Death of Ur-Nammu* text, where at least Gilgamesh is counted among the deities of the underworld to whom sacrifices are given.

[180] Wayne Pitard, "The Ugaritic Funerary Text RS 34.126," 67; Levine and de Tarragon, "Dead Kings and Rephaim," 654.

[181] Another question involves the number of the Rephaim. In *KTU* 1.161, four *rpim qdmym* are mentioned by name and two recently deceased kings follow them in the list. If the dead kings are not Rephaim then only four are mentioned, but seven sacrifices are mentioned in lines 27–30. In the *Death of Ur-Nammu*, seven "*gutug* who had died" are mentioned as deities in the underworld and sacrifices are presented to them by Ur-Nammu (seven sacrifices to seven "gods of the netherworld" plus two spouses). In the Rephaim text *KTU* 1.20 i 1–3 and 1.20 ii 1, according to Theodore Lewis's reconstruction, the Rephaim may be "seven" (or eight?) in number:

rp]um.tdbḥn	[the Rep]aim will feast
[š]bʿd.ilnym	[the s]even spirits
[šbʿ.bbty]	[the seven in my house]
tmn.bqrb.hkly	the eight in the midst of my palace

These texts allude to the number of the underworld deified dead/Rephaim. The number seven should not be taken to be a fixed number (as above in *KTU* 1.20 ii, "seven . . . eight"), but rather the entire complement of Rephaim, symbolized by the number seven and seven sacrifices offered to them. Unfortunately, only if one counts *Sdn* and *Rdn* as two separate Rephaim can one come up with seven in *KTU* 1.161: *Ulkn, Trmn, Sdn-wa-Rdn, Tr ʿllmn, ʿmttmr*, and *Nqmd III.* It is possible here, and suggestive considering the seven sacrifices of this text and the formulaic nature of the "seven" Rephaim mentioned in others, but beyond this it is not possible to say for certain.

then I suggest we ought to assume some sort of sympathetic ritual rather than a *kispu* style feeding of the dead—the sacrifices offered in the funeral ritual summon the Rephaim and invoke them to accept the recently arrived king Niqmaddu.

Levine and de Tarragon and other commentators assume that the Rephaim are here being invoked into the presence of the celebrants at the funeral ritual, at which the dead ancestors are fed. This assumption must be questioned, however. Nowhere in the text are the ancient Rephaim or more recently deceased kings said to be present at the ritual as it is being performed. Indeed, the Rephaim do not appear to have been brought up to the surface in the manner of the witch of Endor at all. Even after being "commanded" or "invoked," the Rephaim and/or recently deceased kings are *still* to be found in the underworld! See lines 22–26:

> Below is Sdn wa-Rdn
> Below is Ṯr ʿllmn
> Below are the most ancient Rephaim
> Below is Ammishtamru the king
> Below is also Niqmaddu the king

My suggestion is that something similar is going on here to what happens in the *Death of Ur-Nammu*, discussed in chapter two above: the ancient spirits and inhabitants of the underworld are roused to greet Ur-Nammu when he arrives there, to welcome him and help him take his place as a king in their midst. It is also noteworthy that the dirge parodied in Isa 14 does not reflect such a feeding of the dead.

Of course, this is not to suggest that there was not a widespread cult of the dead, with a *kispu* style banquet offered by their descendants and relatives.[182] Indeed, the Rephaim are noteworthy for the number and sumptuousness of the feasts in which they participate. In the Rephaim texts mentioned previously, the Rephaim are invited to a feast by ʾEl, possibly in response to Danʾel's need for an heir. In the *Keret* text, Keret is blessed by ʾEl (to have children!) "in the midst of the *rpi.arṣ*" during a banquet. There is also no question that ancestors were provided with food and drink. It is to say that such a practice is not recorded as part of the Ugaritic royal funeral dirge.

---

[182] There are many scholarly treatments of this phenomenon. Among some of the more recent are Miranda Bayliss, "The Cult of Dead Kin in Assyria and Babylonia," *Iraq* 35 (1973): 115–125; Paolo Matthiae, "Princely Cemetery and Ancestors' Cult at Ebla During Middle Bronze II: A Proposal of Interpretation," *UF* 11 (1979): 563–569; J. de Moor, "The Ancestral Cult in KTU 1.17:I.26–28," *UF* 17 (1986): 407–409; Matitiahu Tsevat, "Eating and Drinking, Hosting and Sacrificing in the Epic of Aqht," *UF* 18 (1986): 345–350; and Theodore J. Lewis, *Cults of the Dead in Ancient Israel and Ugarit*.

The fourth question, the function of the deity Šapšu, centers on whether Šapšu functions as a "psychopomp" (one who ferries the dead to the underworld on a nightly sojourn there) in Ugaritic literature as Šamaš does in Mesopotamian literature. Obviously, the position this analysis takes is that she did indeed so act. Pertinent to this discussion are the texts *KTU* 1.161 19–26, *KTU* 1.5 vi 1–1.6 i 31, and *KTU* 1.6 vi 44–47. It is important to ascertain the position of Šapšu relative to the dead in Ugaritic literature in order to make as clear a connection as possible between Levantine, Mesopotamian, and biblical (i.e., Isa 14:4b–21) traditions about the descent and possible ascent of dead kings in the ancient Near East. It is Šapšu/Šamaš who makes the journey possible.

First, in *KTU* 1.161, Šapšu cries out, "After your lord, to his throne, after your lord, go down to the underworld." If *ʾṯr* here means "after," following most recent commentators, then Šapšu is exhorting someone to follow "your lord." Unfortunately, both the one being exhorted and the lord to be followed are not clear in the text. The "lord" to be followed could be 1) the god *bʿl hd*, Baʿal Hadad, who himself dies, goes to the underworld, and was eventually exalted; 2) the Niqmaddu or Ammishtamru (grandfather and great-grandfather of Niqmaddu III, respectively) mentioned in the text; 3) Šapšu; or 4) Niqmaddu III himself. Likewise, who is expected to "go down" "after" this lord? Presumably, following my earlier analysis, it is the recently deceased Niqmaddu III being expedited to the underworld via Šapšu as psychopomp, but other possibilities include 1) ʿAmmurapi (as the next king, who will inevitably "follow his lord" and father Niqmaddu to the underworld); 2) the mourners, who will figuratively follow their dead lord Niqmaddu with weeping; and 3) the *ksi*, the throne of Niqmaddu, which mourns for its lord and will descend to give him royal status in the underworld.

The first alternative for the lord, *bʿl hd*, makes some sense but there is lacking any prior mention or allusion in the text of *KTU* 1.161 to *bʿl* as someone who ought to be followed to the underworld. The second, Ammishtamru or Niqmaddu, again makes sense, but the implication in this case must be that one or both have been summoned to the ritual and will return to the *arṣ*, taking Niqmaddu III with them. The third, Šapšu, is unlikely in the extreme, as we would expect *bʿlt* rather than *bʿl* with reference to this female deity. Likewise, that which follows the lord to the underworld is unlikely to be the throne, even though dead kings often possess thrones in the underworld in ancient Near Eastern literature and in Isa 14. Thrones are never said to "descend," but are granted the deceased king upon his appropriate entrance into the realm of the dead. This leaves the mourners gathered for the ritual and ʿAmmurapi the new king. We do not need to decide between these for the reasons given below.

The "lord" must be Niqmaddu III. First, there are texts which demonstrate that it is the deceased himself who provokes the exclamation "I/we will go down to the earth after him" from the mourners. A biblical analogy to this expression occurs, as several commentators have noticed, when Jacob received the news of Joseph's death in Gen 37:34–35:

> Jacob tore his garments, and put sackcloth on his loins, and mourned for his son many days. . . . He refused to be comforted and said, "No, I shall go down to Sheol to my son, mourning." Thus his father bewailed him.

He, as the mourner, would follow his son to Sheol, although this does not literally occur for some years. In this text we see the visible manifestation of mourning (as in *KTU* 1.161 and *KTU* 1.5 vi–1.6 i) and the refrain concerning going down to the underworld after the deceased (as in *KTU* 1.161, *KTU* 1.5 vi–1.6 i, Ezek 32). The account ends, "Thus he bewailed him," suggesting again the formulaic nature of this refrain.

Second is the text *KTU* 1.5 vi 1–1.6 i 31, the hunt for *bʿl* in the land of the dead. Pidray and Tallay have searched and found *bʿl* dead in the "fields of the shore of death." Upon hearing this, ʾEl mourned by pouring dust on his head, putting on sackcloth, and gashing himself with a flint. He then cried out,

my.lim.bn.dgn	"What (will happen) to the people of the son of Dagan?
my.hmlt	What of the multitude?
a<u>t</u>r.bʿl.ard.barṣ	After Baʿal I will go down into the earth." [183]

The ritual nature of this exclamation is made evident by the fact that ʾEl does not actually "go down to the earth." He rather fades from the action until later. Anat then searches for Baʿal and finds him by the shores of death. She also mourns and gashes her body, then repeats the refrain of ʾEl quoted above. Finally, Anat calls upon Šapšu to lift the body of Baʿal, who places it upon Anat's shoulders, whereupon she carries it to Saphon and gives it proper burial. Sacrifices then ensue for him.

There are several points of contact with *KTU* 1.161. First, a group of mourners lament the death of a king. Second, two mourners say they will go down to the earth after Baʿal. Third, Šapšu makes an appearance in *KTU* 1.161 as the psychopomp of the dead to the underworld. In the case of *KTU* 1.6, why would Šapšu be needed to lift up Baʿal, since Anat was already there? It is for no other reason than that Šapšu was needed to ferry the dead to the underworld, but also to the realm of the deities of the heavens, where Anat takes Baʿal and buries him.[184] Finally, sacrifices in multiples of seven follow. Contra L'Heureux

---

[183] "Baal and Mot," *KTU* 1.5 vi 23–25 (in Gibson, *Canaanite Myths and Legends*, 74).

[184] J. N. Ford has also made this point in his article "The Living Rephaim," 95.

and Gibson, Baʿal is depicted as clearly in the underworld, *lkbd arṣ, lkbd šdm, šd [šḥl] mmt*. He is there, however, without throne or status and without proper burial. Šapšu is needed in this account because Anat is unable to bring Baʿal up from the shores of death without her aid. Indeed, it is not even necessary to assume Anat herself went to the underworld, although the text is unclear. We can say with certainty that she "found" him there and with Šapšu's help was able to recover Baʿal and give him proper burial.

We must conclude, therefore, that it is ʿAmmurapi and the assembled mourners of Ugarit, gathered for the funeral ritual of Niqmaddu, who mourn and are exhorted to "follow their lord" Niqmaddu to the underworld.

A connection can also be made at this point with Isa 14. In the mock funeral dirge depicted there, Hêlēl ben Šaḥar is jeered instead of mourned and has no proper burial to ensure status in the underworld. The sun god, Šamaš, plays no role here, nor should we expect such in a text which is even restrained in its portrayal of Sheol and the Rephaim. Note how he is reported to have "gone down" in the text,[185] with no hint of mourners "following after him" to Sheol. He aspired to ascend to the highest heavens (even in death Baʿal was taken here, at least partially by Šapšu), but in reality his body lay exposed and maggot eaten.

VI. Summary and Conclusion

There are several conclusions which are justified from the analysis above. While the great differences in the cosmologies of ancient Near Eastern cultures must not be minimized, there are several points at which the Egyptian, Mesopotamian, and Syro-Palestinian conceptions of the cosmos are quite similar. First, the sun god travels a course through the heavens but also goes into the underworld at night and performs various functions. In the case of Egypt, of course, the dead pharaoh is himself associated with the sun god and is said to rule in the underworld. Second, dead kings retain status and thrones in the underworld in all three cultures. Third, dead kings are identified with stars, at least in the cases of the Egyptians and the Sumerians. Information is lacking relative to the Levantine cultures and later Assyro-Babylonian monarchs. The particular stars mentioned are *nṯr dwꜣ(w)* (Venus), *sbꜣ ḏꜣ* (probably Venus), and *Wsir* (Venus) for Egypt and Amaušumgalanna (Agru) or Aries for Sumer. It is possible that Hêlēl ben Šaḥar was a star associated with the king in some Levantine cultures. I would suggest that Hêlēl and Šaḥar were deities which figured in funerary rituals, as Isa 14 and the Emar *maš'artu* text attest. It is not possible at present to identify this star unequivocally. Almost certainly, the star

[185] The pharaoh is commanded to do so in Ezek 32.

was not Venus, as this star was associated apparently with ʿAṯtar/Ištar. Perhaps it was a star in close proximity to Venus, as was the case with Amaušumgalanna, but we cannot be certain. Finally, in the case of (the parody in) Isa 14 and the Sumerian lamentations mentioned above, cedar trees are part of the expediting of the dead king on his journey in the afterlife.

The mythological images, then, of Isa 14 are congruent with numerous texts from throughout the ancient Near East. The poem may furthermore be understood as a parody of a royal funeral dirge, utilizing numerous images from such funeral laments. The ascent to heaven section may be understood as a reference to literature or rituals pertaining to the death of kings, or else may be a reference to the king's hubris, as in the case of Etana, in attempting literally to rise above the limitations of his prerogatives.

We come now to an exegesis of Isa 14:4b–21, with particular reference to the dirge form, mythological themes, and the reuse of these themes and forms in the *mashal*.

Chapter 5
A New Reading of Isaiah 14:4b–21

I. Introduction

In the preceding chapters we have surveyed mythology and its relationship to Isa 14:4b–21, the form and function of the *mashal* and the royal dirge, and mythological motifs which may lie behind the poem. It remains to explain the text of Isa 14:4b–21 in light of the dirge forms and mythological motifs. Following the translation of the text I will examine the literary structure of the dirge and the major sections of the poem based upon that structure. I will conclude with a discussion of the identity of the king.

II. Translation

How the oppressor has ceased, the tyranny[1] has stopped!
The Lord has broken the staff of the wicked, the rod of rulers—

---

[1] מדהבה is notoriously difficult. Two lines of reasoning have generally been followed relative to this word. The first is that the ד should be emended to a ר, producing an understandable מרהבה with the sense of "one who acts boisterously, an arrogant one." The other line of reasoning is that the text is not corrupt, but that we no longer know exactly what the term means. Harry Orlinsky ("Madhebah in Isaiah 14:4," VT 7 [1957]: 202–203) suggests that the parallel root *nāgaś* signifies strength. He cites as further evidence the discovery of the Ugaritic root *db'*, which he suggests means "to be strong, mighty." He suggests there may be a reflex of the root *db'* in *madhēbāh* even though it is missing the third radical (א) and that "it may be that the ancients recognized in דאב, דבא, and דהב the common דב element, with the meaning "strong" (p. 203). Orlinsky's first argument from context does not follow, because *nāgaś* does not mean "strong," but rather "drive" or "oppress." The supposed common דב element in Semitic languages is speculative, based on similarity of sound rather than actual roots. It is possible that מדהבה is the best reading on other grounds. First is the principle of *lectio difficilior*. This is clearly the most difficult reading and so ought not to be dismissed

The one who smote peoples with fury, a never-ceasing blow,
The one who ruled[2] the nations with anger, persecuting[3] without restraint.

All the earth rests (and) is quiet; they have broken forth with a joyous shout.
Even the cypresses rejoice over you, the cedars of Lebanon:
"Since you lay down, no hewer comes up against us!"

Sheol below is agitated for you, to greet your coming;
He rouses[4] the Rephaim for you, all the great ones of the earth,
He raises from their thrones all the kings of the nations;
All of them answer and say to you:
"You also have become weak like us, you have become just like us!
Your majesty has been brought down to Sheol, the sound of your harps.[5]
Under you worms are spread out and your covering is maggots."

How you have fallen from heaven, Hêlēl ben Šaḥar[6]!

---

too readily. Secondly, the term occurs twice in 1QH[a] (3.25 and 12.18), meaning "hardship" and "annihilation," parallel to "turmoil" and "ruin." Vv. 4b and 6a are constructed similarly in that each has a masculine singular participle in the A colon, followed by a feminine abstract noun in the B colon. While we do not know the exact meaning of the term, "tyranny" or "oppression," parallel to "oppressor" in v.4b, seems indicated.

[2] *Rādāh* with ב implies manner of rule, as in Ezek 34:4: "You have ruled them with force and harshness."

[3] Read מְרַדֵּף along with most commentators. מֻרְדָּף is not otherwise attested.

[4] The verb is a Polel perfect or a Polel infinitive absolute. If an infinitive, the disagreement in gender with Sheol, usually feminine, is not an issue. The bi-colon, however, uses הֵקִים, hiphil perfect, suggesting that עוֹרֵר in the first colon may be a masculine perfect and therefore a conflict in gender with Sheol. It is possible, on the other hand, that הֵקִים should be emended to the infinitive הָקִים. If Rephaim is the subject, then it does not agree with the verb in number. If Sheol is the subject, then it does not agree in gender. Nowhere else in the twenty-eight occurrences of the term Rephaim in the Old Testament, when it is the subject of a clause, does it have a singular predicate. Job 26:6 indicates that in at least one other instance Sheol is a masculine noun. In any event, Sheol does the rousing of the Rephaim. In this instance either Sheol is depicted as masculine, or both verbs, הֵקִים and עוֹרֵר, should be infinitives.

[5] *Hemyah* is a *hapax legomenon*, possibly meaning "noise," or "sound." See Isa 5:11–14 for an example of arrogant people engaging in feasts with musical instruments who are said to go down to Sheol.

[6] The word Hêlēl has given translators and commentators difficulty for many years. E. König suggested as far back as 1895 that it is cognate with Arabic *hilāl*, "new moon" and therefore the god or divine epithet suggested by the term Hêlēl is the new or crescent moon (see E. König, *Historisch-kritisches Lehrgebäude der hebräischen Sprache, II 1* [Leipzig: J. C. Hinrichs, 1881–97], 106). L. Koehler and W. Baumgartner (*The Hebrew and Aramaic Lexicon of the Old Testament 1* [Leiden: E. J. Brill, 1994], 248) have continued to make this association and it has recently been proposed again by Marjo C. A. Korpel (*A Rift in the Clouds: Ugaritic and Hebrew Descriptions of the Divine* [UBL 8; Münster: Ugarit-Verlag, 1990], 575–576). W. Gallagher has suggested that הֵילֵל is cognate with the Mesopotamian

You have been cut down to the earth, helpless[7] on your back[8]!
You have said in your heart, "I will ascend to heaven, above the stars of ʾEl
I will raise my throne,
And I will sit down in the mount of assembly, in the heights of Saphon,
I will ascend above the heights of the cloud, I will become like ʿElyôn!"
But you are brought down to Sheol, to the depths of the pit!
Those who see you stare, they look at you closely:
"Is this the man who made the earth tremble, who made kingdoms shake?

God *Illil* (Sumerian EN.LIL; Gallagher, "On the Identity of Helel ben Sahar," 137). Gallagher explains the change in spelling reasonably enough, but falters in finding any explanation for *Illil* as the "son of Dawn," surely important to understanding the identity of Hêlēl in Isa 14. P. Grelot ("Sur la vocalisation de הילל (Is. XIV 12)," VT 6 [1956]: 303–304) suggests that the word is derived from the Hebrew הלל, "to shine," and is cognate with Akkadian *ellu*, "brilliant." He suggests that through a complex phonological process, *ellu* in Akkadian becomes הֵילֵל in Hebrew, much as *ekallu* in Akkadian becomes הֵיכָל in Hebrew.

His analysis falters in several ways. First, *e* in Akkadian does not become *hē* in Hebrew, as for example, Akkadian *alāku* becomes *hālak* in Hebrew. Second, his analogy with הֵיכָל/*ekallu* does not follow: *ekallu* is from Sumerian E.GAL and is not even a Semitic term. Third, he leaves the impression that Hêlēl is really an East-Semitic term, and presumably an East-Semitic divine epithet or deity, brought over into West-Semitic through a complex process of vocalic changes and the disappearance/reappearance of the consonant ה. I would suggest that *ellu* and Hêlēl have their own histories of development and, as an epithet of deity, *hll* is found in West-Semitic contexts, Ugarit and Israel. The etymology and vocalization must, therefore, remain a question for the time being.

[7] *Hôlēš* has often been taken to mean "to bring or lay low," "to make prostrate," etc. The usual meaning in the G stem is "to be prostrate, feeble, helpless." The H stem does not otherwise exist in biblical Hebrew for this verb, although it does occur in post-biblical Hebrew and causative meanings are attested in Aramaic. Otto Kaiser (Isaiah 13–39 [OTL; Philadelphia: Westminster, 1974], 28) assumed such a causative meaning in his commentary on Isaiah: "You who laid the nations low." It is difficult to understand in such a construction how the *ʿal* functions, irrespective of problems of classification. The most compelling argument is provided by Raymond C. van Leeuwen ("Isa 14:12, Hôlēš ʿal GWYM and Gilgamesh XI, 6," JBL 99 [1980]: 173–184), who suggests by analogy with Gilgamesh tablet 11 that the original wording of the text is *hôlēš ʿal gēwîm*, "helpless on your back," following an earlier, and similar, suggestion by Gunkel (*Schöpfung und Chaos in Urzeit und Endzeit*, 133). Van Leeuwen quotes an almost identical expression in Gilgamesh tablet 11, 6: [*ina nid*]*i a-ḫi nadāta e-lu ṣe-ri-ka* (Van Leeuwen, 182). See comments below on *gēwîm.*

[8] Van Leeuwen, "Isa 14:12, Hôlēš ʿal GWYM," 174–175, suggests that the MT and the versions have all misread the original word as *gôyîm*. 1QIsa[a] is the only ancient witness which still preserves the original meaning: it reads גוי minus the ם, which van Leeuwen understands to mean "back." He suggests that *gēwî(m)* is a reasonable word for "back" as follows: *gĕwiyyāh* means "corpse, torso," a reasonable term to use for "back" (or flat on one's torso). One can suppose the existence of a noun *gĕwî* by analogy with a number of other feminine nouns and shorter forms of those nouns as in *ʾŏniyyāh*/*ʾŏnî*, *šĕbiyyāh*/*šĕbî*, etc. The מ he takes to be a simple enclitic ending. Van Leeuwen asserts that the copier of 1QIsa[a] understood the meaning "back, torso," but did not understand the presence of the enclitic *mem*, so it was dropped. Read with van Leeuwen.

Who made the world like a wilderness, and tore down its cities, (who) did not let his prisoners go home?'[9]

All the kings of the nations, all of them[10] lie in glory, each in his house,
But you are cast out from your grave, like an abhorrent plant,[11]
Clothed with[12] the slain, those who were pierced with the sword,

---

[9] *Pātaḥ* re-pointed to *pittaḥ*, along with most commentators and the LXX (ἔλυσεν). It is the release of prisoners "to home," not the opening of houses, which is in view.

[10] כֻּלָּם should not be stricken either here or in 10a. In 10a it precedes the speech of the Rephaim and in 18a it immediately follows their second speech, thus framing the speeches of the Rephaim.

[11] LXX reads ὡς νεκρὸς ἐβδελυγμένος, "like a disgusting corpse." F. Schwally, "Miscellen," *ZAW* 11 (1891): 257, Watts, *Isaiah 1–33*, 207, and Kaiser, *Isaiah 13–39*, 29 all read *nēp̄el*, "aborted fetus" for *nēṣer*, "sprout." *Nēp̄el* occurs only three times in the MT, all of which seem to refer to an "aborted fetus" or an "untimely birth": Job 3:16, Ps 58:9, and Eccl 6:3.

Aborted fetuses or untimely births seem to be buried immediately in the Old Testament, not "cast forth from their graves" (see Job 3:16, "Why was I not buried like an untimely birth?"; Eccl 6:3 is even clearer: "If he [a man] has no burial, I say a *nēp̄el* is better than him"). In support of the MT, it is possible that a *nēṣer* may be considered abhorrent on a couple of grounds. First, Isaiah is replete with botanical imagery, particularly those which describe warriors or kings as trees. Ezek 31:18 likewise uses such imagery when he describes the trees of Eden going down to Sheol. Seth Erlandsson (*The Burden of Babylon: A Study of Isaiah 13:2–14:23* [CB, Old Testament Series 4; Lund: CWK Gleerup, 1970], 37) suggests that some such meaning is present in Isa 18:5–6, which describes the Lord pruning off branches. Secondly, *nēṣer* is found only three times in the Old Testament and in each case it has to do with a king, and not specifically with trees.

Besides biblical occurrences of the term *nēṣer* there are extra-biblical occurrences of such terminology as applied to kingship. The first occurs three times in the Deir ʿAlla inscription, comb. II, lines 5, 12, and 14. J. Hoftijzer and G. van der Kooij (*Aramaic Texts from Deir ʿAlla* [Leiden: E. J. Brill, 1977], 80) translate *nǒr* as "blinded one." J. Hackett (*The Balaam Text from Deir ʿAlla* [HSM 3; Chico: Scholars Press, 1984], 57) translates it more appropriately by "scion," as line 13 says *mlkn yḥzw*, which even Hoftijzer admits must mean "kings will see." This phrase is preceded and followed by *nǒr*, in the context of that *nǒr*'s death, suggesting the possibility that royalty, a "scion," is intended. Also, kingship terminology follows the occurrences of *nǒr*. Line 15 certainly, and line 16 possibly according to Hoftijzer, mention *mlk* as well. One other passage from the *Gilgamesh Epic* is worthy of note relative to the terminology of kingship. Enkidu encourages Gilgamesh to slay Huwawa at the Cedar Forest upon their arrival and refers to him as the "offshoot of Uruk." Biblical and extra-biblical materials, therefore, attest to the possibility that the king of Babylon is an "abhorrent branch," or "disgusting scion."

[12] LXX says "with many of the dead," μετὰ πολλῶν τεθνηκότων, possibly due to the difficulty the translator had with a literal translation. The one Old Testament passage which treats the clothing of the dead is Job 7:5, "my flesh is clothed with worms and dirt," a description which fits admirably in this context, considering v. 11b. In this connection, see also Deir ʿAlla comb. II, line 8. In the context of death and the underworld and the *byt ʿlmn*, the text reads *wrmh mngdš*, "and worms from the grave." The reference here in Isaiah is

Who go down to the stones[13] of the pit like a trampled corpse;
You will not be joined with them in burial,
For you destroyed your land, you slew your people!
Let the offspring who do evil not be called out forever!

Prepare a slaughtering-place for his sons, on account of the iniquity of their fathers,
Let them not arise and possess the earth, or fill the face of the world.[14]

III. Exegesis of Isaiah 14:4b–21 in Light of the Dirge and Mythological Motifs

A. The Extent of the Poem

Most commentators recognize that the dirge begins in v. 4b with the dirge exclamation *ʾêk*. The end of the poem is not so obvious. Some commentators, notably Kissane, have included vv. 22–23 within the poem.[15] There are, however, several reasons for separating these verses from the body of the poem. First, they comprise a speech by the Lord, who otherwise makes no appearance in the body of the dirge. Second, these verses are prosaic and depart from the fairly consistent 3/4 *qînāh* meter of the poem. Third, many have noted the late, non-Isaianic character of the terminology found in these verses. Finally, if the poem is a parody of the royal dirge, as I have suggested, the offering of sacrifices and/or the calling out of the name of the new king, consistent with *KTU* 1.161 and the *Death of Ur-Nammu*, are a fitting end to the poem.

---

probably to the king's body lying dead on the field of battle, covered with corpses of the slain.

[13] MT says *yōrĕdê ʾel ʾabnê bôr*, "those who go down to the stones of the pit." LXX simply says καταβαινόντων εἰς ᾅδου, "who go down to Hades," translating the sense if not the words of the text. "Stones of the pit" is difficult, but not impossible: 1) burial pits had stones cast down to block them up; 2) Lam 3:9 suggests that the person in Sheol is blocked from escape by huge stones (*gāzît*); 3) in Ezek 28, the king of Tyre walks about among the "stones of fire," an even more obscure allusion, but possibly the heavenly analog to the *ʾabnê bôr*.

[14] The term "cities" interrupts an otherwise good parallelism. Considering that the Masoretic tradition gives three accented syllables in each stich without the *ʿārîm*, and *tēbēl* is parallel to *ʾāreṣ*, it appears as though *ʿārîm* may be a very early explanatory word, as the second stich appears to have no object. Because the succession is in view here, including dynastic legitimation and the right to inherit and expand imperial territory, the line reads better without *ʿārîm*.

[15] Edward J. Kissane, *The Book of Isaiah: Translated from a Critically Revised Hebrew Text with Commentary, Vol. 1* (Dublin: Richview, 1960), 159.

There is some question whether the poem should end at v. 20a or v. 21. Verse 20a ends the section 7–20a, which refers to the king in the second person. According to some commentators, 20b–21 refers to the king in the third person and is therefore separate from the body of the dirge. Such a position fails to account for the fact that the introduction to the dirge, vv. 4b–6, also refers to the king in the third person and does not directly address him. Thus, on the basis of structural similarity to the royal dirge, as well as coherence in the alternation in perspective, the limits of the poem should be vv. 4b–21.

B. THE STRUCTURE OF ISAIAH 14:4b–21

Most commentators have found five sections or strophes in the poem, although there is little agreement as to the exact boundaries. Edward Kissane[16] and George Gray[17] represent one extreme. They suggest that the poem was originally composed of five strophes of seven poetic lines each. In order to arrive at this symmetry, Kissane had to count vv. 22–23 as part of the poetic text, clearly prosaic and redactional according to most commentators.[18] Gray was more restrained, suggesting that the first three sections (4b–8, 9–11, and 12–15) were originally composed of seven "distichs" each, but that the fourth section, 16–20, had become corrupt in vv. 17, 19, and 20. He nevertheless reconstructed this section based upon the supposition that the first four strophes, at least, were originally of uniform length. The fifth section he labels "miscellaneous" and does not reconstruct it in seven lines, but does suggest the original may have been this length.[19]

One ought to compare Isa 14 with other "complete" dirges in the Old Testament relative to this issue. 2 Sam 1 does not demonstrate such consistency of form. After a single bi-colon introducing the dirge (v. 19) and a bi-colon introducing the dirge refrain ("how"), two bi-cola follow which exhort silence about the death in Philistia. Three bi-cola and a tri-colon (?) exhort the mountains of Gilboa not to rain or drop dew because the shield, bow, and sword of Jonathan and Saul were stilled "there." V. 23 is difficult to divide, but is either a bi- or tri-colon which introduces both Saul and Jonathan, followed by separate treatments of each: v. 24 appears to be a tri-colon relating to Saul's goodness and vv. 25 and 26 relate to Jonathan, much lengthier than the section relating to Saul. Alternatively, it is possible to divide the poem in the middle, at v. 23.

---

16 Kissane, *The Book of Isaiah*, 158.

17 George B. Gray, *A Critical and Exegetical Commentary on the Book of Isaiah, Vol. 1* (ICC; Edinburgh: T & T Clark, 1912), 247–250.

18 Kissane, *The Book of Isaiah*, 159.

19 George Gray, *Isaiah*, 247–248.

Vv. 19–22 relate to the death of Saul and Jonathan on the mountains of Gilboa, while vv. 23–26 relate to their goodness. These two sections do not scan equally in terms of cola, stress, or syllable count. Regardless how one divides the poem, the notion of perfect strophic symmetry in this poem has little to commend it.

Otto Kaiser organizes the dirge in Isa 14 more or less by shift in perspective: vv. 4b–8 (earth's celebration—the nations and trees—at the death of the tyrant); vv. 9–11 (the reaction of the shades in the underworld); vv. 12–15 (the disastrous attempt by the king to reach the highest heaven); vv. 16–19a (back on earth, the response of the onlookers); and 19b–21 (the utter ruin of the tyrant).[20] Kaiser is not sensitive to the form of the dirge.[21] He does not consider the refrain-like character of the lines beginning with *ʾêk* and, therefore, lumps vv. 7–8, the rejoicing of trees, with the introductory comments in vv. 4b–6. Likewise, he does not account for the ideology of the descent of the dead king to Sheol when he suggests that the perspective shifts back to the earth in vv. 16–19a. The point is, all the kings of the nations rest in glory in their sepulchers, while the tyrant's body lies in the open, unburied. We have not suddenly made the shift out of mythopoeic/cosmological thought; it is more likely that the parody of the mythology of the death of kings holds true throughout and we are dealing with something not unlike prince Baʿal lying unburied in the fields of death.[22] The perspective is not that of a radical disjunction between the land of the living and that of the dead. Likewise, there is no discernible strophic structure to Isa 14:4b–21, rather changes in perspective, person, or thematic content which provide the dramatic shifts in the poem.

An interesting, but idiosyncratic, approach to the structure of the poem is that of John D. W. Watts. He understands the taunt song not to begin until v. 8, where the trees express their relief at the tyrant's demise.[23] The taunt is in four sections, according to Watts: vv. 8–10 (response of trees and dead kings), 11–14 (the fall of the tyrant to Sheol), 16–17 (the thoughts of the onlookers, viewing the body of the king), and 18–20a (a "contrast to the usual royal funeral").[24] Watts does not discuss the characteristic imagery or structure of the dirge, so begins this section where he understands the taunt to begin. If the taunt is a parody of the dirge form, then one should pay careful attention to the form

---

[20] Kaiser, *Isaiah 13–39*, 33–43.

[21] Kaiser, *Isaiah 13–39*, 32. He does not discuss the form of the dirge at all, and only lightly deals with its characteristic terminology.

[22] "Poems about Baal and Anath," translated by H. L. Ginsberg (*ANET*, 139).

[23] Watts, *Isaiah 1–33*, 207.

[24] Watts, *Isaiah 1–33*, 207–208.

of the dirge and its constituent parts and imagery. This Watts does not do and therefore divides the dirge in its middle.

Marvin Sweeney has recently suggested a more nuanced structure for the dirge. He divides it into five sections: 1) 4b–6 (introductory dirge); 2) 7–8 (reaction of earth, including trees); 3) 9–17 (reaction of Sheol); 4) 18–20 (denial of the king's legacy); and 5) 21–23 (concluding command to sacrifice the king's sons).[25] I accept Sweeney's approach in broad strokes, but his addition of vv. 22–23 to the dirge, probably redactional and clearly a change of perspective from the dirge proper to a command by the Lord, is inappropriate.[26] Also, Sweeney has correctly understood that vv. 7–8 comprise a section different from the introduction in vv. 4b–6. His characterization of this section as the "reaction from the earth," however, does not account for its cosmological and metaphorical character.[27] As I noted in chapter four above, the cedars and cypresses refer to the Cedar Forest, a holy precinct and garden of the gods, and are not mentioned here simply to report the reaction of trees to being cut down. See the analysis below for further commentary. In this case, vv. 7–8 begin a major section relating to the divine realm and the underworld (note that ארץ often refers to the underworld in the Old Testament; see especially Ezek 31:16). Sweeney correctly notices that the "cosmology" section continues through v. 17, including the rousing of the Rephaim (vv. 9–11), the king's plan to ascend to the heavens and his subsequent fall to Sheol (vv. 12–15), and the reaction of the Rephaim to his demise in 15–17. Sweeney does not recognize that the section on Sheol is not over until v. 20a, the comparison of the burials of the Rephaim with the non-burial of the tyrant. He separates vv. 18–20 under the heading "denial of the king's legacy," but in reality the perspective and subject matter (the death of the king and his burial) do not change until v. 20b. See further on these structural issues below.

Isaiah 14:4b–21 is difficult to analyze structurally. On the one hand, the dirge clearly possesses traditional elements of the common dirge, including the exclamation, the memory of past glory, present reality, and the personification of inanimate objects. On the other hand, it resembles the royal dirge in terms of its imagery and even the sequence of those images. It appears that the poem is a combination of the royal dirge, known outside of the Bible and only twice in the Old Testament in parody form, and the common dirge form, well-attested in the Old Testament. It is possible that the author has taken the royal dirge, with its attendant imagery and order of events, and set it within a more typically Israelite

---

[25] Marvin Sweeney, *Isaiah 1–39, with an Introduction to Prophetic Literature* (FOTL 16; Grand Rapids: Eerdmans, 1996), 225.

[26] Sweeney, *Isaiah 1–39*, 225.

[27] Sweeney, *Isaiah 1–39*, 225.

dirge style. Several lines of evidence converge to suggest such a possibility: 1) Isa 14 possesses elements of both the royal dirge (descent of the king, rousing the citizens of the netherworld, sacrifices, and proclaiming the new king) and the common dirge (the exclamation “How!”, the comparison of present state with former glory). This combination of elements makes for an interesting and complex structure, for which the sum is greater than the parts: the resulting dirge transcends both dirge forms in beauty and complexity. 2) Other examples of the royal dirge—Ezek 32 and *KTU* 1.161—do not possess the comparison between the past glory and present lamentable state. It is not a typical part of the royal dirge pattern or ideology. 3) The refrain/exclamation “How!” does not appear in the examples of the royal dirge we have attempted to isolate. Though the royal dirge is a communal ritual lament, its intent is not so much to bewail the unfortunate state of the departed king as to expedite his arrival in the netherworld and provide for the transfer of power to the king’s son.

In light of its complexity, perhaps the best way to organize the poem is by means of thematic shifts of character or perspective, rather than attempt to adhere more strictly to the typical pattern of the royal dirge or the common dirge, difficult in any event in this poem. It appears, then, that the text falls into three major sections, with the middle section subdivided into four sub-sections: vv. 4b–6, vv. 7–20a [vv. 7–8, vv. 9–11, vv. 12–17, vv. 18–20a], and vv. 20b–21. 4b corresponds to the exclamation of lament and introduction to the dirge, beginning with אֵיךְ. Vv. 5–6 correspond to the “memory of past glory,” except in this parody the king is presented not as glorious in battle and beautiful in life, but as arrogant and cruel. Note also that the tyrant is referred to in the third person in this section: the “oppressor” (נֹגֵשׂ, preceded by the third person perfect שָׁבַת), the “one who smote,” the “one who persecuted,” but in the following section he is referred to in the second person. Vv. 7–20a deal with the realm of the gods in the Cedar Forest (7–8), Sheol (vv. 9–11, 12, 15–20a), and the heavens (vv. 13–14). Thus the three parts of the cosmos are reflected in the poem: the heavens, the underworld, and the surface of the earth. Vv. 7–8 present the attitude of the trees of the garden of God (rejoicing rather than weeping over the death). In vv. 9–11 the scene shifts to Sheol (the Rephaim roused not to greet the newcomer but to mock him). This scene displays affinity with the royal dirge (the rousing of the Rephaim) as well as the common dirge (the Rephaim compare his present low estate with his earlier glory). V. 12 is a mock exclamation of lament (“How you have fallen from heaven!”), followed by the memory of the king’s arrogant aspirations of ascending to the heavens (vv. 13–14), but the present reality of his pitiful state in Sheol (vv. 15–17). Vv. 18–20a depict the status of the dead kings in Sheol. They received proper burial and have their own sepulchers, while the tyrant is “cast forth from his grave” and “will not be joined with them in burial.” Vv. 20b–21 return the reader to the surface of the earth and to the ritual. They contain admonitions not to call out the name of the descendant of the king and to prepare for the slaughter of his sons. Note also that the person changes back from second to third: "you have destroyed your land, you have slain your people" in v. 20a, to "prepare a slaughtering-place for his sons" in v. 21. This is the same shift in perspective we saw between the first and second sections above.

There is one further consideration pertaining to structure which has generally been overlooked. The initial section of the poem, referring to the tyrant in the third person, also clearly introduces the dirge and depicts the situation on the earth: the persecuting tyrant has ceased his persecuting and his power has been broken by the Lord. The second person address begins in v. 7 and does not return to the third person until v. 20b. It is my suggestion that vv. 7–20a represent cosmological imagery with close ties to the royal dirge. First, the cedars of Lebanon figure in ritual laments for the death of kings. As the trees on the mountains of the sunset, they represent a sacred place understood by Wildberger and others as the "garden of the gods." The trees rejoice because the tyrant will no longer desecrate the sacred precincts. The other section often not understood as containing cosmological imagery is 18–20a. Some scholars have understood vv. 16–17 to pertain to "onlookers" on the surface of the earth who view the dead, discarded body of the king and give their reaction. More sense is maintained, as well as logical flow to the poem, if the speech in vv. 16b–17 is ascribed to the Rephaim, who have been roused at the king's coming. Vv. 18–20a, then, pertain to their privileged status in the underworld and their comfortable burial shrines, while the king has no such privilege, comfort, or status, but lies unburied, "cast from his grave" (v. 19). The "cosmological" section, dealing with the heavens and the underworld, the descent and ascent of the king, ends with v. 20a, whereupon we once again shift perspective back to the surface of the earth. The king is now referred to in the third person, as he was in vv. 4b–6, and the dirge parody is complete with the command for the participants in the dirge to sacrifice the king's sons rather than proclaim the name of his heir.

C. STRUCTURAL OUTLINE OF ISAIAH 14:4b–21

In light of these considerations of structure, the following is a structural outline of the dirge. The poem demonstrates inner thematic consistency and subtle structuring. In regard to the former, the entire poem contains the themes and images, and to some degree the ordering, of the royal dirge, exemplified in *KTU* 1.161 and the *Death of Ur-Nammu.* In regard to the latter, the poem is structured around events surrounding the death of the king and his succession on the earth and exhortations to the participants in the dirge (vv. 4b–6, 20b–21) and the scene portrayed in the underworld and its portals (vv. 7–20a). As has been suggested long ago, the center of the poem is the dramatic sequence in vv. 12–15, the fall of the tyrant from heaven. In light of the shifts in perspective and "location" within the dirge, the poem exhibits careful structuring with the king's "fall from heaven" at its center: A–A': Vv. 4b–6 and 20b–21 refer to the tyrant in the third person and report/exhort from the viewpoint of "the nations" and, apparently, the dirge participants on the earth. B–B': Vv. 7–8 and 18–20a deal with the entrance of the king into the underworld. The cedars and cypresses in vv. 7–8, sacred trees on the mountains of the sunset, send the king off with rejoicing that he is gone forever. The king enters the underworld more overtly and less courteously in vv. 18–20a. C–C': The Rephaim deliver mocking speeches in vv. 9–11 and 15–17. "Those who see you" cannot be those on earth who view his discarded body. The immediate antecedent is "But you are brought down to the depths of the pit." Only then comes, "Those who see you stare." The only ones on hand to stare at the king are the Rephaim, who also delivered the previous speech. D–E–D': The fall, rise, and fall of the king. Vv. 12 and 15 (D and D') frame the "ascent to heaven" motif (vv. 13–14), which occurs only once in the poem.

I. Introduction to the dirge (vv. 4b–6).

A. Dirge exclamation, "How the oppressor has ceased!" (v. 4b).

B. Judgment by the Lord on the tyrant who had oppressed the nations (**A**; first description of the situation on earth and God's judgment) (vv. 5–6).

II. The cosmos (הָאָרֶץ) and the fall of the tyrant (vv. 7–20a).

A. The rejoicing of the cosmos and the Cedar Forest (vv. 7–8).

1. All the earth rejoices: introduction to the "cosmological section" (v. 7).

2. The trees of the garden of God/cedars of the western sunset express relief that there will no longer be any to desecrate them (**B**; entrance into the divine realm/realm of the dead—"since you lay down") (v. 8).

B. The rousing of the Rephaim (vv. 9–11).

1. Sheol prepares for the coming of the king and rouses the Rephaim from their thrones (v. 9).

2. The Rephaim express astonishment at the tyrant's pathetic state. (**C**; first speech by the Rephaim) (vv. 10–11).

C. The ascent and descent of the king (vv. 12–17).

1. The desire of the king to ascend to heaven (vv. 12–14).

a) Dirge exclamation, acknowledgement of the king's fall from heaven (**D**; the king falls from heaven to Sheol) (v. 12).

b) The king's attempt to rise to the highest heaven (**E**) (vv. 13–14).

2. The king's fall to Sheol (vv. 15–17).

a) The reality of the king's fall to the depths of the "pit" (**D'**; the king falls from heaven to Sheol) (v. 15).

b) The Rephaim once again express their astonishment at the demise of the tyrant and his low estate (**C'**; second speech by the Rephaim) (vv. 16–17).

D. The comparison of the king's unburied corpse with the dead kings/Rephaim in their sepulchers (vv. 18–20a).

1. The burial of the Rephaim; their comfort and repose (v. 18).

2. The tyrant's non-burial, descent to the lowest depths of the underworld, and the reason for his fate (**B'**: the king's entrance into the underworld) (vv. 19–20a).

III. Exhortation to the dirge celebrants (A'; second scene on the earth and judgment on the king's sons) (vv. 20b–21).

A. Command not to "call out" the name of the king's successors (vv. 20b).

B. Command to slaughter the king's sons (v. 21).

If this analysis is correct, this poem is carefully constructed around a traditional dirge for the death of an ancient Near Eastern monarch. It also possesses several of the motifs of the traditional Israelite dirge, as exemplified by 2 Sam 1:19–27 (dirge exclamation, the contrast motif), but these do not provide the structure for the poem as do the motifs of the royal dirge. This dramatic parody of the royal dirge is constructed around the supreme arrogance of the tyrant, who sought power and immortality ("I will ascend to the heavens, above the stars of ʾEl I will raise my throne) in vv. 13–14," but is brought to lowest depths of the underworld in disgrace ("But you are brought down to Sheol, to the depths of the pit").

We will look at each of the three major sections in turn in order to determine how each relates to the dirge as a whole and also to understand how the mythological images surveyed in chaps. 2–4 fit into this mock dirge. As the middle, cosmological section is lengthy, we will look at each of its four sections as well.

D. EXEGESIS OF ISAIAH 14:4b–21

1. Introduction to the Dirge (vv. 4b–6)

The introduction to the dirge is v. 4b, beginning with the typical dirge exclamation "How!" This exclamation generally begins dirges in the Old Testament and its presence may indicate that a dirge will follow.[28] The beginning of the dirge introduces its thematic content. In the case of 2 Sam 1:19, we are

---

[28] 2 Sam 1:19 begins with the statement, "Your beauty, O Israel, is slain upon your high places," immediately followed by the exclamation, "how!" See Jer 9:19, 49:25, 51:41, Ezek 26:17, etc. for examples of dirges or dirge-like prophetic speeches which begin with

told that the "beauty of Israel," Saul and Jonathan, are slain and that this has occurred on the high places of Israel. These high places, the "mountains of Gilboa" where Saul and Jonathan were cut down, are further admonished to receive neither rain nor dew in v. 21. Saul and Jonathan are described in greater detail as the "beauty" or "honor" of Israel in vv. 22–24: their bow and sword never returned unblooded (v. 22); they were beloved and pleasant, swifter than eagles and stronger than lions (v. 23); and they clothed the daughters of Israel in scarlet and gold (v. 25). Even the command not to speak of the death in Philistia in v. 20 relates to the introductory statement: mighty warriors have been struck down on the mountains by the Philistines, who must not be allowed to gloat over their victory.

In the same manner, Isa 14:4b–6 introduces us to the thematic content of the dirge. It is the mock dirge to be sung over the death of a mighty tyrant who has been brought low:

> "How the oppressor has ceased, the tyranny has stopped!"

We are introduced to the dual themes of the poem: that the ruler is guilty of arrogance (later in the poem this arrogance is manifested as a desire for God-like rule and even divine status) and that this ruler has been humiliated and defeated:

> "The Lord has broken the staff of the wicked, the rod of rulers."

It appears that the introductory lines of the common dirge were intended to introduce the reader in broad strokes to the major themes developed in the dirge.

On the level of the *mashal*, this section serves to introduce the themes of the poem (the one who arrogated to himself supreme power and sovereignty has been stopped and broken), but also serves to let the reader know that this will be a parody of a dirge. Rather than eulogize the dead king or call for general lament over a great loss, as one would expect in a dirge (such as in 2 Sam 1), the introduction to the *mashal* signals that this "dirge" is to be sung on an occasion for great rejoicing.

These verses do not simply introduce the parody, however. While most commentators see in this section a simple reference to historical realities, the *mashal* functions throughout vv. 4b–6 on a metaphorical level. The Lord has not simply broken the arrogant ruler. The Lord has broken the rod (מַטֵּה) and the staff (שֵׁבֶט) of the wicked ruler. The rod and staff imagery here is related not only to symbols of royal authority (see, for example, Ps 125:3), but also to

---

אֵיךְ. It is not essential for אֵיךְ to begin the dirge; it will follow soon after the opening in any case (see, for example, Mic 2:4).

the use of such authority to punish and wound (see Isa 10:5). In Isa 14:6 the wicked ruler smote the peoples with unceasing wrath, but the rod the ruler used in dispensing such punishment (v. 5) has now been broken by the Lord. While many passages in Isaiah use metaphorical language, the *mashal* lends itself particularly well to the use of metaphor. Both invite the reader to compare the metaphorical world, where myth and symbol operate, to the referential world, the world of political and social realities.

2. The Cosmos and the Fall of the Tyrant (vv. 7–20a)

a. The Trees of the Cedar Forest (vv. 7–8)

Most commentators have understood the trees rejoicing because the cutter would no longer hew their branches to be a reference to campaigns by an Assyrian or Babylonian monarch to recover cedar timber from the mountains of Lebanon. Even this literal approach has to account for the personified nature of the trees rejoicing and speaking. Another possibility is that the language is metaphorical and could refer to something other than literal trees. Finally, Wildberger has suggested that the myth of the garden of the gods in the Lebanon is reflected in vv. 7–8 (see chapters 1 and 4 above).

Most have understood this to be a reference to Assyrian tree-gathering campaigns. One such incident is recorded in Isa 37:24, paralleled in 2 Kgs 19:23:

> By your servants you have mocked the Lord, and you have said, With my many chariots I have gone up the heights of the mountains, to the far recesses of Lebanon; I felled its tallest cedars, its choicest cypresses; I came to its remotest height, its densest forest.

Indeed, such activities are very well-documented on the part of Assyrian monarchs. Note these inscriptions of Tiglath-Pileser I:

> Its cracks I smoothed over, with cedar and . . . -logs, (for) which, at the command of Assur and Anu, the great gods, my lords, I went [to the Lebanon mountains] (where) I cut down, and (whence) I brought these splendid beams of the temple of . . ., where the great gods, my lords, continually abide.[29]

> To Ṃount Lebanon I went. Logs of cedar for the temple of Anu and Adad, the great gods, my lords, I cut and brought away. . . . At the command of Anu and Adad, the

[29] "Sargon," *Ancient Records*, 2:86–87.

> great gods, my lords, I went (and) cut logs of cedar for the temple of Anu and Adad, the great gods, my lords, and I brought (them to Assyria).[30]

Note also this inscription by Assurnasirpal II:

> I climbed up to Mount Amanus (and) cut down logs of cedar, cypress, *daprānu*-juniper, (and) *burāšu*-juniper. . . . I transported cedar logs from Mount Amanus and brought (them) to Ešarra to my temple the shrine.[31]

At the time of Isaiah of Jerusalem, several of the Assyrian kings either went to the Lebanon to cut wood, or received timber as tribute:

> With ivory, ebony, boxwood, sissoo wood, cypress wood, In[dian wood . . . and] juniper—the tribute of the kings of the land of Hatti and the Aramean and Chaldean princes, whom I subdued with mighty courage—[I decorated them] (and) filled (them) with splendor . . . With long beams of cedar, a product of Am[anus], Lebanon, and Anti-Lebanon, which are as sweet to smell as the scent of *hašurru* wood, I roofed them, demonstrating appropriate care.[32]

Sennacherib says the following about his construction of his "palace without a rival":

> Beams of cedar, the product of Mt. Amanus, which they dragged with difficulty out of (those) distant mountains, I stretched across their ceilings.
>
> I sent the order to the kings of Amurru, all of them, who had submitted to me . . . Great cedar beams they felled in Mt. Amanus, dragged them to Nineveh, and roofed (my palaces with them).[33]

There is no problem whatsoever with the historical verisimilitude of vv. 7–8 and its relationship to a Mesopotamian ruler. There is even no problem with the possibility of such a ruler devastating stretches of forest in the Lebanon to provide for building projects, as the more accessible, lower-lying forests seem to have been. Indeed, Isa 37:24 has often been interpreted as suggesting that Sennacherib was engaged in just such an enterprise in remote mountain stretches of Lebanon. As K. Nielsen has suggested, a literal/historical understanding of 14:7–8 does not require a crude literalism, but that the trees depicted are personified

---

[30] "Sargon," *Ancient Records*, 2:98.

[31] Albert Kirk Grayson, *Assyrian Rulers of the Early First Millennium BC I (1114–859 BC)* (RIMA 2; Toronto: University of Toronto Press, 1991), 219.

[32] Hayim Tadmor, *The Inscriptions of Tiglath-Pileser III King of Assyria* (Jerusalem: The Israel Academy of Sciences and Humanities, 1994), 173.

[33] Daniel D. Luckenbill, *The Annals of Sennacherib* (Chicago: University of Chicago Press, 1924), 96, 132.

with human characteristics in much the same way as trees "sing for joy" in Ps 96:12.[34]

Nielsen has suggested that the second option, that the trees are metaphorical images of political realities, is the most satisfying. She suggests that most tree or wood terminology in Isa 1–39 is not to be understood literally, but in a political, metaphorical sense.[35] Indeed, as a *mashal* one would expect that the images present in the poem will *not* be intended to be taken literally, but in a metaphorical or mythopoeic sense. Not all of the wood or tree images Nielsen identifies in Isaiah are pertinent to the present discussion. We will deal only with those images which portray trees personified as human beings.

1) Isa 2:12–13:

> For the Lord of hosts has a day against all that is proud and lofty, against all that is lifted up and high; against all the cedars of Lebanon, lofty and lifted up; and against all the oaks of Bashan. (RSV)

Nielsen is right in suggesting that the surrounding oracle makes it quite clear that this has little to do with trees and much to do the arrogance of rulers, depicted as tall and stately trees.[36] Note Isa 2:11–12:

> The haughty eyes of people are brought low,
> And the pride of people humbled,
> And the Lord alone will be exalted in that day.
>
> For the Lord of Hosts has a day against all that is proud and uplifted,
> And against anything raised and it shall be brought low.

The image here is obviously not one which intends to portray the Lord's disdain for trees. It intends rather to depict human pride in graphic metaphors pertaining to political realities. Those who are "brought low" and "humbled" (2:9) are those who "strike hands with foreigners" (v. 6), and fill their land with silver and gold (v. 7), implements of war (v. 7) and idolatry (v. 8). The refrain in v. 9 pertaining to humbling and abasing arrogance is repeated with slight variations in vv. 11 and 17.

2) Isa 10:18–19:

> And the glory of his forest and his fruitful land, both soul and body, he will destroy, and it will be as when a sick man wastes away.

---

[34] Kirsten Nielsen, *There is Hope for a Tree: The Tree as Metaphor in Isaiah* (JSOTS 65; Sheffield: Sheffield Academic Press, 1989), 172.

[35] Nielsen, *There is Hope for a Tree*, 71.

[36] Nielsen, *There is Hope for a Tree*, 178.

And the remnant of the trees of his forest will be so few that a child can write them down.

As with 2:7–8, the oracle in 10:5–19 makes it quite clear that the references to trees and forests involve political realities. This oracle is in two sections: 5–12, which deals with Assyria's selection by God to punish Judah, but their subsequent going beyond the imposed limits of destruction, and 13–19, their impending destruction for arrogance and presumption. The forest imagery in this oracle deals at least partially with the Assyrian military. Note v. 16:

Therefore the Lord YHWH of Hosts will send leanness on his "stout ones"
And under his glory a burning will be kindled, like the burning of fire.

The word מִשְׁמָן, "stout ones," can refer to rich land, as it does in Dan 11:24. In this case, we are simply dealing with the Lord's judgment on and devastation of the land of Assyria, as the land of Judah is devastated in chapter 7:23–25, although this devastation deals with depopulation of the land rather than deforestation. It is also possible that the מִשְׁמַנָּיו, "his stout ones," is an agricultural metaphor refering to people. First, as Nielsen has pointed out, this section is replete with wood and tree imagery.[37] Verse 15 uses metaphorical language to describe the incomprehensibility of the arrogance of the king of Assyria: it is as incomprehensible as a rod attempting to lift its lifter. The wood metaphor continues in the next two verses. The Lord was going to send a "wasting" on his "stout ones" and burn the arrogant wood with fire. In v. 17, the flame from the "Holy One" would devour "thorns and briers," the true character of the "stout ones." Vv. 19–20 complete the tree imagery in this section. The Lord was about to destroy "the forest and the fruitful land (כַּרְמֶל)," both soul (נפשׁ) and body (בשׂר), never said of trees. Finally, Ps 78:31 may also shed light on the meaning of מִשְׁמַנָּיו. In this psalm, מִשְׁמָן is a reference to soldiers and not to fertile land:

The anger of God rose against them and he slew their stout ones (מִשְׁמַנֵּיהֶם), And laid low the elite of Israel (בַּחוּרֵי יִשְׂרָאֵל).

It is likely, therefore, that the wood and tree imagery in vv. 15–19 is also metaphorical. What is in view is the Assyrian king, leaders, and/or military.

3) Isa 10:33–34:

The Lord, YHWH of hosts is lopping off the boughs with terror;
The lofty are hewn down, and the high are brought low.
He will strike off the thickets of the forest with iron,
And Lebanon with its noble (trees?) will fall.

[37] Nielsen, *There is Hope for a Tree*, 191–193.

As with the preceding analysis, this passage has to do with the arrogance of the political leaders of Assyria. 10:33–34 bears closest resemblance to 9:17: "For wickedness burns like fire, and consumes thorns and briers, and it kindles the thickets of the forest and they mount upwards in a column of smoke." In 9:17 the metaphorical language is clear: *wickedness* burns like fire and consumes thorns and briers. In 10:33–34 the tree imagery is consistent, while its metaphorical nature is less obvious but equally important to perceive. Nowhere is the metaphorical artistry of the passage more apparent than in the choice of the term אַדִּיר, "noble" or "majestic." This term can be applied to trees, as in Ezek 17:23 and Zech 11:2, but is also used of water, the gods, the Lord God, and, most commonly, noblemen.

Ezekiel 17 refers to the allegory of the eagle as a *mashal* and one of the most prominent images in it is that of the cedar of Lebanon, whose topmost branch (the king of Judah), is carried away by the eagle (the king of Babylon). The cedar is called אַדִּיר as in 10:34. The language has been specifically chosen because it allows more than one meaning. On the one hand, the trees are simply trees and "majestic" is an adjective describing them. On the other hand, trees and their branches in Ezek 17 represent the the king of Judah and, at least, its nobles (אַדִּירִים; compare with Jer 14:3 and 25:34). Tree imagery used of the nobility or monarchy is common throughout the Old Testament and particularly in Isaiah. Note especially Isa 6:13, 11:1, 4:2, and Dan 4. As we saw in chapter two, the *mashal* uses metaphorical language in making comparisons. This is the case in Ezek 17 and I will argue that it is also the case in Isa 14:7–8. Isaiah 10:33–34 does not specifically identify itself as a *mashal*, but the imagery and specific terminology used is quite similar to that of Ezek 17 and Isa 14:7–8, which do. The tree imagery in 10:33–34 is consistent, with just a hint in the term אַדִּיר that more is going on than simply the use of arboreal language. When one compares the use of images in these verses with others in Isaiah and elsewhere, it becomes clear that metaphorical/cosmological language is being used.

4) Isa 37:24–25:

> By the hand of our servants you have taunted the Lord and you have said, "With the multitude of my chariotry I have ascended the height of the mountains, the remotest parts of Lebanon, and I cut its highest cedars, its choicest cypresses, and I came to its remotest height, its most fruitful forest;
>
> I dug (wells) and I drank water and I dried up with the sole(s) of my feet all the streams of Egypt."

Most commentators have understood this passage to be a reference to Sennacherib's literal timber-gathering expeditions to the Lebanon. While I have been unable to identify in Sennacherib's writings such timber-gathering expeditions (as we have seen particularly with Tiglath-Pileser I and Assurnasirpal II above), tribute of cedar and cypress was taken from the Lebanon. It is also possible that Sennacherib's armies and/or work crews went into the Lebanon on such expeditions—note "by the hand of your servants" in v. 24. This passage reflects the common practice of Assyrian and Babylonian kings.

There is also reason to suggest that more is going on in this passage than lumbering. First, these two verses cannot be entirely literal. Sennacherib never invaded Egypt or "dried up the streams of Egypt" by crossing them with his armies (the "soles of his feet"?), as many commentators have noted. The drying up of the streams is rather an image of political and cosmic sovereignty. Isaiah 19:4–7 depicts such a drying of the rivers of Egypt, a judgment of God on Egypt by the hand of a "harsh master" (אֲדֹנִים קָשֶׁה):

> I will stop up Egypt by the hand of a harsh master and a strong king will rule over them, says the Lord YHWH of Hosts.
>
> And water from the sea will be dry and the river will be parched and dry.
>
> And the rivers will stink (?) and the streams of Egypt will diminish and dry up, (and) reeds and rushes will decay.
>
> (There will be) bare places by the Nile, by the mouth of the Nile, and all of the sown land of the Nile will dry up, be driven under, and be no more.

Metaphorical elements are strong in this passage. The streams are said to be dried up *by* the hand of the "harsh ruler," whom the Lord will bring against Egypt. The land and people of Egypt will suffer judgment at the hand of this ruler in the exercise of his (delegated) sovereignty, portrayed by means of graphic political/cosmological imagery.

This language is reminiscent of the cosmological/creation imagery in Exod 14 and the "Song of the Sea" in Exod 15. These passages reflect the imagery of the primeval *Chaoskampf* as many commentators have noted.

Kings personified as trees and the violation of the Cedar Forest are also metaphors for the exercise of sovereignty. Gilgamesh and Enkidu's foray into the Cedar Forest was a supreme act of hubris and presumption on their part, resulting in the death of Huwawa, the guardian of the forest. It may be that the account of Solomon's building the "House of the Forest of Lebanon" in 1 Kgs 7:2–3 is driven as much by cosmological imagery as by the fact that its columns were made of cedar. Ezekiel 32 and Dan 4 depict kings as trees, their expansive foliage providing shelter for birds and beasts, a transparent reference to a great king providing shelter and sustenance for lesser kings and kingdoms. Likewise, loss of power and dominion is portrayed in Ezek 17:4 and Dan 4:14 and 23 as the hewing down of the tree or the breaking of its branches.

Therefore, while Isa 37:24 may reflect the longstanding tradition of Mesopotamian rulers campaigning for lumber in the Lebanon, this fact pales before the more significant metaphorical use of the tree imagery. Isa 14:7–8 reflects not so much literal tree-cutting as it does the metaphor of presumed sovereignty, the removal and destruction of kings and princes of the Levant, and the relief of the petty nations at the news of the death of the "king of Babylon" in this passage. Mythopoeic language is metaphorical language, based in the primordium with continuing and constitutive significance for the society of a later day.

K. Nielsen has alerted us to the use of metaphorical tree imagery in 14:7–8[38] and she has noticed the relationship between metaphor and myth in Isaiah and elsewhere. She, along with most commentators, however, has not considered how the cedar/cypress image figures in the dirge form. The "cedar mountains" were understood from the standpoint of Mesopotamia to be mountains of sunset, where the sun god entered the netherworld on his daily course through the heavens, ferrying the dead. In the *tigi* hymn for Inanna, the dead king is ushered over the "mountains of aromatic cedar" to be united as Amaušumgalanna with Inanna, twin stars in the heavens. In some conceptions of Near Eastern cosmology, therefore, the cedar mountains figure in hymns pertaining to the death of kings. We have already seen above how kings are often portrayed in the image of a tree, especially cedar, or the topmost portion of a tree in Old Testament literature. It is not surprising that cedars figure in the dirge for the king in Isa 14 also.

The third approach is the "mythological approach." We have already dealt with the idea of a myth fragment about a divine Cedar Forest in the Lebanon. The image of the "cutter" coming against the divine forest is analogous to Gilgamesh's foray into the Cedar Forest and usurpation of divine privileges. As such, the trees rejoice that they need not fear such destruction any longer.

If the poem is based upon a royal dirge, thoroughly permeated with mythopoeic images and references, then there is probably not a single myth or myth fragment lying behind vv. 7–8. We have seen above in chapters three and four how the cedars and the mountains of the Lebanon, the "mountains of the sunset," figure in ancient mythological narratives (the *Gilgamesh Epic*) and ritual texts (the *tigi* hymn for Inanna and the *eršemma* lament). The images pertaining to the death of the king in the *tigi* hymn were 1) The king has died; 2) the king appears like the sun coming forth over the mountains of cedar after his death; 3) he becomes the consort of Inanna and ascends as a star, with daily

[38] Nielsen, *There is Hope for a Tree*, 162.

and monthly cycles of appearance. Relative to the *eršemma* of Ninḫursag, these themes were isolated: 1) the king has ignominiously and tragically died; and 2) the death of the king causes the earth to tremble like "a forest fragrant with cedars." Of these elements, only the death of the king and the response of the trees is unambiguous in vv. 7–8. Other elements have been transformed by the *mashal*: rather than "set the earth atremble like a forest fragrant with cedars" at the death of the king, the earth is "quiet" and the trees "rejoice." Rather than ascend like the sun or a star over the mountains of cedar, the king "lies down" in death. It is possible that these images, incorporated in dirges for dead kings, also provided imagery for the parody of the dirge in Isa 14.

It is likely, therefore, that several mythical/cosmological allusions lie behind vv. 7–8. On the one hand, the "cutter" is an image of the king who trespasses on sacred space and violates it for his own glory. On the other hand, the response of the cosmos and the trees to the death of the king is at variance with liturgical texts which indicate how they are *supposed* to react; these elements have been transformed by the *mashal* parody.

b. Rousing the Rephaim (vv. 9–11)

Vv. 9–11 recount the rousing of the Rephaim from their repose in the underworld to greet the king on his arrival. This motif occurs in all four examples of the royal dirge discussed in chapter 2 (*KTU* 1.161, *Death of Ur-Nammu*, Ezek 32:20, and Isa 14:9). In *KTU* 1.161, the *Rapiʾūma* are explicitly invoked at the funeral of Niqmaddu. In the *Death of Ur-Nammu,* the inhabitants of the netherworld greet the king upon his arrival, along with various dignitaries who had died. In Ezek 32, the "rams of the warriors" address the "multitude of Egypt." [39] The Rephaim are also invoked in Isa 14, to greet the king "at his coming." Rephaim do not rouse themselves for just any recently deceased person. They do not appear in non-royal dirges.

The purpose for the rousing of the Rephaim is so that the recently deceased king may be welcomed into their company. While it is difficult to be certain about the exact identity of the Rephaim, they did at least consist of the dead kings of the past, some of whom were understood outside of Israel to be the deified dead. Ur-Nammu and Niqmaddu are welcomed by dead officials and earlier kings. In Ezek 32:20, Pharaoh or his "multitude" are addressed by the

[39] אֵלֵי here is certainly a defective spelling for אֵילֵי, "rams" or leaders, parallel to "goats" or leaders in Isa 14:9. The "rams" will speak to "him," unclear as to antecedent, but likely a reference to the הֲמוֹן מִצְרַיִם, the "multitude of Egypt," in v. 18. Furthermore, these "rams" speak from the midst of Sheol and may themselves be "his helpers," referring to Sheol, although it is not entirely clear to whom עזריו refers.

ʾēlê gibbôrîm, parallel to the *ʿattûdê ʾāreṣ* of Isa 14:9, clearly the Rephaim. It is interesting that in the two biblical parodies of the royal dirge, the Rephaim/*ʾēlîm* do not greet the fallen as one of their own. In Ezek 32, they announce the destruction of the various nations. When Pharaoh of Egypt arrives, he will be "consoled" in the depths of the pit along with all the other uncircumcised slain. In Isa 14, the Rephaim are incredulous that the great king is now in such a pitiable state.

It is clear that in Isa 14 the king is depicted as one who has no proper burial. The Rephaim are surprised that the great ruler has worms and maggots for his final resting-place and burial clothes. This point is again underscored, and the comparison with the Rephaim made even clearer, in vv. 19–20, where the Rephaim are buried in regal splendor in their sepulchers while the king is cast out on the ground. We have already seen the unenviable lot of those with no proper burial: Baʿal on the fields of death in the *Baʿal Epic* and Enkidu's description of those who die in the open field or have none to attend to their ritual needs after death.[40]

The Rephaim say, "You have become just like us," even though they have retained royal status (thrones and titles, v. 9) and possess regal burial "houses" (v. 18), while the tyrant possesses none of these things. It is possible that this simply means that the king is weak and ephemeral, as are the Rephaim. It is more likely that these words are put on the mouths of the Rephaim by way of comparison with the king's own plan to ascend "above the heights of the clouds." In this manner, the Rephaim are dumbfounded that one who aspired to greatness should now be dead, as they are, but worse, given the lowest possible status in the "depths of the pit." His pride or majesty (גָּאוֹן), which prompted him to desire to rise to the heavens (v. 13), is his undoing and has brought him down to Sheol. It is interesting in this regard that neither in Ezek 32 nor in Isa 14 are the Rephaim given divine status as is the case in some extra-biblical inscriptions. At best, they are deceased kings, "helpers" of Sheol, with some degree of status in the netherworld.

On the metaphorical level, these verses demonstrate a connection between Isa 14 and other dirges for dead kings. The Rephaim are roused to greet the newly arrived king as they do in the Ur-Nammu text and Ezek 32 and as they are exhorted to do in the Niqmaddu text. The normally expected welcoming committee of deceased notables does indeed show up, but only to gape and stare. Being a parody of the dirge, and not a true one, this "welcoming committee" does not truly welcome, but by their words and attitudes further add to the taunt heaped upon the king.

---

[40] "Poems about Baal and Anath" (*ANET*, 139) and "The Epic of Gilgamesh" (*ANET*, 97–99).

On the referential level, the Rephaim supply the comparison: “You have become just like us (אֵלֵינוּ נִמְשָׁלְתָּ)”! “Like us” refers to being weak and ephemeral (חוּלֵּיתָ כָמוֹנוּ), in other words, dead. This king’s death, however, is not an honorable event. He has died, no one mourns him, and he now possesses no status, neither on earth nor in the netherworld.

c. The Ascent and Descent of the King (vv. 12–17)

I will address this section in two parts: the desire of the king to ascend (vv. 12–14) and then his descent into Sheol (vv. 15–17a). In each part I will begin with a discussion of how the dirge and the mythological themes discussed in the previous chapters help us understand the imagery in Isa 14, followed by a discussion of these parts in relation to the whole dirge in Isa 14.

i. *The Ascent of the King (vv. 12–14)*

The ascent into the heavens is explicitly stated as a plan of the tyrant in Isa 14:13 (“I will ascend to the heavens, above the stars of ’El I will raise my throne”). The ascent to heaven as a star is a feature of some ritual congregational laments (the *eršemma* of Ninḫursag, the *tigi* hymn of Inanna), many of which were composed or at least copied until late in the first millennium B.C.E., and clearly was part of the ideology of kingship of ancient Sumer. Some of these were evidently intended to be sung upon the death of the king and the mountains of cedars and the ascent into heaven figure prominently in at least two of these compositions. That at least some kings aspired to achieve the same levels as their legendary forebears during the time of Isaiah must be seen as a distinct possibility. At least the imagery of such descent texts may be borrowed in the *mashal* of Isa 14.

That the *Gilgamesh Epic* reached its final form during the Neo-Assyrian period may also be witness to the continuing ideology of divine kingship, though in a back-handed, critical manner. Gilgamesh is himself two-thirds god and one-third human. He aspires to scale the Cedar Mountain and cut down the divine forest. Even with a predominance of godhood, however, Gilgamesh does not succeed in his quest. He is still partially human, enough to disqualify him from his quest to achieve immortality. How much less can fully human kings hope to aspire to godhood?

Isaiah borrows stock ideology from Near Eastern ritual texts concerned with the death of kings and uses these to mock the tyrant. We have seen in vv. 7–8 above that imagery pertaining to the Cedar Forest is used to mock the tyrant’s attempt to achieve the level of the gods and that imagery is connected with mythology about the gods and with ritual texts pertaining to the death of kings. In vv. 13–14, he again borrows from the ideology of the death of kings and combines it with another, oblique reference to the Cedar Mountain in the Lebanon. I will address these issues in order.

First, the author tips his hand that he is using imagery from the ideology of kingship by his use of the epithet Hêlēl ben Šaḥar. As we saw in chapter three, Hêlēl is terminology with astral connotations.[41] I have suggested previously that Hêlēl is a star in the constellation Š/Sinūnūtu, the Swallow, in close proximity to the Ištar star, Annunītu. We saw above that there is evidence for suggesting the identity of Ištar and Šaḥar, at least in some references. Hêlēl, I suggested, may have been the "son" of Ištar in the same manner that Amaušumgalanna and Ištar were stars in close proximity in the Sumerian conception. In the ideology of kingship of the third-second millennia, some Mesopotamian kings, upon their death, became transformed into a star in the constellation Swallow, near Aries and Annunītu. This image in the dirge does not require that *first millennium* kings were thought to be deified, nor that Isaiah thought this of Mesopotamian ideology. It does mean that traditional dirge imagery relating to dead kings was used by Isaiah in the *mashal* parody.

This conception of ascent does not negate the descent of the king into the netherworld: in the Egyptian as well as early Mesopotamian understanding, the king could both "ascend to heaven as a star" and descend to the netherworld with regal status. One way this could be accomplished was by following Šamaš/Šapšu on his/her daily course through the heavens and the netherworld, as the stars were said to do in any event. The ascent of the king and the descent into the netherworld are not two mutually exclusive movements. As the heavenly bodies sank into the western horizon, they necessarily entered the underworld, which in some conceptions may have been the mountains of the west or the Cedar Mountains.

Not all kings became stars, even in the third millennium. Most Mesopotamian kings were probably not deified, although it seems to have been the norm with Ur III kings. By the first millennium, the practice of deifying kings seems to have become unusual, or at least we do not read much about it other than in the late ritual compositions in Sumerian. It may also be that the funerary practice for kings became so standardized that ancient ritual laments were used *de riguer* for any dead king.

In any event, the tyrant is said to have planned in his heart to set his throne above all of the stars. In the astral form of *hll snnt*, the king would enjoy primacy as one of the three primary stars in the "field of Enlil." He would indeed, in a more Western conception, be "above the stars of ʾEl." In the words

---

[41] See the multiple mention of *hll snnt* in *KTU* 1.24, *Nikkal and the Kotharat*, drawing attention to Hêlēl's astral character.

of the *mashal*, he sought primacy not only on earth, but in the heavenly realm: he sought to be like ʿElyôn, he wished to ascend above the "heights of the cloud," to be enthroned above all other astral bodies or deities.

Another image of ascent which may lie behind these verses is the myth of *Etana*, analyzed in the previous chapter. This myth depicts the human king Etana, indeed the model and exemplar of human kingship as he was understood to be the first one, attempting to rise above his station to the highest heaven, and so was "cut down to the earth." The myth depicts the king in a manner perhaps not too different from *Gilgamesh*. These kings had access in some measure to divine realms. Etana is able to ascend to the lower heavens and visit some of the gods by means of the eagle. Gilgamesh is able to enter the Cedar Forest and traverse the "path of the sun." They both attempt, however, to achieve a status not ordained for human kings: to come to the highest heaven (Etana) and to achieve immortality (Gilgamesh). The king in Isa 14 likewise desires, in the words of the *mashal*, to achieve divine status in the highest heavens, not allowed to human kings. So his fall is catastrophic, as is the fall of Etana from his aborted attempt.

At first glance, these images appear contradictory. On the one hand, the dead king is depicted as a star in the heavens in the words of the *tigi* hymn and the *eršemma*. On the other hand, the king who reaches for divinity is denied and suffers repercussions (Etana, Gilgamesh). In another sense, however, both Etana and Gilgamesh are depicted as extraordinary human beings with limited access to divine beings and locations. In both these cases, it is their attempt to rise above their allotted station which results in disaster.

There is another manner in which these conflicting images may be understood. The *Etana* and *Gilgamesh* epics are both Neo-Assyrian in their final form and both are critical of kings who usurp authority or aspire for divinity. The *mashal* in Isa 14 also depicts the hubris of the king in his desire for divinity. It may be that the kind of ideology reflected in the congregational laments (the astral character of the dead king), is criticized or negated by such writings as *Gilgamesh* and *Etana*. Isaiah 14 also criticizes such impulses in the words of the *mashal*. It is, finally, impossible to say which images of ascent to heaven by the king lie behind vv. 12–14. It is at least suggestive that we have two dirge-like laments which demonstrate similar images. It is my suggestion that these laments, the *Etana* epic, and perhaps many other writings provide the backdrop in terms of available imagery for use in the ideology of kingship and its critique.

The second image is one of enthronement upon the holy mountain. More than one depiction of the divine world is operative in the poem. Mount Saphon, the mountain of the assembly of the gods in Canaanite mythology, is mentioned in v. 13. The *Gilgamesh Epic* combined the images of the Cedar Forest and the

Cedar Mountain/abode of the gods into one coherent image. We are also given information as to the location of the Cedar Forest: Saria (Sirion) and Lebanon tremble at the felling of the cedars and the death of Huwawa.[42] It is possible that the cedar forest mentioned in Isa 14:7–8 and the mountain of assembly in v. 13 denote the same location: the Cedar Forest and the mountain home of the gods. If this is the case, then we are not really dealing with the felling of simple timbers at all, but with the storming of the divine garden and mountain of the gods. Note that in the same verse the king intends to sit on the mountain of assembly and ascend to the heavens. These are not mutually exclusive categories. In the same ritual text (the *Pyramid Texts*), the pharaoh of Egypt can both ascend to heaven and enter the underworld. Similarly, Gilgamesh and Enkidu enter the Cedar Forest, the home of Ištar and the other deities, which mortals could not enter. This location is upon the earth (Lebanon and Sirion), but at the same time transcends the mundane. It is possible that the Cedar Forest is at once the most sacred site located on the earth (after all, it is the home of the gods, whether in Canaanite mythology or in the Neo-Assyrian version of the *Gilgamesh Epic*) and the point at which the earth, underworld, and heavens meet. If this is so, then the texts which mention the Cedar Forest, the death of kings, and the ascent to heaven in the same context suddenly make sense. These are not mutually exclusive, but relate to Near Eastern cosmology, the course of the heavenly bodies, and the ideology of death. Likewise, the tyrant is depicted in the *mashal* of Isa 14 as both planning to ascend into the heavens as a star and storm the gates of the divine abode in the Cedar Mountains of the west. The extent of his hubris becomes clear. According to the images of the *mashal*, he intends to achieve divine status, possibly like one of the legendary kings of old, and to achieve immortality by invading the sacred mountain like Gilgamesh.

This is not to say that the king literally aspired to deity, nor a throne in the underworld. The poem is a *mashal*. Its images are a comparison of the divine realm and a ritual of kingship with the reality of human affairs by means of a parody of that ritual. It is uncertain and immaterial to this thesis whether the Assyrian kings ever literally aspired to some form of divinity. The *mashal*, however, depicts the king's hubris and vaunted self-importance as akin to that which a deity might possess. His cruel persecution, harsh rule, and usurpation of authority was tantamount to that which a god might inflict on humanity, yet he was no god. Like Etana and Gilgamesh, he failed in his attempt and fell. Unlike the star of the king, Hêlēl ben Šaḥar, to which he is compared in his arrogance, his "star" fell to the earth in disgrace.

The referent is, then, to the king and his arrogance. Isaiah is full of references to pride and arrogance, particularly on the part of rulers (see especially

---

[42] "The Gilgamesh Epic—Additions," (*ANET*, 504).

the "arrogant boasting" of the king of Assyria in 10:12–15!). In the case of the king in Isa 14, his boasting and presumption led to his total demise. In the case of the boasting of the king of Assyria in chapter 10, the Lord would so destroy his armies that few would remain.

ii. *The Descent of the King (vv. 15–17)*

The descent of the king is much less problematical in terms of its function in the poem and the royal dirge. That the king descends to the underworld in the royal dirge is clear. There he was to be greeted by the kings and notables who had preceded him in death and to take his place in their midst. In terms of the mechanics of descent, we have seen that Šapšu probably functions as a psychopomp (*Baʿal Epic*, *KTU* 1.161) to ferry the dead to their abode in the underworld. In the *tigi* hymn of Inanna, the king comes forth each month at the time of the new moon over the mountains "like the sun," a probable reference to the cyclical course of the heavenly bodies through the heavens and the underworld. In Isa 14, there is neither psychopomp nor periodic course of the heavenly bodies. Instead of a psychopomp, there is the characteristic reluctance of the Hebrew text to deify or give personality to natural processes by means of circumlocution, the use of the passive voice to avoid granting agency to such processes: the king is "brought down" to Sheol (תּוּרָד/הוּרַד, vv. 11 and 15); he is "cut down" (נִגְדַּעְתָּ, v. 12); and he is "cast" from his grave (הָשְׁלַכְתָּ, v. 19). In Isa 14, the only reference to the ascension to heaven and course through the cosmos as a star is the aborted plan of the king in vv. 13–14.

Besides the actual descent to the netherworld, the arrival in Sheol is not the expected one from the royal dirge. Similar to Ezek 32, the king is cast into the lowest pit, where there is no position, honor, or privilege. Similarly, he has no throne, sepulcher, burial slab, or grave clothes as do the Rephaim. Rather than being greeted enthusiastically by his peers, the Rephaim stare at him and are incredulous at his situation.

V. 12 alludes to the twin themes of ascent to heaven and violation of the Cedar Forest by means of negative references. First, the plan of the king to storm the divine realm (Hêlēl ben Šaḥar, vv. 12–13) results in his "fall" (נָפַלְתָּ), an appropriate image for one who wishes supreme authority but whose real place is in the depths of the pit. Second, the king is "hewn down" (נִגְדַּעְתָּ, said of trees, specifically majestic trees of Lebanon, in Isa 10:33 and elsewhere). This is a provocative statement in light of the quote of the cedars of Lebanon in vv. 7–8: the one who cut (כֹּרֵת) their branches has now laid down (שָׁכַבְתָּ). This last is not a reference to "being laid low," as the RSV has it, but to "lying down," a reference to the king's death and his bed in the grave. The one who wished to cut the trees of the sacred forest has himself been hewn down like those trees. The one who wished to ascend to the highest heaven has fallen to the lowest pit, in the words of metaphor.

Vv. 15–17a once again report the reaction and words of the Rephaim, as we saw in the first speech in vv. 9–11. Vv. 12–14 are probably not a continuation of the words of the Rephaim. The particle *ʾêk* does not otherwise begin a quote within a dirge. Second, the extent of the quote becomes problematical if it is viewed as extending past v. 11. The king's speech within his heart then would become a quote within a quote. Also, "Your seers" in v. 16 introduces another quote, further complicating the extent of the Rephaim's speech. Furthermore, the verse immediately preceding "your seers" is "You are brought down to Sheol, to the depths of the pit" in v. 15, suggesting that it is those who are in Sheol who are his viewers. Finally, v. 10 and its introduction to the Rephaim's speech parallels that of v. 16: "All of them will speak and say to you, 'You too'" in v. 10 is parallel to "Those who see you will stare at you, they will ponder over you:' Is this the man?'" in v. 16.

The Rephaim, then, have a second speech in which they continue their response of incredulity after the interlude of the king's desire to ascend to heaven but subsequent fall to Sheol. In light of the king's power and sovereignty over the nations and the destruction and terror he caused, the dead kings, his predecessors, are justifiably amazed that such power should be brought so low.

The metaphor relates, as we saw in the preceding speech of the Rephaim, to the ideology of kingship, the death of kings, and the greeting provided by the notables in the underworld. The image is a graphic one relating to the sort of welcome a supreme monarch might anticipate in the underworld: royal peers, a throne, repose, and recognition. Instead the king is cast into the lowest pit, without honorable burial, shroud, or slab, and his body slain in battle is worm-eaten: see Ezek 32 relative to kings and their armies who die in battle and are relegated to the lowest pits of Sheol!

The referent is probably to the actual death of the king on the field of battle (see section d). The contrast motif, characteristic of dirges, is employed here: how is it one so mighty and powerful should be so utterly destroyed? How is it that one who aspired to such absolute sovereignty is now king of nothing in the lowest pit? The immediate antecedent of the onlookers is the Rephaim, but need not exclude those on the earth who actually see the king's dead body, lying exposed. On the referential level, the scene depicts those who once marveled at the king's power, now equally marveling at his demise.

d. The Burials of the Rephaim and the Tyrant Contrasted (vv. 18–20a)

Vv. 18–20a return to a description of the king's lack of burial, first suggested in v. 8 ("since you lay down") and mentioned in the Rephaim's first speech in vv. 9–11 ("Under you worms are spread out and your covering is maggots"). The Rephaim are captives in Sheol, but the passage does not dwell on the negative aspect of their captive status. It rather seeks to draw attention to the comparison between the Rephaim's privileged status, appropriate burial in sepulchers, and their security with this arrangement. Their sanctity and position are not violated, but they all lie in glory. Opposed to the honor and security which they experience, the tyrant is cast out (הָשְׁלַכְתָּ), far from a grave, clothed with dead bodies rather than burial garments (לְבוּשׁ הֲרֻגִים), along with all those who die by the sword without proper burial. V. 20a ends this section pertaining to the lack of burial for the king and the entire cosmological section from vv. 7–20a. The king will not be joined with "them" in burial. This must refer to the Rephaim and not to those slain by the sword, who receive no burial. The only antecedent which makes sense is the Rephaim, who have just been described as having exemplary burials and underworld status.We then are given the reason for such negative treatment of the tyrant: he has slain his own people and has annihilated his own land.

The reference, as in the previous section, is to the king's death on the field of battle, his covering with corpses, and lack of grave, graveclothes, slab, or other appurtenances of an honorable burial. The contrast motif is once again used to depict the difference between those who receive honorable burial and the one who, though supremely arrogant, is cast out on the ground without the benefits of a grave, proper care for the dead, and a proper funeral.

3. The Sacrifice of the King's Sons (vv. 20b–21)

The final section is the briefest. It returns us to the scene on earth, at the mock funeral ceremony for the king. The perspective changes from second person address to the king to a direct address to the mock dirge participants, as the celebrants are exhorted to sacrifice in *KTU* 1.161, with a corresponding narrative about the king in the third person. As we saw in chapter two above, in three of the four examples of the royal dirge surveyed, sacrifices are offered towards the end of the dirge (or narrative, in the case of the *Death of Ur-Nammu*). In *KTU* 1.161 a series of seven sacrifices is offered to the gods. Vv. 20b and 21 are the necessary ending of the dirge in Isa 14. They describe a sacrifice as well, but this sacrifice is the sacrifice of the king's sons. The name of the royal heir is proclaimed in *KTU* 1.161 to end the ritual with an official proclamation concerning the throne succession. In Isa 14, the celebrants are exhorted that the offspring (זֶרַע) who do evil should never be "called out" (יִקָּרֵא). In the Niqmaddu text, the Ugaritic verb *qra* is used repeatedly for the invocation of the *rapi'ūma*, presumably by the dirge celebrants. In Isa 14, Sheol invokes the Rephaim while the dirge celebrants are exhorted not to "call out" the "offspring who do evil." The Niqmaddu text "calls out" or names (*qra*) the dead kings Niqmaddu and Ammishtamru, as well as the son of Niqmaddu and heir to the throne, ʿAmmurapi. Descendants of the king or heirs to the throne are often referred to as the "seed" in the Old Testament. זֶרַע is a collective noun which may refer to a single descendant (2 Sam 4:8, Ishbosheth and Saul), or to multiple descendants (2 Sam 22:51, "to David and to his offspring forever"). זֶרַע מְרֵעִים also occurs in Isa 1:4:

> Ah, sinful nation, a people laden with iniquity, offspring who do evil (זֶרַע מְרֵעִים), sons who deal corruptly! They have forsaken the Lord, they have despised the Holy One of Israel, they are utterly estranged. (RSV)

Israel is clearly the "sons" of God who have rebelled in 1:4. In Isa 14, the reference may be to the King of Babylon, in which case the plural ("who do evil") is difficult to explain. Another possibility is that the dynasty as a whole is in view, including not only the king, but also his potential successors. This would explain the use of "offspring" (זֶרַע) in v. 20, as well as the command to slaughter the sons because of the guilt of the father in v. 21.

On the metaphorical level, the children provide the sacrifice for the mock dirge ceremony. Their names are not to be proclaimed in the succession of kings: the dynasty, in the *mashal*, ends with the dead "king of Babylon." Both the sacrifices and the naming of the new king are prominent elements of the Niqmaddu text.

The referent is to the death of the king and the hope and exhortation that all potential heirs, who possess their father's evil pedigree, be exterminated, so that the king might not live on in his descendants and continue to tyrannize the world through his posterity. The mock dirge ends with the exhortation that the descendants of evildoers, in this case evil and oppressive kings, might not be proclaimed for kingship.

IV. The Identity of the Tyrant in Isa 14:4b–21

Two issues remain to be addressed, both of which have produced very different approaches and suggestions: whether the king depicted is alive or dead and what the identity of that king is. I will look at each of these issues in turn.

Relative to the question of whether the king parodied in the dirge is alive or dead, K. Nielsen has suggested that the king must be alive for the imagery in the poem to be effective.[43] Others have suggested that the king in the poem must be dead and therefore the *mashal* is a taunt to ridicule him after his demise. Evidence in the poem in support of his demise having occurred already includes 1) the predominant use of perfect forms in the poem, depicting the death of the king and rejoicing of the nations as an accomplished fact; 2) dirges are always sung after, and not before, a death occurs; and 3) the introduction to the poem (vv. 3–4a) is late and non-Isaianic, so its projection of the events of the poem into the future may be discounted for understanding the contents and background of the poem itself. Most scholars have adopted this position and then looked for evidence of an Assyrian or Babylonian king who dies in the manner apparently depicted in the poem: without burial, "clothed with the slain" (i.e., covered with dead corpses on the field of battle), etc. The king who comes most readily to mind in this regard is Sargon II, who was slain on the field of battle and left unburied.

Some scholars, such as Nielsen, are not as convinced by this evidence.[44] True dirges, of course, are sung at the occasion of an actual death (2 Sam 1, 3), but dirges in prophetic literature are, in Westermann's words, judgment speeches with dirge-like elements. These dirge-like judgment speeches may reflect events which have already occurred, or they may present events which have yet to occur as if they have already. The dirge fragment in Amos 5:2–3, for example, clearly presents the death of Israel as a present reality ("Fallen, no more to rise is virgin Israel"), yet Israel just as clearly has not yet fallen. Likewise, Ezek 32 presents pharaoh as alive (see v. 2, the command to raise a *qînāh*), and yet, also in v. 2, the recognition of the king as very alive. In the same way, the use of the perfect verbal form in the poem is inconclusive, as prophets often use such forms to depict the certainty of a coming event, as in Amos 5:2. Nielsen suggests also that the *mashal* requires that the king referred to in the poem be alive in order for it to communicate irony and metaphors relating to the downfall of the king.[45] Finally, contra Clements,[46] vv. 3–4a, which suggest the poem is to be sung in the future and is a *mashal*, are replete with Isaianic terminology and it is at least arguable that these verses are attributable to Isaiah himself.

Fortunately, this issue need not be finally resolved in order to understand the *mashal* or for it to function effectively. Whether the king is alive or dead, his aspirations to greatness and supremacy are ridiculed and his utter demise and loss of all privilege, authority, and position may be clearly seen. The dirge

---

[43] Nielsen, *There is Hope for a Tree*, 159.

[44] Nielsen, *There is Hope for a Tree*, 160–161.

[45] Nielsen, *There is Hope for a Tree*, 159.

[46] Clements, *Isaiah 1–39*, 139–140.

form, whether as a parody of a funeral ritual in celebration of that demise or in anticipation of the certainty of its occurrence, still effectively condemns and ridicules the king.

The second issue, in some respects related to whether, or how, the king died, is the question of his identity. The king in Isa 14:4b–21 is anonymous. In the redactional introduction to the poem (vv. 3–4a), he is referred to as the "king of Babylon." I take 3–4a to be by the same author as the dirge in 4b–21. The use of terminology is similar and there is no reason to assign these verses to another author. The "king of Babylon," therefore, is the designation of choice for the tyrant in the poem.

Because Babylon was fighting for its life at the time of Isaiah, it is unlikely that a native Babylonian king is in view, since the tyrant is described as a world ruler and full of hubris and divine pretensions. From the time of Tiglath-Pileser III on, however, Assyrian kings were crowned king of Babylon and referred to themselves by that title. It is much more likely that such an Assyrian king is in view, particularly if the poem was written during the time of Isaiah of Jerusalem. Since Sennacherib is referred to in 37:24 as violating the Lebanon and its forests, some have suggested him as the most likely candidate for the king in the dirge. He also died violently, apparently at the hand of his sons, but did not die in battle and apparently his body was not exposed.

If the poem was written during the time of Isaiah of Jerusalem, there are other possible candidates. Sargon II, who died in battle and whose body was exposed on the open field (see v. 19!), has often been mentioned as the king. Tiglath-Pileser III also qualifies, as he was the first to take the title "king of Babylon" and was a great and tyrannical empire-builder of Assyria. On the other hand, he was not "cast out from his grave" and exposed on the field of battle as was Sargon II, nor did he meet a violent end as Sennacherib did. Clements has even suggested Shalmaneser V as the king, although the inscriptions of Shalmaneser are few and fragmentary and he does not appear in the book of Isaiah.

One bit of evidence has generally been overlooked. This is the oracle against Philistia in 14:28–32. It has several affinities with the terminology of the tyrant in the dirge in 14:4b–21: "your smiter" (מַכֵּךְ), "the rod" (שֵׁבֶט) which is broken (נִשְׁבָּר), and judgment on a "shoot" or "branch" (שֹׁרֶשׁ, possibly parallel to נֵצֶר). Furthermore, there is an intriguing parallel in v. 31: here, הֵילִילִי שַׁעַר, "wail, O gate!," is a virtual homophone of הֵילֵל בֶּן שַׁחַר. Furthermore, Philistia is mocking the death of a tyrant in a similar way that the tyrant is mocked after his death in 14:4b–21. These similarities suggest that the "rod" of the dirge is the "rod" who also smote Philistia. The question of the identity of this rod and of the setting for the oracle is another matter.

Its superscription would seem to date the oracle clearly, "In the year of the death of king Ahaz came this oracle." Some, however, have suggested that the superscription is not original and useless for dating the oracle.[47] A second problem is the identity of the "rod" which smote Philistia, but is now dead. If a Judean king, is it Ahaz or Hezekiah? If an Assyrian, Tiglath-Pileser III, Shalmaneser V, or Sargon II could qualify. The third problem is related to the second. We are unsure about the year of Ahaz's death: J. Begrich has suggested 725[48] while J. Bright and W. F. Albright have suggested 715,[49] a significant period of time during which the three Assyrian kings mentioned above reigned.

In response to the first question, attempts to emend בִּשְׁנַת הַמּוֹת הַמֶּלֶךְ׃ אָחָז falter because the only other analogy to this superscription is the one in 6:1, where the name of the king who has died is given and the failure in chapter 14 to give the name of the king would be curious. Furthermore, this proposed emendation is not attested in ancient versions and manuscripts. It may still be a later editorial addition totally lacking in historical value, but for the time being it is the only time referent we possess. We will, therefore, withhold judgment and look at other evidence which may or may not corroborate the historical verisimilitude of the superscription. In response to the second problem, kings of Judah are never called the "rod which smites," or the "rod of God's anger" in the book of Isaiah. This terminology is reserved for Assyrian kings (see 9:3, 10:5, 15, 24, 26, 14:5), God's punishment (see 28:27, 30:31-32), and once for the righteous punishment to be inflicted on the wicked by the coming messianic king (see 11:4). Whatever the meaning of the serpent terms might be in v. 29b, it is unlikely that the "rod" refers to the king of Judah. In response to the third problem, one needs to verify that the possible candidates did indeed oppress the Philistines. There is no question of this in the case of Tiglath-Pileser III,[50] Sargon II,[51] and Sennacherib.[52] In the case of Shalmaneser V, we do not possess enough of his inscriptions to make a judgment one way or another.

If the superscription is correct, then one would expect rejoicing of the Philistines not long after the death of the Assyrian king had occurred and at

---

[47] Kaiser, *Isaiah 13–39*, 51.

[48] Joachim Begrich, "Jesaja 14, 28–32: Ein Beitrag zur Chronologie der israelitisch-judäischen Königszeit," in *Gesammelte Studien zum Alten Testament, Herausgegeben von Walther Zimmerli* (TB 21; Munich: Chr. Kaiser, 1964), 128.

[49] John Bright, *A History of Israel* (3rd ed.; Philadelphia: Westminster, 1981), 281, 292 and William F. Albright, "The Chronology of the Divided Monarchy of Israel," BASOR 100 (1945): 22.

[50] Tadmor, *The Inscriptions of Tiglath-Pileser III*, 39, 177–179, etc.

[51] "Sargon," *Ancient Records*, 2:31.

[52] "Sennacherib," *Ancient Records*, 2:119.

least close to the time of the death of Ahaz. This limits our possibilities to two: Tiglath-Pileser III, who died in 725 and was succeeded by Shalmaneser V, or Shalmaneser V, who died in 722 and was succeeded by Sargon II. Shalmaneser is attractive as the king who died in 14:28, as already noted by Clements, followed by a stronger king (Sargon) who would invade them from the North. This Sargon did decisively in 711. We do not know, however, the circumstances surrounding Shalmaneser's death. It is difficult to cast him in the role of Hêlēl ben Šaḥar, if the king mentioned in 14:4b–21 and the one in vv. 28–32 refer to the same person. He could qualify as hated by the nations in the Levant, as he was instrumental in the destruction of Samaria, but he apparently did not die on the field of battle with his body left exposed. Nor, conceivably, was he king long enough to engender the hatred which we see portrayed in the metaphor and myth of Isa 14.

It is more likely that the superscription is an erroneous attribution, attached by a later redactor who was left without an introduction to this oracle. If the superscription is erroneous, then it is possible that Sargon II is the king referred to in both 14:4b–21 and vv. 28–32. There is no question of the hatred he generated, nor that he died in battle. If v. 28 refers to the same person, then the worse scourge that was to succeed him could easily be Sennacherib. Further evidence for this may be Isa 20:1, the notice that Ashdod has fallen to Sargon II, underscoring the seriousness of the plight of the Philistines and Judah. If the superscription is correct, on the other hand, then the king in v. 28 must still be Sargon, unless Begrich's dating of Ahaz' death to 725 is accurate. We are left with a several year hiatus between the deaths of Tiglath-Pileser III or Shalmaneser V and Ahaz if the 715 date for his death is correct. Of course, it is also possible that the king in vv. 4b–21 is different from the one in vv. 28–32 and that the similar language used in both is formulaic or coincidental. Given the difficulties involved in determining the identity of the king, it is impossible for the time being to be certain. It is my suggestion, nevertheless, that Sargon II satisfies more of the characteristics of the king in Isa 14 than do the other Assyrian kings during Isaiah's prophetic ministry.

V. Summary and Conclusion

In this chapter I have attempted to demonstrate the coherence between various ancient Near Eastern dirges for dead kings and Isa 14:4b–21. A detailed outline of the poem was offered, further underscoring the connections between elements in the cosmology of dirges and the poem. In the examination of each section of the poem, it has been necessary to demonstrate not only how these elements and allusions are reflected, but also how they function as metaphors in the *mashal*. Finally, I made a suggestion relative to the identity of the king and the occasion for the mock dirge.

Chapter 6
Myth and Meaning in Isaiah 14:4b–21

That the poem in Isa 14:4b–21 is one of the greatest literary achievements in the Hebrew Bible has long been recognized. What has not been so readily recognized is that it has a literary and cosmological/mythopoeic coherence which add to its beauty and subtlety. It is coherent literarily because it borrows from the themes of ancient Near Eastern dirge forms and uses them to create a consistent and highly structured unit. It is coherent in terms of cosmology because the images of the poem relate to the ideology of, and rituals pertaining to, the death of kings. Finally, it is a coherent piece because all of these complex images have been transformed by the *mashal*. They no longer serve the same function that they did in the ritual dirge. They now serve to mock and taunt the king. The *mashal* uses metaphorical and cosmological imagery in order to assign the king in the most graphic way possible to his eternal "reward." The *mashal* uses accepted images and forms and endows them with new meaning by means of the literary comparison or analogy. So the dirge is not a true dirge. Its intent is to point away from the ritual and myth to political, social, and religious realities. It is an indictment and condemnation of an arrogant king who tyrannized the world and whose actions and hubris suggested divine pretensions.

In the previous chapters we have surveyed the complex relationship between myth, ritual, and *mashal* in the literature and theology of Isa 14:4b–21. In chapter one we examined several ways in which myth has been understood to function in the poem, followed by a survey of the phenomenon of myth in general and its relationship to ritual. In chapter two we examined the literary form of the poem, concluding that the entire work is a single dirge for a dead king. It is also, however, a *mashal*, which uses the language of metaphor and myth in order to make points about, and draw analogies with, the world of Isaiah's day. In chapters three and four we examined several of the cosmological/mythological motifs imbedded in the poem. The first, and most controversial, is the figure of Hêlēl ben Šaḥar. Chapter three explored the cosmological background to this terminology and provided clarity relative to the terminology used and its relationship to kingship in the ancient Near East. Chapter four explored other mythological motifs found in the poem: the ascent and descent of the king, the Cedar Forest of Lebanon, and the Rephaim. Chapter five provided a translation of the text and the literary structure of the unit. This was followed by a suggestion for a new way to read the text based on the analysis of myth, *mashal*, and liturgical dirge found in the preceding chapters. My conclusion was that mythological imagery related to kingship, especially dirges for dead kings, was borrowed and significantly transformed by the *mashal* in order to mock the tyrant and expedite him to the lowest possible pit in Sheol, where he would enjoy neither position, nor authority, nor even royal regalia or comfort. I ended the analysis by tentatively concluding that Sargon II most nearly fits the characteristics and possible historical setting for such a king as described in Isa 14.

It is perhaps fitting that this analysis end the way it began. If Isa 14:4b–21 pertains to political realities of Isaiah's day, and parodies Near Eastern myth by means of the *mashal*, how could the Church later apply this passage to the fall of Lucifer, or Satan, from heaven? While the passage does not relate specifically to a myth of the primordial fall of one of the members of the divine court, there are points of contact between the historical/mythological setting and its later theological appropriation by Church and Synagogue. If the "king of Babylon" personified arrogance, presumption, and usurpation of the gods' prerogatives, how much more are these attributes characteristic of Satan, the great accuser of the Lord's elect and tyrannizer of creation?

> And the great dragon was thrown down, that ancient serpent, who is called the Devil and Satan, the deceiver of the whole world—he was thrown down to the earth, and his angels were thrown down with him.
>
> And I heard a loud voice in heaven, saying, "Now the salvation and the power and the kingdom of our God and the authority of his Christ have come, for the accuser of our brethren has been thrown down, who accuses them day and night before our God." (Rev 12:9–10)

Bibliography

Abusch, Tzvi. "Ascent to the Stars in a Mesopotamian Ritual: Social Metaphor and Religious Experience." Pages 15–39 in *Death, Ecstacy, and Other Worldly Journeys*. Edited by John J. Collins and Michael Fishbane. Albany: State University of New York Press, 1995.

———. "The Demonic Image of the Witch in Standard Babylonian Literature: The Reworking of Popular Conceptions by Learned Exorcists." Pages 27–58 in *Religion, Science, and Magic: In Concert and in Conflict.* Edited by Jacob Neusner, Ernest Frerichs, and Paul V. M. Flesher. New York: Oxford University Press, 1989.

———. "An Early Form of the Witchcraft Ritual *Maqlû* and the Origin of a Babylonian Magical Ceremony." Pages 1–57 in *Lingering Over Words: Studies in Ancient Near Eastern Literature in Honor of William L. Moran.* Edited by Tzvi Abusch, John Huehnergard, and Piotr Steinkeller. Harvard Semitic Monographs 37. Atlanta: Scholars Press, 1990.

———. "Ritual and Incantation: Interpretation: Interpretation and Textual History: A Consideration of *Maqlû* VII:58–105, IX:152–59." Pages 367–380 in *"Sha'arei Talmon": Studies in the Bible, Qumran, and the Ancient Near East Presented to Shemaryahu Talmon.* Edited by M. Fishbane and E. Tov. Winona Lake: Eisenbrauns, 1991.

———. "The Ritual Tablet and Rubrics of *Maqlû*: Towards the History of the Series." Pages 233–255 in *Ah, Assyria: Studies in Assyrian History and Ancient Near Eastern Historiography Presented to Hayim Tadmor.* Edited by Mordecai Cogan and Israel Eph'al. Scripta Hierosolymitana 33. Jerusalem: Magnes, 1991.

Ackerman, Robert. *The Myth and Ritual School: J. G. Frazer and the Cambridge Ritualists.* New York: Garland, 1991.

Albright, William F. "The Chronology of the Divided Monarchy of Israel." *Bulletin of the American Schools of Oriental Research* 100 (1945): 16–22.

———. *Yahweh and the Gods of Canaan: A Historical Analysis of Two Contrasting Faiths.* Garden City: Doubleday, 1968.

Alfrink, Bernhard. "Der Versammlungsberg im aüssersten Norden." *Biblica* 14 (1933): 41–67.

Alster, Bendt. "A Dumuzi Lament in Late Copies." Acta Sumerologica Japonesa 7 (1985): 1–9.

———. "A Sumerian Poem about Early Rulers." Acta Sumerologica Japonesa 8 (1986): 7.

Arnaud, Daniel. *Recherches au pays d'Aštata: Emar 6.3 and 6.4, textes Sumeriens et Accadiens.* Synthèse 18. Paris: Editions Recherches sur les Civilisations, 1986.

Augustine. *St. Augustine on the Psalms*. Translated by S. Hebgin and F. Corrigan. 2 vols. Ancient Christian Writers 30. New York: Newman, 1961.

Batto, Bernard F. *Slaying the Dragon: Mythmaking in the Biblical Tradition*. Louisville: W/JKP, 1992.

Bayliss, Miranda. "The Cult of Dead Kin in Assyria and Babylonia." *Iraq* 35 (1973): 115–125.

Begrich, Joachim. "Jesaja 14, 28–32: Ein Beitrag zur Chronologie der israelitisch-judäischen Königszeit." Pages 121–131 in *Gesammelte Studien zum Alten Testament, Herausgegeben von Walther Zimmerli*. Vol. 21 of Theologische Bücherei: Neudrucke und Berichte aus dem 20. Jahrhundert. Munich: Chr. Kaiser, 1964.

Bergerhof, K., Manfried Dietrich, and Otto Loretz. "Baal RPU in KTU 1.108; 1.113 und nach 1.17 VI 25–33." *Ugarit-forschungen* 12 (1981): 171–182.

Bertolucci, Jose M. "The Son of the Morning and the Guardian Cherub in the Context of the Controversy between Good and Evil." Th. D. diss., Andrews University, 1985.

Black, Jeremy and Anthony Green. *Gods, Demons, and Symbols of Ancient Mesopotamia: An Illustrated Dictionary*. Austin: University of Texas Press, 1992.

Bordreuil, Pierre and Dennis Pardee. " Le rituel funèraire Ougaritique RS 34.126." *Syria* 59 (1982): 121–128.

Bost, Hubert. "Le chant sur la chute d'un tyran en Esaïe 14." *Etudes théologiques et religieuses* 59 (1984): 3–14.

Boutflower, Charles. *The Book of Isaiah Chapters I–XXXIX in the Light of the Assyrian Monuments*. London: Society for Promoting Christian Knowledge, 1930.

Bright, John. *A History of Israel*. 3rd ed. Philadelphia: Westminster, 1981.

Brinkman, John A., Miguel Civil, Ignace J. Gelb, A. Leo Oppenheim, and Erica Reiner, eds. *Š*. Vol. 17 of *The Assyrian Dictionary*. Chicago: University of Chicago Press, 1992.

Burns, John B. "Ḥôlēš ʿal in Isaiah 14:12: A New Proposal." *Zeitschrift für Althebräistik* 2 (1989): 199–204.

Cagni, Luigi. *The Poem of Erra*. Sources and Monographs on the Ancient Near East 1/3. Malibu: Undena, 1977.

Calvin, John. *Commentary on the Book of the Prophet Isaiah*. Translated by William Pringle. Calvin's Commentaries 7. Grand Rapids: Baker, 1979.

Caquot, Andre. "Le dieu ʿAṯtar et les textes de Ras Shamra." *Syria* 35 (1958): 45–60.

———. "Les Rephaim Ougaritiques." *Syria* 37 (1960): 75–93.

———. "Report." *Annuaire du Collège de France* 75 (1975): 427.

Carmignac, Jean. "Six passages éclairés par Qumran (Isaïe 14:11, 21:10, 22:5, 25:4, 26:3, 50:6)." Pages 37–46 in *Bibel und Qumran*. Edited by H. Bardtke. Berlin: Evangelische Hauptbibelgesellschaft, 1968.

Cassirer, Ernst. *Language and Myth*. New York: Harper & Brothers, 1946.

———. *The Myth of the State*. New Haven: Yale University Press, 1946.

———. *The Philosophy of Symbolic Forms. Vol. II: Mythical Thought*. New Haven: Yale University Press, 1955.

Castellino, G. R. *Two Šulgi Hymns (BC)*. Studi Semitici 42. Rome: Istituto di Studi del Vicino Oriente, 1972.

Childs, Brevard S. *Myth and Reality in the Old Testament*. Studies in Biblical Theology 27. London: SCM, 1960.

Civil, Miguel, Ignace J. Gelb, A. Leo Oppenheim, and Erica Reiner, eds. *L*. Vol. 9 of *The Assyrian Dictionary*. Chicago: University of Chicago Press, 1973.

Clements, Ronald. *Isaiah 1–39*. New Century Bible. Grand Rapids: Eerdmans, 1980.

Clifford, Richard. *The Cosmic Mountain in Canaan and the Old Testament*. Harvard Semitic Monographs 4. Cambridge: Harvard University Press, 1972.

Cohen, Mark. *The Canonical Lamentations of Ancient Mesopotamia*. Potomac: Capital Decisions Limited, 1988.

———. *Sumerian Hymnology: The Eršemma*. Hebrew Union College Annual: Supplement Series 2. Cincinnati: Hebrew Union College, 1981.

Cooper, Jerrold. *The Curse of Agade*. Baltimore: Johns Hopkins University Press, 1983.

Craigie, Peter C. "Helel, Athtar and Phaeton." *Zeitschrift für die alttestamentliche Wissenschaft* 85 (1973): 223–225.

Dalley, Stephanie. *Myths from Mesopotamia*. Oxford: Oxford University Press, 1989.

Dietrich, Manfried and Otto Loretz. "Baal *RPU* in KTU 1.108; 1.113 und nach 1.17 VI 25–33." *Ugarit-forschungen* 12 (1980): 171–182.

———. "Rapiʾu und Milku aus Ugarit: Neuere historische-geographische Thesen zu rpu mlk ʿlm (KTU 1.108: 1) und mt rpi (KTU 1.17 I 1)." *Ugarit-forschungen* 21 (1989): 123–131.

Dietrich, Manfried, Otto Loretz, and Joaquín Sanmartín. *The Cuneiform Alphabetic Texts from Ugarit, Ras Ibn Hani, and Other Places*. 2nd, enl. ed. Abhandlungen zur Literatur Alt-Syrien-Palästinas und Mesopotamiens 8. Münster: Ugarit-Verlag, 1995.

———. "Die ugaritischen Totengeister RPU(M) und die biblischen Rephaim." *Ugarit-forschungen* 8 (1976): 45–52.

Dijkstra, M. "The Legend of Danel and the Rephaim." *Ugarit-forschungen* 20 (1988): 35–51.

Dobbs-Allsopp, F. W. *Weep, O Daughter of Zion: A Study of the City-Lament Genre in the Hebrew Bible*. Biblica et Orientalia 44. Rome: Pontifical Biblical Institute, 1993.

Eichrodt, Walther. *Der Herr der Geschichte: Jesaja 13–23, 28–39*. Stuttgart: Calwer, 1967.

Eissfeldt, Otto. *Der Maschal im Alten Testament*. Beihefte zur Zeitschrift für die alttestamentliche Wissenschaft 24. Gießen: Alfred Töpelmann, 1913.

Eliade, Mircea. *Myth and Reality*. New York: Harper & Row, 1963.

Erlandsson, Seth. *The Burden of Babylon: A Study of Isaiah 13:2–14:23*. Coniectanea biblica: Old Testament Series 4. Lund: CWK Gleerup, 1970.

Erman, Adolf. *Life in Ancient Egypt*. London: MacMillan, 1894.

Fales, F. M. and J. N. Postgate, *Imperial Administrative Records Part 1: Palace and Temple Administration*. State Archives of Assyria 7. Helsinki: Helsinki University Press, 1992.

Falkenstein, A. "Untersuchungen zur sumerischen Grammatik (Fortsetzung)." *Zeitschrift für Assyriologie* 48 (1944): 105–118.

Faulkner, R. O. *The Ancient Egyptian Book of the Dead*. New York: Limited Editions Book Club, 1972.

———. *The Ancient Egyptian Coffin Texts, Volume 1: Spells 1–354*. Warminster: Aris & Phillips, 1973.

———. *The Ancient Egyptian Pyramid Texts*. Oxford: Oxford University Press, 1969.

———. "The King and the Star Religion in the Pyramid Texts." *Journal of Near Eastern Studies* 25 (1966): 153–161.

Fischer, Johann. *Das Buch Isaias, I. Teil, Kapitel 1–39. Die Heilige Schrift des Alten Testaments* 7. Bonn: Peter Hanstein, 1937.

Fleming, Daniel E. *The Installation of Baʿal's High Priestess at Emar: A Window on Ancient Syrian Religion*. Atlanta: Scholars Press, 1992.

Ford, J. N. "The Living Rephaim of Ugarit: Quick or Defunct?" *Ugarit-forschungen* 24 (1993): 73–101.

Foxvog, Daniel. "Astral Dumuzi." Pages 103–108 in *The Tablet and the Scroll: Near Eastern Studies in Honor of William W. Hallo*. Edited by Mark Cohen, et al. Bethesda: CDL, 1993.

Frankfort, H. and H. A. et al. *Before Philosophy: The Intellectual Adventure of Ancient Man.* Chicago: University of Chicago Press, 1946.

Frazer, James. *The Golden Bough: A Study in Magic and Religion.* New York: MacMillan, 1922.

Gallagher, William R., "On the Identity of Helel ben Sahar of Is. 14:12–15." *Ugarit-forschungen* 26 (1995): 131–146.

Gaster, Theodore H. *Myth, Legend, and Custom in the Old Testament: A Comparative Study with Chapters from Sir James G. Frazer's Folklore in the Old Testament.* New York: Harper & Row, 1969.

———. *Thespis: Ritual, Myth, and Drama in the Ancient Near East.* Garden City: Doubleday, 1961.

———. "Ugaritic Mythology." *Journal of Near Eastern Studies* 7 (1948): 184–193.

Gelb, Ignace J., Benno Landsberger, and A. Leo Oppenheim, eds. *I/J.* Vol. 7 of *The Assyrian Dictionary.* Chicago: University of Chicago Press, 1960.

Gelb, Ignace J., Thorkild Jacobsen, Benno Lansberger, and A. Leo Oppenheim, eds. *Ḫ.* Vol. 8 of *The Assyrian Dictionary.* Chicago: University of Chicago Press, 1956.

Geyer, John B. "Mythology and Culture in the Oracles against the Nations." *Vetus Testamentum* 36 (1986): 129–143.

Gibson, John. *Canaanite Myths and Legends.* Edinburgh: T & T Clark, 1977.

Good, R. McClive. "Geminated Sonants, Word Stress, and Energic in, -nn/, -.nn in Ugaritic." *Ugarit-forschungen* 13 (1981): 118–119.

Gowan, Donald E. *When Man becomes God: Humanism and Hubris in the Old Testament.* Pittsburgh Theological Monographs 6. Pittsburgh: Penguin, 1975.

Gray, George B. *A Critical and Exegetical Commentary on the Book of Isaiah, Vol. 1.* International Critical Commentary. Edinburgh: T & T Clark, 1912.

———. "The Desert God ʿAṯtar in the Literature and Religion of Canaan." *Journal of Near Eastern Studies* 8 (1949): 72–83.

Gray, John. "DTN and RP'UM in Ancient Ugarit." *Palestine Exploration Quarterly* 84 (1952): 39–41.

———. "The Rephaim." *Palestine Exploration Quarterly* 81 (1949): 127–139.

Grayson, Albert Kirk. *Assyrian Rulers of the Early First Millennium BC I (1114–859 BC).* The Royal Inscriptions of Mesopotamia, Assyrian Periods 2. Toronto: University of Toronto Press, 1991.

Green, M. W. "The Eridu Lament." *Journal of Cuneiform Studies* 30 (1978): 127–161.

———. "The Uruk Lament." *Journal of the American Oriental Society* 104 (1984): 253–279.

Grelot, Pierre. "Isaïe XIV 12–15 et son arrière-plan mythologique." *Revue de l'histoire des religions* 149 (1956): 18–48.

———. "Sur la vocalisation de הילל (Is. XIV 12)." *Vetus Testamentum* 6 (1956): 303–304.

Gunkel, Hermann. *Schöpfung und Chaos in Urzeit und Endzeit: eine religions-geschichtliche Untersuchung über Gen. 1 und Ap. Joh. 12.* Göttingen: Vandenhoeck & Ruprecht, 1894.

Hackett, Jo Ann. *The Balaam Text from Deir ʿAlla.* Harvard Semitic Monographs 31. Chico: Scholars Press, 1984.

Hallo, William W., ed. *Monumental Inscriptions from the Biblical World.* Vol. 2 of *The Context of Scripture.* Leiden: E. J. Brill, 2000.

———. "The Death of Kings: Traditional Historiography in Contextual Perspective." Pages 148–165 in *Ah, Assyria: Studies in Assyrian History and Ancient Near Eastern Historiography Presented to Hayim Tadmor.* Edited by Mordecai Cogan and Israel Eph'al. Scripta Hierosolymitana 33. Jerusalem: Magnes, 1991.

———. "Royal Ancestor Worship in the Biblical World." Pages 381–401 in "*Sha'arei Talmon": Studies in the Bible, Qumran, and the Ancient Near East Presented to Shemaryahu Talmon.* Edited by Michael Fishbane and Emanuel Tov. Winona Lake: Eisenbrauns, 1992.

Hamborg, G. R. "Reasons for Judgment in the Oracles against the Nations of the Prophet Isaiah." *Vetus Testamentum* 31 (1981): 145–159.

Handy, L. *Among the Host of Heaven: The Syro-Palestinian Pantheon as Bureaucracy.* Winona Lake: Eisenbrauns, 1994.

Hanson, Paul D. "Rebellion in Heaven, Azazel, and Euhemeristic Heroes in 1 Enoch 6–11." *Journal of Biblical Literature* 96 (1977): 195–233.

Hayes, John H. "The Oracles against the Nations in the Old Testament: Their Usage and Theological Importance." Th. D. Diss., Princeton Theological Seminary, 1964.

———. "The Usage of Oracles against Foreign Nations in Ancient Israel." *Journal of Biblical Literature* 87 (1968): 81–92.

Healey, John F. "MLKM/RP'UM and the Kispum." *Ugarit-forschungen* 10 (1978a): 89–91.

———. "The Last of the Rephaim." Pages 33–44 in *Back to the Sources: Biblical and Near Eastern Studies.* Edited by K. Cathcart and J. Healey. Dublin: Glendale, 1989.

———. "Ritual Text KTU 1.161—Translation and Notes." *Ugarit-forschungen* 10 (1978b): 83–88.

———. "The Sun Deity and the Underworld: Mesopotamia and Ugarit." Pages 239–242 in *Death in Mesopotamia.* Edited by Rencontre assyriologique internationale. Mesopotamia 8. Copenhagen: Akademisk, 1980.

———. "The Ugaritic Dead: Some Live Issues." *Ugarit-forschungen* 18 (1986): 27–32.

Heidel, Alexander. *The Gilgamesh Epic and Old Testament Parallels.* Chicago: University of Chicago Press, 1946.

Heimpel, Wolfgang. "A Catalog of Near Eastern Venus Deities." *Syro-Mesopotamian Studies* 4 (1982): 9–22.

———. "The Sun at Night and the Doors of Heaven in Babylonian Texts." *Journal of Cuneiform Studies* 38 (1986): 127–151.

Herbordt, Suzanne. *Neuassyrische Glyptik des 8.–7. Jh. v. Chr.* State Archives of Assyria Studies 1. Helsinki: Helsinki University Press, 1992.

Hermisson, Hans Jürgen. *Stüdien zur israelitischen Spruchweisheit.* Wissenschaftliche Monographien zum Alten und Neuen Testament 28. Neukirchen-Vluyn: Neukirchener Verlag, 1968.

Hess, Richard. *Amarna Personal Names.* Winona Lake: Eisenbrauns, 1993.

Hoftijzer, J. and G. van der Kooij. *Aramaic Texts from Deir 'Alla.* Leiden: E. J. Brill, 1977.

Hooke, S. H., ed. *The Labyrinth.* New York: Macmillan, 1935.

———, ed. *Middle Eastern Mythology.* Baltimore: Penguin, 1963.

———. *Myth and Ritual: Essays on the Myth and Ritual of the Hebrews in Relation to the Culture Pattern of the Ancient East.* London: Oxford University Press, 1933.

———, ed. *Myth, Ritual, and Kingship: Essays on the Theory and Practice of Kingship in the Ancient Near East and in Israel.* Oxford: Clarendon, 1958.

———. *Origins of Early Semitic Ritual.* London: Oxford University Press, 1938.

Huffmon, Herbert. *Amorite Personal Names in the Mari Texts.* Baltimore: Johns Hopkins University Press, 1965.

Hunger, Hermann. *Astrological Reports to Assyrian Kings.* State Archives of Assyria 8. Helsinki: Helsinki University Press, 1992.

Hunger, Hermann and David Pingree. *MUL.APIN: An Astronomical Compendium in Cuneiform.* Beihefte, Archiv für Orientforschung 24. Horn: Ferdinand Berger & Söhne, 1989.

Jacobsen, Thorkild. *The Harps that Once . . .: Sumerian Poetry in Translation*. New Haven: Yale University Press, 1987.

———. *The Sumerian King List*. Assyriological Studies 11. Chicago: University of Chicago Press, 1939.

———. *The Treasures of Darkness: A History of Mesopotamian Religion*. New Haven: Yale University Press, 1976.

Jahnow, Hedwig. *Das hebräische Leichenlied im Rahmen der Völkerdichtung*. Gießen: Alfred Töpelmann, 1923.

Janzen, Waldemar. *Mourning Cry and Woe Oracle*. Beihefte zur Zeitschrift für die alttestamentliche Wissenschaft 125. Berlin: Walter de Gruyter, 1972.

Jeppesen, Knut. "You are a Cherub, but No God." *Scandinavian Journal of the Old Testament* 1 (1991): 83–94.

Jeremias, Joachim. *The Parables of Jesus*. 2nd ed. New York: Charles Scribner's Sons, 1972.

Jerome. *The Letters of St. Jerome*. Translated by Charles Mierow. 2 vols. Ancient Christian Writers 33. New York: Newman, 1963.

de Jirku, A. "Rapa'u, der Fürst der Rapa'uma—Rephaim." *Zeitschrift für die alttestamentliche Wissenschaft* 77 (1965): 82–83.

Johnson, Aubrey. "The Rôle of the King in the Jerusalem Cultus." Pages 71–111 in *The Labyrinth*. Edited by S. H. Hooke. New York: MacMillan, 1935.

———. *Sacral Kingship in Ancient Israel*. Edited by S. H. Hooke. Cardiff: University of Wales, 1955.

Kaiser, Otto. *Isaiah 13–39*. Old Testament Library. Philadelphia: Westminster, 1974.

Keown, Gerald L. "A History of the Interpretation of Isaiah 14:12–15." Ph. D. Diss., Southern Baptist Theological Seminary, 1979.

Kissane, Edward J. *The Book of Isaiah: Translated from a Critically Revised Hebrew Text with Commentary, Vol. 1*. Dublin: Richview, 1960.

Kitchen, Kenneth A. "The King List of Ugarit." *Ugarit-forschungen* 9 (1977): 131–142.

Klein, Jacob. "The Coronation and Consecration of Šulgi in the Ekur (Šulgi G)." Pages 292–313 in *Ah, Assyria: Studies in Assyrian History and Ancient Near Eastern Historiography Presented to Hayim Tadmor*. Edited by Mordecai Cogan and Israel Eph'al. Scripta Hierosolymitana 33. Jerusalem: Magnes, 1991.

———. "A New Nippur Duplicate of the Sumerian King List in the Brockman Collection, University of Haifa." *Aula Orientalis* 9 (1991): 128–129.

———. *The Royal Hymns of Shulgi King of Ur: Man's Quest for Immortal Fame*. Transactions of the American Philosophical Society 71. Philadelphia: American Philosophical Society, 1981.

———. "Šulgi and Išme-Dagan: Originality and Dependence in Sumerian Royal Hymnology." Pages 65–136 in *Bar-Ilan University Studies in Assyriology*. Edited by Jacob Klein and Aaron Skaist. Ramat-Gan: Bar-Ilan University Press, 1990.

———. *Three Šulgi Hymns: Sumerian Royal Hymns Glorifying King Šulgi of Ur*. Ramat-Gan: Bar-Ilan University Press, 1981.

Koefoed, Aase. "Gilgames, Enkidu, and the Netherworld." Acta Sumerologica Japonesa 5 (1983): 17–23.

Koehler, Ludwig and Walter Baumgartner. *The Hebrew and Aramaic Lexicon of the Old Testament*. Vol. 1. Leiden: E. J. Brill, 1994.

König, E. *Historisch-kritisches Lehrgebäude der hebräischen Sprache*. Leipzig: J. C. Hinrichs, 1881–97.

Korpel, Marjo C. A. *A Rift in the Clouds: Ugaritic and Hebrew Descriptions of the Divine*. Ugaritisch-biblische Literatur 8. Münster: Ugarit-Verlag, 1990.

Kramer, Samuel N. "BM 88318: The Ascension of Dumuzi to Heaven." Recueil de travaux et de communication de l'association des Études du Proche-Orient Ancien 2 (1984): 5–9.

———. "BM 98396: A Sumerian Prototype of the Mater Dolorosa." *Eretz-Israel* 16 (1982): 141*–146*.

———. "CT XXXVI: Corrigenda et Addenda." *Iraq* 36 (1974): 98–99.

———. "The Death of Ur-Nammu and His Descent to the Netherworld." *Journal of Cuneiform Studies* 21 (1967): 104–122.

———. "The Lamentation Over the Destruction of Nippur." Acta Sumerologica Japonesa 13 (1991a): 1–26.

———. *The Sacred Marriage Rite: Aspects of Faith, Myth, and Ritual in Ancient Sumer.* Bloomington: Indiana University Press, 1969.

———. "Solomon and Šulgi: A Comparative Portrait." Pages 189–195 in *Ah, Assyria: Studies in Assyrian History and Ancient Near Eastern Historiography Presented to Hayim Tadmor*. Edited by Mordecai Cogan and Israel Eph'al. Scripta Hierosolymitana 33. Jerusalem: Magnes, 1991.

———. *Two Elegies on a Pushkin Museum Tablet: A New Sumerian Literary Genre*. Moscow: Oriental Literature, 1960.

L'Heureux, Conrad. "El and the Rephaim: New Light from Ugaritica V." Ph. D. Diss., Harvard University, 1972.

———. *Rank Among the Canaanite Gods: El, Baʿal, and the Rephaʾim.* Harvard Semitic Monographs 21. Missoula: Scholars Press, 1979.

———. "The Ugaritic and Biblical Rephaim." *Harvard Theological Review* 67 (1974): 265–274.

Labat, R. *Manuel d'epigraphie Akkadienne*. 6th ed. Paris: Guethner, 1988.

Lambert, W. G. "Babylonian Astrological Omens and Their Stars." *Journal of the American Oriental Society* 107 (1987): 93–96.

———. "Old Testament Mythology in its Ancient Near Eastern Context." Pages 124–143 in *Congress Volume, Jerusalem.* Edited by John Emerton. Supplements to Vetus Testamentum 40. Leiden: E. J. Brill, 1988.

Landes, Geoge M. "Jonah: A Māšāl?" Pages 137–146 in *Israelite Wisdom: Theological and Literary Essays in Honor of Samuel Terrien.* Edited by John Gammie et. al. Missoula: Scholars Press, 1978.

Langdon, S. *The Legend of Etana and the Eagle, or the Epical Poem "The City They Hated."* Paris: Guethner, 1932.

Leeuwen, Raymond C. van. "Isa. 14:12: Hôlēš ʿAl Gwym and Gilgamesh XI, 6." *Journal of Biblical Literature* 99 (1980): 173–184.

Lévi-Strauss, Claude. *The Naked Man*. Chicago: University of Chicago Press, 1971.

———. *Structural Anthropology.* New York: Basic Books, 1963.

Levine, Baruch and de Tarragon, Jean-Michel. "Dead Kings and Rephaim: The Patrons of the Ugaritic Dynasty." *Journal of the American Oriental Society* 104 (1984): 649–659.

Lewis, Theodore. *Cults of the Dead in Ugarit and Israel.* Harvard Semitic Monographs 39. Atlanta: Scholars Press, 1989.

———. "Toward a Literary Translation of the Rapiʾūma Texts." Pages 115–149 in *Ugarit: Religion and Culture, Proceedings of the Edinburgh International Conference 20–23 July 1994, Studies in Honor of John Gibson.* Ugaritisch-Biblische Literatur 12. Münster: Ugarit-Verlag, 1996.

Livingstone, Alasdair. *Court Poetry and Literary Miscellanea.* State Archives of Assyria 3. Helsinki: Helsinki University Press, 1989.

Loretz, Oswald. "Der kanaanäisch-biblische Mythos vom Sturz des Saḥar-Sohnes Hêlēl (Jes 14, 12–15)." *Ugarit-forschungen* 8 (1976): 133–136.

Luckenbill, Daniel D. *Ancient Records of Assyria and Babylonia.* 2 vols. London: Histories and Mysteries of Man, 1989.

———. *The Annals of Sennacherib.* Chicago: University of Chicago Press, 1924.

Luther, Martin. *Lectures on Isaiah, Chapters 1–39.* Translated by Jaroslav Pelikan. Luther's Works 16. St. Louis: Concordia, 1969.

Malinowski, Bronislaw. *Argonauts of the Western Pacific.* New York: E. P. Dutton, 1961.

———. *Myth in Primitive Psychology.* New York: W. W. Norton, 1926.

Margalit, Baruch. *A Matter of 'Life' and 'Death': A Study of the Baal-Mot Epic (CTA 4–5–6).* Neukirchen-Vluyn: Neukirchener Verlag, 1980.

Matthiae, Paolo. "Princely Cemetery and Ancestors' Cult at Ebla During Middle Bronze II: A Proposal of Interpretation." *Ugarit-forschungen* 11 (1979): 563–569.

McKane, William. *Proverbs: A New Approach.* Old Testament Library. Philadelphia: Westminster, 1970.

McKay, J. W. "Helel and the Dawn-Goddess: A Re-examination of the Myth in Isaiah XIV 12–15." *Vetus Testamentum* 20 (1970): 451–464.

Meier, Gerhard. *Die assyrische Beschwörungssammlung Maqlû.* Beihefte, Archiv für Orientforschung 2. Osnabrück: Biblio-Verlag, 1967.

Michalowski, Piotr. "The Death of Šulgi." *Orientalia* New Series 46 (1977): 220–225.

———. *The Lament Over the Destruction of Sumer and Ur.* Winona Lake: Eisenbrauns, 1989.

Moor, Johannes C. de. "The Ancestral Cult in KTU 1.17:I.26–28." *Ugarit-forschungen* 17 (1986): 407–409.

———. "Rāpiʾūma—Rephaim." *Zeitschrift für die alttestamentliche Wissenschaft* 88 (1979): 325–329.

Morgenstern, Julian. "The Mythological Background of Psalm 82." *Hebrew Union College Annual* 14 (1939): 29–126.

Moscati, Sabatino. *An Introduction to the Comparative Grammar of the Semitic Languages: Phonology and Morphology.* Wiesbaden: Otto Harrassowitz, 1964.

Mowinckel, Sigmund. "Die Sternnamen im Alten Testament." *Nederlands theologisch Tijdschrift* 29 (1928): 1–77.

Mullen, E. Theodore. *The Assembly of the Gods: The Divine Council in Canaanite and Early Hebrew Literature.* Harvard Semitic Monographs 24. Chico: Scholars Press, 1980.

Neugebauer, O. and Richard Parker. *Egyptian Astronomical Texts, Vol. 1: The Early Decans.* London: Lund Humphries, 1960.

Niditch, Susan. *Folklore and the Hebrew Bible.* Minneapolis: Fortress, 1993.

Nielsen, Kirsten. *There is Hope for a Tree: The Tree as Metaphor in Isaiah.* Journal for the Study of the Old Testament: Supplement Series 65. Sheffield: Sheffield Academic Press, 1989.

O'Connell, Robert H. "Isaiah 14:4b–23: Ironic Reversal Through Concentric Structure and Mythic Allusion (Gilgamesh XI)." *Vetus Testamentum* 38 (1988): 406–418.

Oldenburg, Ulf. "Above the Stars of El: El in Ancient South Arabic Religion." *Zeitschrift für die alttestamentliche Wissenschaft* 82 (1970): 187–208.

Olmo Lete, G. del. "Ug. ṯʿ, ṯʿy, ṯʿt: Nombre Divino y Accion Cultual." *Ugarit-forschungen* 29 (1988): 27–33.

Orlinsky, Harry. "Madhebah in Isaiah 14:4." *Vetus Testamentum* 7 (1957): 202–203.

Oswalt, John. *The Book of Isaiah, Chapters 1–39.* New International Commentary on the Old Testament. Grand Rapids: Eerdmans, 1986.

Otzen, Benedikt, Hans Gottlief, and Knud Jeppesen. *Myths in the Old Testament*. London: SCM, 1980.

Parker, Simon, "Shahar." Page 1425 in *Dictionary of Deities and Demons in the Bible.* Edited by Karel van der Toorn et al. Leiden: E. J. Brill, 1995.

———. "The Ugaritic Deity Rapiʾu." *Ugarit-forschungen* 4 (1972): 103–104.

Parpola, Simo. *The Correspondence of Sargon II.* State Archives of Assyria 1. Helsinki: Helsinki University Press, 1987.

Pitard, Wayne. "RS 34.126: Notes on the Text." *Maarav* 4 (1987): 75–86.

———. "The Ugaritic Funerary Text RS 34.126." *Bulletin of the American Schools of Oriental Research* 232 (1978): 65–75.

Polk, Timothy. "Paradigms, Parables, and Mešālîm: On Reading the Māšāl in Scripture." *Catholic Biblical Quarterly* 45 (1983): 564–583.

Pope, Marvin H. *El in the Ugaritic Texts*. Leiden: E. J. Brill, 1955.

———. "Notes on the Rephaim Texts from Ugarit." Pages 163–182 in *Essays on the Ancient Near East in Memory of Jacob Joel Finkelstein.* Edited by Maria de Jong Ellis. Vol. 19 of Memoirs of the Connecticut Academy of Arts and Sciences. Hamden: Archon, 1977.

Pope, Marvin H. and W. Röllig. "Šaḥar and Šalim." Pages 306–307 in *Wörterbuch der Mythologie.* Band 1, 1 Abteilung. Stuttgart: Ernst Klett, 1965.

Prinsloo, Willem S. "Isaiah 14:12–15: Humiliation, Hubris, Humiliation." *Zeitschrift für die alttestamentliche Wissenschaft* 93 (1981): 432–438.

Pritchard, James. *Ancient Near Eastern Texts Relating to the Old Testament*. 3rd ed. Princeton: Princeton University Press, 1969.

Procksch, Otto. *Jesaia I.* Leipzig: A. Deichertsche, 1930.

Quell, Gottfried. "Jesaja 14, 1–23." Pages 131–157 in *Festschrift Friedrich Baumgärtel zum 70. Geburtstag, 14 Januar 1958.* Edited by Johannes Hermann. Erlangen: University of Erlangen Press, 1959.

Rad, Gerhard von. *Wisdom in Israel*. London: SCM, 1972.

Ratosh, Y. "'עבר' במקרא או ארץ העברים." *Beth Mikra* 16 (47) (1972): 549–568.

Reiner, Erica. *Šurpu: A Collection of Sumerian and Akkadian Incantations.* Beihefte, Archiv für Orientforschung 11. Osnabrück: Biblio-Verlag, 1970.

Reiner, Erica and David Pingree. *Babylonian Planetary Omens, Part 2: Enūma Anu Enlil, Tablets 50–51*. Bibliotheca Mesopotamica 2/2. Malibu: Undena, 1981.

Roberts, J. J. M. *Nahum, Habakkuk, and Zephaniah: A Commentary*. Old Testament Library. Louisville: W/JKP, 1991.

Rodgers, Richard and Oscar Hammerstein II. *Oklahoma! A Musical Play*. New York: Williamson Music, 1943.

Robinson, Theodore. "Hebrew Myths." Pages 179–180 in *Myth and Ritual: Essays on the Myth and Ritual of the Hebrews in Relation to the Culture Pattern of the Ancient East.* Edited by S. H. Hooke. London: Oxford University Press, 1933.

Rochberg-Halton, Francesca. *Aspects of Babylonian Celestial Divination: The Lunar Eclipse Tablets of Enūma Anu Enlil.* Beihefte, Archiv für Orientforschung 22. Horn: Ferdinand Berger & Söhne, 1988.

Rogerson, John W. *Myth in Old Testament Interpretation*. Berlin: Walter de Gruyter, 1974.

Sawyer, John F. A. "From Heaven Fought the Stars (Judges V 20)." *Vetus Testamentum* 31 (1981): 87–89.

Shaffer, Aaron. "Gilgamesh, the Cedar Forest, and Mesopotamian History." *Journal of the American Oriental Society* 103 (1983): 307–313.

Schmidt, J. *Studien zur Stylistik der atlttestamentlichen Spruchliteratur*. alttestamentliche Abhandlungen 13. Münster: Aschendorffschen, 1936.

Schneider, N. *Die Götternamen von Ur III*. Rome: Pontifical Biblical Institute, 1939.
Schwally, F. "Miscellen." *Zeitschrift für die alttestamentliche Wissenschaft* 11 (1891): 253–260.
Scott, R. B. Y. "Isaiah 1–39." Pages 151–380 in vol. 5 of *Interpreter's Bible*. Edited by George A. Buttrick et al. 12 vols. Nashville: Abingdon, 1956.
Segert, Stanislav. *A Basic Grammar of the Ugaritic Language*. Berkeley: University of California Press, 1984.
Seow, C. L. *Myth, Drama, and the Politics of David's Dance*. Harvard Semitic Monographs 44. Atlanta: Scholars Press, 1989.
Sjöberg, Åke. "The First Pushkin Museum Elegy and New Texts." *Journal of the American Oriental Society* 103 (1983): 315–320.
Smith, Mark. "Baal in the Land of Death." *Ugarit-forschungen* 17 (1985): 311–314.
Soden, Wolfram von. "Vokal färbungen im Akkadischen." *Journal of Cuneiform Studies* 2 (1948): 291–303.
Speiser, E. A. "The Gilgamesh Epic." Pages 72–99 in *Ancient Near Eastern Texts Relating to the Old Testament*, Edited by James B. Pritchard. 3rd, ed. Princeton: Princeton University Press, 1969.
Spronk, Klaas. *Beatific Afterlife in Ancient Israel and in the Ancient Near East*. Alter Orient und Altes Testament 219. Neukirchen-Vluyn: Neukirchener Verlag; Kevelaer: Butzon & Bercker, 1986.
Steinmann, Jean. *Le prophète Isaïe: sa vie, son oeuvre, et son temps*. Paris: Cerf, 1955.
Stolz, F. "Die Baüme des Gottesgartens auf den Libanon." *Zeitschrift für die alttestamentliche Wissenschaft* 84 (1972): 141–156.
Strenski, Ivan. *Four Theories of Myth in Twentieth-Century History: Cassirer, Eliade, Lévi-Strauss and Malinowski*. London: MacMillan, 1987.
———. *Malinowski and the Work of Myth*. Princeton: Princeton University Press, 1992.
Suter, David. "Māšāl in the Similitudes of Enoch." *Journal of Biblical Literature* 100 (1981): 193–212.
Sweeney, Marvin. *Isaiah 1–39, with an Introduction to Prophetic Literature*. Forms of Old Testament Literature 16. Grand Rapids: Eerdmans, 1996.
Tadmor, Hayim. *The Inscriptions of Tiglath-Pileser III King of Assyria*. Jerusalem: The Israel Academy of Sciences and Humanities, 1994.
Talmon, Shemaryahu. "Biblical Repha'îm and Ugaritic rpu/i(m)." *Hebrew Annual Review* 7 (1983): 235–249.
Taylor, J. Glen. "A First and Last Thing to Do in Mourning: KTU 1.161 and Some Parallels." Pages 151–177 in *Ascribe to the Lord: Biblical and Other Studies in Memory of Peter C. Craigie*, Edited by L. Elsinger and J. Glen Taylor. Journal for the Study of the Old Testament Supplement Series 67. Sheffield: Sheffield Academic Press, 1988.
Theodoret of Cyrus. *Theodoret of Cyrus on Divine Providence*. Translated by Thomas Halton. Ancient Christian Writers 49. New York: Newman, 1988.
Tigay, Jeffrey. *The Evolution of the Gilgamesh Epic*. Philadelphia: University of Pennsylvania Press, 1982.
Tsevat, Matitiahu. "Eating and Drinking, Hosting and Sacrificing in the Epic of Aqht." *Ugarit-forschungen* 18 (1986): 345–350.
Virolleaud, Charles. "Les Rephaîm: Fragments de Poèmes de Ras-Shamra." *Syria* 22 (1941): 1–30.
———. "Report." Comptes rendus de l'academie des inscriptions et belles lettres (1939): 638–639.
Waerden, B. L. van der. "Babylonian Astronomy II: The Thirty-six Stars." *Journal of Near Eastern Studies* 8 (1949): 6–26.

Walker, C. B. F. and Hermann Hunger. "Zwölfmaldrei." Mitteilungen der Deutschen Orient-Gesellschaft 109 (1977): 27–34.

Watson, P. J. and Horowitz, W. B. *Catalogue of Cuneiform Tablets in Birmingham City Museum. Vol. 1: Neo-Sumerian Texts from Drehem.* Warminster: Aris & Phillips, 1991.

———. "Further Notes on Birmingham Cuneiform Tablets, Volume 1." Acta Sumerologica Japonesa 13 (1991): 409–417.

Watson, W. G. E. "Helel." Pages 747–748 in *Dictionary of Deities and Demons in the Bible.* Edited by Karel van der Toorn et al. Leiden: E. J. Brill, 1995.

Watts, John D. W. Isaiah 1–33. Word Biblical Commentary 24. Waco: Word, 1985.

Westenholz, Joan G. *Legends of the Kings of Akkade: The Texts.* Mesopotamian Civilizations 7. Winona Lake: Eisenbrauns, 1997.

Westermann, Claus. *Lamentations: Issues and Interpretation.* Minneapolis: Fortress, 1994.

Whybray, R. N. *Proverbs.* New Century Bible. Grand Rapids: Eerdmans, 1994.

Wildberger, Hans. *Jesaja, Kapitel 13–39.* Biblischer Kommentar 10.2. Neukirchen-Vluyn: Neukirchener Verlag, 1980.

Wilson, J. V. Kinnier. *The Legend of Etana: A New Edition.* Warminster: Aris & Phillips, 1985.

Wiseman, D. J. *Chronicles of Chaldean Kings (626–556 B. C.) in the British Museum.* London: The Trustees of the British Museum, 1956.

Wyatt, Nicolas. "ʿA̲ttar and the Devil." Transactions of the Glasgow University Oriental Society (1973–74): 85–97.

———. "Cosmic Entropy in Ugaritic Religious Thought." *Ugarit-forschungen* 17 (1985): 383–386.

———. "Killing and Cosmogony in Canaanite and Biblical Thought." *Ugarit-forschungen* 17 (1985): 375–381.

Yee, Gale A. "The Anatomy of Biblical Parody: The Dirge Form in 2 Samuel 1 and Isaiah 14." *Catholic Biblical Quarterly* 50 (1988): 565–586.

Yoshikawa, Mamoru. "an–šè–a (= šè/e_{11}) 'to die'." Acta Sumerologica Japonesa 11 (1989) 353.

Young, Edward J. *The Book of Isaiah: Volume 1, Chapters 1–18.* New International Commentary on the Old Testamentt. Grand Rapids: Eerdmans, 1965.

Indexes

Index of Ancient Texts

Author Index

Index of Proper Nouns and Technical Terms

S

T

U

V

W

Y

Z

Scripture Index

Proverbs

Ecclesiastes

Isaiah

Jeremiah

Lamentations

Index of Ancient Languages

Akkadian

Sumerian